True Crime Philadelphia

From America's First Bank Robbery to the
Real-Life Killers Who Inspired Boardwalk Empire

Kathryn Canavan

Guilford, Connecticut

An imprint of Globe Pequot, the trade division of
The Rowman & Littlefield Publishing Group, Inc.
4501 Forbes Blvd., Ste. 200
Lanham, MD 20706
LyonsPress.com

Distributed by NATIONAL BOOK NETWORK

British Library Cataloguing in Publication Information available

Library of Congress Cataloging-in-Publication Data

Names: Canavan, Kathryn, author.
Title: True crime Philadelphia : from America's first bank robbery to the
  real-life killers who inspired Boardwalk empire / Kathryn Canavan.
Description: Guilford, Connecticut : Lyons Press, [2021] | Includes
  bibliographical references and index. | Summary: "A tour through
  Philadelphia that highlights the locations within each neighborhood
  where crime occurred"— Provided by publisher.
Identifiers: LCCN 2021017897 (print) | LCCN 2021017898 (ebook) | ISBN
  9781493036158 (hardback) | ISBN 9781493036165 (epub)
Subjects: LCSH: Crime—Pennsylvania—Philadelphia—History. |
  Criminals—Pennsylvania—Philadelphia—Biography. | Philadelphia
  (Pa.) —History. | Philadelphia (Pa.) —Biography.
Classification: LCC HV6795.P5 C36 2021 (print) | LCC HV6795.P5 (ebook) |
  DDC 364.9748/11—dc23
LC record available at https://lccn.loc.gov/2021017897
LC ebook record available at https://lccn.loc.gov/2021017898

To my wonderful parents, Pearl and Clarence Canavan,
keen newspaper readers who, no doubt,
followed some of these crimes in the headlines as they happened,
long before arsenic widows and celebrity bank robbers slipped into history.

Contents

Foreword

THINGS DON'T ALWAYS GO EXACTLY ACCORDING TO PLAN FOR CRIMINALS in Philadelphia. More often than not, even celebrated crooks like Al Capone and H. H. Holmes have proved no match for the ordinary citizens of Philadelphia.

This book raises a glass to the clever, heroic, and quietly confident everyday Philadelphians who have tripped up criminals for more than 300 years.

Curious pipefitters. Nosy neighbors. Dogged detectives. Bold patrolmen. Heroic homemakers. Fearless mechanics. Take-charge delivery boys. And, always, sharp-eyed passersby.

When bank robber Willie Sutton tunneled out of prison and popped up out of a hole along Fairmount Avenue in broad daylight in 1945, it was an unshakeable average citizen who foiled his escape.

When Octavius Catto was assassinated on South Street on Election Day, 1871, a 61-year-old brickmaker jumped off a trolley car and chased down the 21-year-old shooter.

When a former madam fell from a mansion window on leafy Pine Street in 1868, it was her neighbors who deduced she was killed with a fireplace poker in the sitting room. They pressed the police to arrest her son-in-law on the spot.

America's first kidnapping unfolded in Germantown on July 4 weekend, 1874. Stealing a child was so unheard of that police laughed about it, so the boy's father and uncle followed the clues on their own. Within months, the search for little Charley Ross had spread to three continents.

Whenever you walk city streets, you likely pass places where headline-grabbing crimes happened decades or centuries earlier. Historic crimes happened at every turn here, and, historically, Philadelphians rarely hesitated to break a few rules or step over some lines to save the day.

Singlehandedly or in impromptu groups, Philadelphians are problem solvers who quietly take charge when things break badly.

The most sensational bank robbery in city history is an extreme example of average Philadelphians stepping up with no thought for themselves. Any savvy bettor would have predicted the professional holdup artists would prevail in the Olney Bank and Trust robbery of 1926. They planned the caper for weeks and armed themselves with high-caliber weapons. For a few brief seconds, they were holding a fortune that would be worth almost $1.2 million today—until the people of Philadelphia put their thumbs on the scale.

The robbers didn't count on the extraordinary pluck of the ordinary people of Olney. Instead of running from a hail of bullets, men and women ran out onto the streets to offer any help they could.

Just as the bandits thought they were scot-free, passersby armed themselves with handguns and rifles and knives, and, in one less-successful instance, a broom. It turned into a scene rivaling *It's a Mad, Mad, Mad, Mad World*.

Those who had cars invited police officers and armed strangers to jump in.

A woman in a second-story widow threw an automatic pistol and an ammo clip to a stranger on the street who shouted, "Does anyone have a gun?"

Two men laying a gas pipe decided to join the chase instead.

A boy grabbed the satchel of cash and carried it back to the bank.

A mechanic, a night watchman, and a poultry salesman—all strangers until that morning—tailed the robbers together.

When the mechanic spotted one of the stickup men on Erie Avenue, in a jaw-dropping move, he jammed a borrowed pistol into the back of the bandit's head and shouted, "Drop that gun, or I'll blow your head off."

When it comes to crimes, Philadelphians are a resourceful bunch, whether committing them or stopping them. The city's long history provides plenty of examples:

- The country's first bank robbery came off on Chestnut Street in 1798.

- The first mass murder happened near present-day Citizens Bank Park in 1866, when axes and hammers were the automatic weapons of the day.

- The six Lanzetta brothers, the real-life models for the murderous D'Alessio brothers in HBO's *Boardwalk Empire*, met their ends in stranger-than-fiction fashion on city streets. One's corpse was tied to the running board of a touring car.

- Notorious Chicago serial killer H. H. Holmes met the hangman on Passyunk Avenue in one of the most bizarre executions in state history. Holmes's body, encased in 2,000 pounds of cement to deter graverobbers, rests in Holy Cross Cemetery just over the city line in Delaware County. Despite the cement, it was removed from the ground for 117 days in 2017.

- A chubby-faced tailor masterminded the largest mass murder plot in US history on Passyunk Avenue in the 1930s. His partners in crime were unhappy homemakers. Their weapons were love potions, hexes, the evil eye, and arsenic sprinkled on spaghetti. When the case broke wide open, the usually quiet corridors of City Hall were filled with fortune-tellers, womanizing witch doctors, and a parade of self-made widows in black dresses.

- Harry Wodlinger just wanted his golf clubs when he bounded up the steps to his house on North Camac Street on December 7, 1944. He found Susie, his mop-haired terrier, locked in the basement and barking furiously. Then he discovered his wife, Freeda, in a dark upstairs bathroom. The room was a fight scene. The attractive brunette was sprawled on the floor in a pool of her own blood. The maid did it.

- Thirty-Minute Gertie, a World War II–era housemaid, could strip a new employer's home of valuables in less than a half hour.

- In the 1950s, Philadelphia's top cop spent 10 years trying to prove a burglary case against Lillian Reis, a city showgirl so sultry she was once arrested for lewdness for doing the twist fully clothed. He contended the brunette beauty masterminded the most lucrative house burglary in Pennsylvania history. His case fizzled when one burglary witness was stabbed to death waiting for a bus, one was blown up on Alma Street, and a third was fished out of the Atlantic with a heavy chain padlocked around his torso.

- While the Founding Fathers were hammering out the Constitution's guarantees of life and liberty in 1787, just a few blocks away, a crowd stoned a woman believed to be a witch.
- Catholics and Protestants fought each other with cannons on city streets during the Bible Riots of 1844.
- The line about Max "Boo Boo" Hoff around Philadelphia was "Whatever Boo Boo wants, well, that's what Boo Boo gets." The millionaire bootlegger became so famous that Damon Runyon and James Thurber wrote about him. The district attorney who could never quite nab him crowned him "king of the bootleggers."

Ten of the villains in this book took their last glimpses at the world from atop gallows or buckled into an electric chair. Except for Holmes, whose story was revived in Erik Larson's best-selling *The Devil in the White City*, they are now part of a forgotten Philadelphia.

Although some of these true crime stories stun or startle, this is a work of nonfiction. Every detail and quotation in this book is true and documented in endnotes.

Lillian Reis's Celebrity Room is gone from Juniper Street now. The site of the 1866 axe octo-murder is now a food warehouse. The spot where H. H. Holmes swung from the gallows for 33 minutes is an Acme Market now. The pirates who once plied the Schuylkill are gone, too.

Snatches of the past still exist, though. Al Capone served his first prison term in Philadelphia, and you can visit a reconstructed model of his cell at Eastern State Penitentiary, now a tourist attraction. You can still stroll by the old Sylvania Hotel at 1324 Locust Street, where Boo Boo Hoff had 175 telephones installed in his office in the 1920s. The exterior of Freeda Wodlinger's Camac Street home is largely unchanged.

The site of Octavius Catto's assassination at 812 South Street is dotted with a state historical marker. When you drive down narrow Alma Street, you can slip back to the summer of 1961, when Richie Blaney turned his car key and set off an explosion that sent his sedan's heavy hood soaring over the rowhouse roofs.

If you are from Philadelphia, your own ancestors might have played a part in committing these crimes or solving them. No matter where you're from, your ancestors likely followed these crime stories, because they made headlines coast-to-coast and sometimes worldwide.

CHAPTER ONE

The Lillian Reis Case—The Beauty, the Sugar Daddy, the Tax Cheat, and the Toppled Cop

LILLIAN REIS WAS SO BEAUTIFUL that conversation would drop to a low hush whenever she walked into a room. Men described her as a "swell-looking dish" and a "capital G glamour girl." She once got arrested for lewd behavior for doing the twist fully clothed.[1]

When Philly's top cop said she was the brains behind a half-million-dollar heist in a coal town she had never set foot in, he set in motion a string of unintended consequences that would upend dozens of lives, including his own.

Mahantongo Street was the swankiest address in Pottsville, Pennsylvania, in 1959. Perched atop one of the coal city's seven hills, the tree-lined stretch was dotted with formal gardens, wrought-iron balconies,

Lillian Reis was still a teenager when she began dancing in chorus lines. One of Lillian Reis's several sugar daddies showered her with more than $150,000 worth of cash and cars and jewels—about $1.3 million today.
SPECIAL COLLECTIONS RESEARCH CENTER, TEMPLE UNIVERSITY LIBRARIES, PHILADELPHIA, PA

I

The burglary crew drove uphill to the back entrance of the Rich mansion on Mah-
antongo Street, the most prestigious street in Pottsville, Pennsylvania.
AUTHOR PHOTO

and Queen Anne porches. It was home to Pottsville society—doctors, lawyers, bankers, and coal barons. Novelist John O'Hara grew up in a six-bedroom Italianate townhouse there. The Yuengling Brewery scion occupied a stately 20-room, turn-of-the-century Tudor. Millionaire John Rich raised his family in a three-story stucco built in 1927 on one of the best corners.[2]

So why were four mooks from out of town cruising up and down Mahantongo in a yellow Lincoln on the picture-perfect high-summer evening of August 7, 1959? And why were they packing a hacksaw, a sledgehammer, and an empty carryall bag?[3]

They came to hunt for negotiable bonds in a stranger's basement. They drove almost 100 miles on an inside tip from Lillian Reis's pot-bellied sugar daddy.

Clyde "Bing" Miller, a one-time college football star at Bucknell, was lovesick over Reis, a curvy chorus girl 25 years his junior. Miller, a paunchy 53-year-old mining engineer, had done business with John Rich of 1801 Mahantongo Street, owner of Gilberton Coal Company.[4]

Rich was aptly named. He was so wealthy he owned the largest dragline strip mining shovel in the world, one with a scoop the size of a one-car garage.[5]

Miller knew Rich routinely stashed bonds in a safe in his basement because he didn't report all his income to the Internal Revenue Service.[6]

Then, by chance, in the first week of August, Miller was admitted to Pottsville Hospital, where he heard chitchat that Rich was vacationing in Italy and wouldn't be home for another three weeks.

He immediately thought of Reis, the cigarette-voiced stunner he had already showered with cash and cars and furs and jewels worth more than $150,000. He paid her rent. He paid for her maid. He bought a mink stole for her and one for her sister. He bought her a garbage disposal, a washing machine, and a full-length fur coat.[7] And, on August 6, he walked to the pay phone in the hospital lobby with 45 cents to make a long-distance call to her.[8]

With that 45-cent call, he set up the most lucrative house burglary in Pennsylvania history.

The next day, the four men in the Lincoln drove roller-coaster roads deep into anthracite coal country to check whether Miller's tip was solid. Two of the men in the Lincoln also had been romantically involved with Reis.

When the Lincoln turned onto Mahantongo Street around 6 p.m., it was still sunny and mild.[9] The occupants didn't know it, but they narrowly missed the caretaker who checked the property daily. The house looked deserted, but their business was best done in the dark, so they headed to a taproom where they ordered beer and sandwiches and waited for the sun to set.[10]

By the time they returned sometime after 8 p.m., darkness enveloped Mahantongo Street. They walked around the back of the house near the swimming pool and broke in through the kitchen door.

Ralph Staino Jr., Reis's broad-shouldered, 27-year-old current flame, walked to a front window to serve as lookout. John Berkery, 30, a handsome oil salesman from New Jersey, headed to the basement to crack the safe with Vincent Blaney, 28, a Philadelphia man with one distinguishing feature, an oversize front tooth. Robert Poulson, 24, followed with a carryall bag for the cash.[11]

As Blaney approached the safe, it was a typical Friday night elsewhere in Pottsville, with couples headed out to the pictures. The musical *South Pacific* was playing at the Capitol Theatre in CinemaScope and high-fidelity stereophonic sound. The Strand was offering a horror double feature—*The Woman Eater* and *The H Man*, the latter with the tame tagline, "It's H on Earth."

Blaney had the safe open in fewer than 15 minutes. He peeled it, removing the outermost layer and the asbestos lining. Then they broke the handle.[12]

In the basement light, it seemed to be stuffed with old newspapers. Then Poulson cried, "It's money!"

They realized they were staring at a large safe jammed tight with US currency. When they recalled it later, they said they could hardly believe their own eyes.

Poulson and Blaney ran upstairs to Staino with fists full of dollars.

The carryall was quickly filled, and someone ran to a bedroom to fetch a pillowcase. Instead, he snatched a large bolster off the bed. In their haste to fill it, they didn't realize the money was falling out on the floor. Bolsters are open on both ends.

Upstairs again, they grabbed two pillowcases and started filling them with cash. One was bulging when they heard a siren. Staino shouted, "Here come the cops!" They ran upstairs so fast they created a traffic jam at the kitchen door.

They huddled on the back porch, watching for a prowl car, but it was a false alarm. The siren had sounded the Friday night curfew for teenagers. Too shook to go back downstairs, they piled into the car with the loot, a diamond bracelet, and at least six bottles of Rich's liquor.[13]

They couldn't believe their luck. Someone had gone off to Europe and left almost a half million dollars unguarded in his basement. At 66, Rich was the second-biggest employer in a coal town where everybody knew everybody for generations. He probably never envisioned an after-dark visit from four outsiders.

By the time the Lincoln left Mahantongo Street, it was carrying $478,000 and burglars so happy they burst out in song. They belted out an Irish drinking song, except for Staino, who was of Italian descent. He didn't want to sing it, so they sang without him. Blaney had $13,000 in his hands and he kept counting it. Staino was so excited he couldn't drive, so Berkery took the wheel for the trip back to Philadelphia. They started joking they'd call themselves the Darby O'Gill Gang, based on the name of a new Disney movie. A euphoric Staino realized that one heist with them had made him rich. "To hell with the Mafia," he said. "I'm with the Darby O'Gill Mob from now on."[14]

They had blundered into a payoff that was bigger than their expectations. They were halfway home when someone realized they had left the bonds on the bottom shelf of the safe. They also had dropped an envelope containing ten $100 bills.

They stopped at Staino's West Philadelphia apartment to count the money. They poured it out on the bed. "It damn near covered the whole bed," Poulson said. They counted it three times, coming up with a different count each time. They got up to $400,000 but were just too tired to count any more.

Blaney took one share to his brother Richie's place in a brown paper bag. He spilled the cash out on the kitchen table to show him. Then he stashed it in Richie's oven and went out to celebrate.[15]

They had made a clean getaway, or at least it seemed that way on that perfect 70-degree night in the summer in the city. In fewer than two years, both Blaney brothers would be dead.[16]

That was how the Rich caper began. Soon the beauty, the burglars, the safecrackers, and the sugar daddy would be joined by the killers, the mastermind, the tax cheat, the stool pigeon, and the legendary detective who met his undoing.

The crime came to light the next day when the caretaker spotted the busted screen door and the open back door. Inside, asbestos footprints covered the kitchen floor. He peered down the basement stairs and saw the mangled safe. Somebody had dropped a necklace on a step. He didn't go downstairs because he feared he'd be a suspect. He called Rich's adult daughter, who called her brother. To the caretaker's surprise, neither of them seemed ruffled. Jack Rich said his father never kept more than $3,000 or $4,000 in the safe. They put in a transatlantic call to their father, but he did not head back to Pottsville. His vacation unspoiled, he spent another three weeks in Italy.[17]

While the coal baron was touring Italy, Berkery bought a new house with Rich's money. He chose a particular suburban New Jersey property because it resembled Rich's home in Pottsville. He had it painted white, like Rich's. He told friends he wanted to be reminded of the biggest score he ever made. He even had it carpeted wall to wall in blue because Rich did. He also had Mrs. Rich's diamonds reset in a nice ring for himself.

Berkery and his wife, Rosalie, took a two-week, $10,000 luxury-hotel vacation to California. He spent another $2,000 on a mink stole for her. They bought $8,000 worth of French provincial furniture for their new house. He bought a red-and-white Edsel for Rosalie, and a gold Lincoln and a blue-and-white cabin cruiser for himself.[18]

Lavish spenders Poulson and Blaney told strippers about their big score upstate.

Staino asked a friend if he would change some bills into hundreds for him. When the man agreed, Staino handed him a shirt box with more than $10,000 inside.

The heist didn't make the papers in Philadelphia, but Capt. Clarence Ferguson, a legendary Philadelphia police detective, heard that some suspects were suddenly spending big, thanks to a heist in the coal country. He called Pottsville police, but they said the take from the Rich robbery was only about $20,000, including the jewelry.

Ferguson was stumped for the moment. As head of the much-publicized unit dubbed Fergy's Boys, the swaggering detective had carte blanche to investigate anything he wanted. He wanted to know where these mooks were getting the money.

Fergy caught a break when Richie Blaney tired of being jailed on a probation violation. In return for early release, Blaney served up his

Richie Blaney, the star witness against Lillian Reis, was blown up in his car on his 27th birthday on July 27, 1961. His killer stacked the dynamite to blow upward, not outward toward the houses on Alma Street. Firemen used an aerial ladder to retrieve Blaney's car hood from the roof of a house more than a football field away.
SPECIAL COLLECTIONS RESEARCH CENTER, TEMPLE UNIVERSITY LIBRARIES, PHILADELPHIA, PA

brother's burglary crew and the $478,000 heist. He had all the details from his brother, Staino, and Berkery. They had even taken him to Pottsville and pointed out the Rich house, hoping he might sign on for a second burglary to steal the forgotten bonds.[19]

Blaney told Fergy the largest share of the half-million-dollar heist went to Lillian Reis, the splashy new owner of the Celebrity Room, who was billed as "Tiger Lil." She hosted up-and-comers like Don Rickles and Johnny Mathis at her popular center-city venue. Her arrest would ensure front page headlines. Fergy set out to prove the $40,000 Reis paid for the Juniper Street club came from Rich's safe. He could draw a line from Reis to the money, but it wasn't a thick line.[20]

By April, nine months after the heist, Fergy had arrested Reis, Staino, Berkery, Miller, Poulson, and Vincent Blaney.

Suddenly, news pages were plastered with headshots of husky Staino, handsome Berkery, jowly Richie Blaney, and "Fergy" in his trademark flat-topped porkpie hat, and full-length shots of leggy "Lil," who favored skin-tight knits and stiletto heels.

Fergy and Lil were masters of public relations. She wooed reporters to her limbo contests. He took them along on police raids. Their disdain for each other was unmistakable.

She scoffed at his claim that she needed to pull a heist to buy her nightclub. "If I really wanted just money, I could go out today and marry one of the many men with money who want to marry me," she said matter-of-factly.[21]

Although his bald head and deeply lined face made Fergy appear older than his 63 years, he quipped to a reporter that the shapely 31-year-old Reis "had some mileage on her."[22]

In the lead-up to the trial, Fergy's Boys turned some of the suspects into state's witnesses. Robert Poulson stopped talking after he was beaten, stabbed, and shot while waiting for a bus. Vincent Blaney was beaten almost senseless on August 1, 1960, but he kept talking until mid-August, when someone put a bullet in the back of his head, padlocked a weighted chain to his torso, and dumped him in the Atlantic near Margate, New Jersey. They knocked out most of his teeth but left the

Club owner Lillian Reis and bouncer Ralph Staino Jr., her long-time boyfriend, appear for booking after a dust-up with police officers.

oversize one in the front for identification. He was fished out on August 23. The *Daily News* dubbed it a "sea-going murder."[23]

Richie Blaney became Fergy's star witness by process of elimination. Blaney idolized Ferguson to the point that he started wearing a porkpie hat like Fergy's trademark topper. Ferguson also seemed to take a shine to his chatty witness, who was bright, funny, an attentive husband, and a doting dad to his three young children. He told people he was doing his best to straighten Blaney out, even taking him to church on Good Friday so he could make his Easter duty.[24]

Still, Fergy gave an unvarnished answer to a reporter who asked what would likely happen to Blaney after the trial: "Someday, when this is all over, he's going to sit in his car, turn on the motor and that'll be the end of him."[25]

Fergy's gruesome hunch came true more quickly than he expected. Neighbors said Richie Blaney routinely looked in the trunk and under the hood of his car to make sure enemies hadn't planted stolen goods there to get him arrested, but, for some reason, he skipped it on his 27th birthday on July 27, 1961.

He woke up late that afternoon, read *Anatomy of a Murder*, ate two eggs, and walked outside in his ironed Bermuda shorts, perfect attire for an 85-degree day with a light breeze. He waved to his three-year-old neighbor, Brenda Kanefsky, and slid into his two-tone sedan.

When he turned the key, he likely had no idea someone had stowed three sticks of dynamite under the hood. The sticks were thoughtfully packed to force the explosion up instead of out toward the rowhomes.

They performed exactly according to plan, breaking Blaney's left leg and jettisoning all 219 pounds of him into different parts of the back seat.

Next door to the Blaneys, retired police detective Ed Byrns had fallen asleep waiting for *American Bandstand*, a popular national dance show broadcast from a studio in West Philadelphia starting at 3 p.m. He was awakened by the sound of his front window shattering.

Inside the Blaney home, Richie's 24-year-old wife, Joanne, holding four-month-old Joseph in her arms, was bending to sit down on the couch when she felt the house tremble. She said she knew instantly because they had received telephone threats.

She ran outside screaming, the baby still in her arms. She cried, "They killed him. They killed him." Pieces of the car lay in the street and her husband's nude body landed in a twisted heap on the back seat. The papers said he was blown to eternity. Police recovered his belt and one shoe.[26]

Daniel Rubenstine dashed outside just in time to watch the hood from Blaney's car fly up over the rowhouse roofs. Firemen used an aerial ladder to retrieve it from the roof of 5945 Alma Street, more than a football field away.[27]

One woman was so flabbergasted she called the fire department and reported that a man exploded.

Neighbors poured out of their homes. One found a car part embedded in the front wall of her brick home. Soon 100 policemen would be on the scene.

Detectives allowed a *Daily News* photographer to shoot a page-one picture of Blaney's lifeless arm extended from the door of his mangled car. It showed his wristwatch, which was still ticking.

Glass as fine as sugar covered the blacktop street. A phalanx of housewives came out with their brooms to sweep it up.[28]

Blaney's demise put Fergy's case in a tailspin. One reporter called him the angriest man in Philadelphia.

Despite his loss of the Blaney brothers, the first trials went Fergy's way.

Jurors convicted Poulson of burglary on March 24. Berkery and Staino were convicted on May 9. When the Staino verdict was read, Reis dabbed her heavily made-up eyes with a pink hanky.

Reis pulled up to the Pottsville courthouse in a black limousine for the first day of her trial—but she arrived 50 minutes late. The standing-room–only crowd inside the courtroom fell silent when she entered in a tan summer dress cinched at the waist and white spike heels.

Reis wore a new outfit every day of her 20-day trial. That got tongues wagging among the female jurors, who were paid $9 a day. She was sometimes spotted shopping in Pottsville stores during the lunch breaks.

Reporters described her outfits daily—"a white sheath that looked as if it had been sprayed on" and "a tight white skirt with a tighter white sweater."[29]

Reis professed not to be interested in making news. "I always wanted to be a headliner, not a headline," she quipped.[30]

John Lavelle, her lawyer, turned the prosecutor's claim that Reis had masterminded the burglary on its head. He said Bing Miller, the government's witness, was the brains of the operation. He told the jurors Miller pinned the blame on Reis to get even with her. Miller was fuming that she threw him over after he lavished more than $150,000 in gifts on her, Lavelle said. He pointed out that Reis had never been to Pottsville, but Miller was a native. Reis didn't know Rich, but Miller had been inside his house. Reis didn't know where the safe was, but Miller did.[31]

He cast Reis as a thrifty gal who saved her salary. Her estranged husband testified he helped her count a hatbox full of money she saved to the tune of $29,950. Her stepfather testified she left $12,000 in an old valise stashed in the boiler room of his Flushing, New York, home. And Lavelle pointed out that she could have paid for the Celebrity Room three times over with just the money Bing Miller gave her.

The prosecutor insisted Reis was implicated up to her neck, but the defense lawyer appealed to the coal country jurors' sense of decency. In his arm-waving, table-pounding, three-hour summation, Lavelle blasted Miller for his "barnyard morality." He knocked Captain Ferguson for already taking $100 from a detective magazine writing about the case. He christened Richie Blaney "the biggest liar to come down the pike since Hitler." He called the case "a bushel of nothing."[32]

The state had one glaring problem with its case. Witnesses claimed $478,000 was taken from Rich's safe, but the victim himself testified 11 times that he never kept more than $4,000 in the safe. To convince them to take the word of the perpetrators over the word of the victim, one prosecutor told the jurors, "Mr. Rich is the second-biggest employer in Pottsville, but that doesn't make him the second-most-honest man."[33]

The male jurors seemed unable to take their eyes off Reis. All five female jurors voted against her. The forewoman broke out in tears when they couldn't reach a verdict. The trial ended in a hung jury.[34]

Reis's second trial opened on St. Patrick's Day, 1964. To mark the holiday, she wore Kelly green eyeshadow. Reis, known for frequently glancing at her first jury of seven men and five women with her big, almond-shaped hazel eyes, may have noticed her second jury was composed of seven women and five men. They found her guilty in just over seven hours.[35]

Like the other convicted defendants, Reis appealed.

Appeals dragged on until a higher court quashed one of the confessions. By 1969, more than 30 prosecution witnesses had died, been killed, moved, or refused to testify again.

The next year, the prosecutors announced they were dropping all charges. The three trials took 10 years, cost $50,000, and netted nothing.

Fergy's unit was disbanded in 1970. He was reassigned after 51 years with the police department.[36]

Soon after, he retired. On his way out, he reminded reporters that he still had the most arrests of any officer in city history.[37]

A newsman reached out to Lillian Reis for a comment on the downfall of her old nemesis. Reis called Fergy "a good cop" and a "nice old guy."[38]

After a brief stint working for a 34-year-old private investigator, Ferguson died in 1971.

He landed back in the headlines quickly, though.

In 1972, his will revealed he had a secret daughter with a beauty parlor owner from the coal country town of Mahanoy City, 13 miles from Pottsville.

Fergy, who had somehow amassed a sizable real estate portfolio on a detective's salary, bequeathed the bulk of his estate to his coal country daughter, 21-year-old Mary Sally Ferguson.

His wife and son in Philadelphia were floored. "I don't know a thing," Rosalie Ferguson told reporters.[39]

Lillian Reis and Ralph Staino, who eventually married, moved to Florida briefly. There they met actor Robert Conrad, star of television's *Wild Wild West*. Conrad wanted to make a movie about Reis's life. Natalie Wood and Lynda Carter, then TV's Wonder Woman, were mentioned for the lead role. It was never made.[40]

Another filmmaker produced a low-budget movie based on Lil's life. *The Block* premiered in 1964. The ads promised "the most sordid story ever to hit the screen." The tagline said, "This is not a travelogue, so don't

Lillian Reis's provocative dancing drew crowds to her club at 254 South Juniper Street. She once was arrested for doing the twist fully clothed.

bring the kiddies. See it all. The violence, the death and the famous Miss Reis do her even more famous version of the twist."[41]

Reis and Staino stayed together 54 years despite long periods of physical separation. When he was imprisoned for 21 years on federal racketeering charges, he sent her three cards and a letter every day. When he hid out from the police in the Dominican Republic, he lived with another woman but he wrote a diary detailing how much he missed Lil: "Boy, do I miss Lillian. Not just for sex. For compassion. For understanding. For conversation. For, above all, love."

He was at her side when she died at age 79, following a stroke, lung disease, and a kidney transplant. "Even when she was dying, she was beautiful," he told a reporter. "She was the love of my life, and we really were dear lovers. She was the most beautiful woman that I've ever seen in my life. She was the most gorgeous thing that was ever in Philadelphia."[42]

The central question about the haul at 1801 Mahantongo Street— was it $3,000 to $4,000 or $478,000?—was finally answered in 1964.

That's when John B. Rich pleaded no contest to three charges of evasion of personal income taxes for the years of 1957, 1958, and 1959.[43]

CHAPTER TWO

The Maid Did It

HARRY WODLINGER, PLAYING HOOKY FROM HIS CENTER CITY OFFICE ON the afternoon of December 7, 1944, bounded up the 12 cement steps to his house on leafy North Camac Street with a package in his hand.[1]

He was making haste to drop off the meat his wife wanted for dinner and snatch his golf clubs so he could play a round with his buddy Irving Weingrad, who was waiting in the car at the curb.

As he climbed the steep steps, an alarm went off in Wodlinger's head. He spotted his front door ajar on a day when the temperature never climbed above 46.

Then he heard Susie, his mop-haired terrier, barking furiously in the basement. The small white pup usually had the run of the house.

The insurance man wasn't certain whether his wife, Freeda, was home. When he had telephoned more than an hour earlier, she told him she was leaving shortly to volunteer at a local settlement house.

He zipped through the house, calling his wife's name. He found her in the dark upstairs bathroom.

The attractive brunette was sprawled on the floor in a pool of her own blood. The room was a fight scene. Her blouse had been ripped off. The strap of her slip had been severed. Her skirt was blood-spattered. Bottles were upended on a shelf. The bathroom curtain rods had been knocked off the wall.

Wodlinger called for a doctor. Then he ran to the car to get Weingrad. They called the police.

After she murdered Freeda Wodlinger, Corrine Sykes walked down these steps and looked for a cab. Minutes later, Harry Wodlinger bounded up them looking for his golf clubs. He found his 44-year-old wife in a pool of blood.
AUTHOR PHOTO

The first detective on the scene said the evidence showed a terrible struggle. Freeda Wodlinger was likely taken by surprise, but she fought hard. The gashes on her hands indicated she probably tried to wrest the large blade from her attacker. The little finger on her left hand was dismembered.[2]

Her attacker tore Freeda's platinum wedding ring and a two-carat diamond from her ring finger. Stab wounds dotted her head, her neck, her face, and her chest. One of the chest cuts punctured a lung. The deepest was directly above her heart. It looked as if her attacker had twisted the blade inside her.[3]

Police told reporters whoever robbed the 45-year-old housewife hacked her unmercifully with a large kitchen knife before fleeing. Such a knife had been missing from its drawer in the Wodlinger kitchen for two days.

Along with the victim's rings, a string of pearls, and $100 cash, the Wodlinger's new live-in maid was missing. Harry Wodlinger last saw her when she had prepared his breakfast that morning.[4]

At 1:50 p.m. the only thing left of her was a discarded purse. Inside it, police found a Social Security card in the name of Heloise T. Parker and 10 help-wanted ads. One was the Wodlingers'.

The search for the maid took off.

Mrs. Benjamin Ginns, who lived next door at 6303, told police she had been preparing lunch for her six-year-old son Robert in her kitchen, directly opposite the Wodlinger bathroom, but she heard no noise, struggle, or outcry. She thought it might be because her storm windows were installed for winter.

Mrs. Ginns did notice the Wodlingers' new housemaid hanging wash on the clothesline earlier that morning. She described her to police as "a little slip of a thing."[5]

Mrs. Ginns said Freeda Wodlinger was overjoyed that she was able to hire the young African American maid just two days earlier. Mrs. Ginns had her own problems with housemaids, but none as dire. She recently had hired Myrtle Voughs, a house robber known to police as 30-Minute Gertie. Voughs stole some rings and cash.[6]

The Wodlingers' maid was nowhere to be found as four uniformed policemen carried the body out of the two-and-a-half-story white stucco home and carefully negotiated the two flights of steps to the street.

Freeda Wodlinger hadn't lived long enough to catch the upbeat war headlines on the front page of Philadelphia's *Evening Bulletin* that afternoon. She never got to read that American tanks were at last rolling into French border towns and routing Germans from the streets.

She missed the story about Mrs. Marie Scafidi of Warnock Street birthing twins 81 hours apart—a boy at 8:15 a.m. Monday and a girl at 5:12 p.m. Wednesday.[7] They were the talk of the town until Mrs. Wodlinger made front-page headlines of her own the next day: "Broker's Wife Slain in Oak Lane Home."[8]

Police figured Freeda Wodlinger had returned early from walking her Sealyham terrier and found her maid ransacking her jewelry drawer. They believed the young woman attacked her boss with the kitchen knife, and the housewife tried to wrest the blade away.

The maid's backstory began to unravel the next day when the real Heloise T. Parker saw her name in the paper and appeared voluntarily at a neighborhood police station. She said her Social Security card had been stolen about a week earlier. Police theorized the killer used it to register with the employment agency.

Meanwhile, a small death notice was placed in the *Evening Bulletin* for Freeda Wodlinger, who, it said, died suddenly.

It was Wodlinger's 14-year-old daughter who gave police the tip that broke the case. Just hours after her mother's body was found, leafing through a police photo book, the girl spotted a mugshot that her father had flipped past. She pointed to 20-year-old Corrine Sykes and said, "Daddy, that's her on the side view. I'm positive."[9, 10]

Sykes landed in the book because she had made off with some jewelry while working as a maid at another address. She served 11 months in the county jail.

The teenager's identification was corroborated by Det. Albert Connors, who had worked through the night, dusting for prints inside the murder house. He found them on a small alarm clock, on two tin cans, on a tomato juice glass, on a plate of fish in the refrigerator, and on the maid's white-enameled bedroom door. They all tallied with the fingerprint record for Sykes.[11]

Then, the observant teenager gave police another lead. She recalled passing down the hall when Sykes was on the telephone to her boyfriend. She overheard Sykes say, "I'll be seeing you, Jaycee." That name was familiar to city police.

After 17 arrests, small-time bootlegger Jaycee Kelly knew a thing or two about talking to police. He gave them the address where Sykes was hiding out. He told them where they might find some of the jewels. And, when they found her blood-soaked sweater at his house, he told them he had no idea she had been involved in a murder when she changed clothes there. "News to me," he said.[12]

Twenty-year-old Corrine Sykes went to the electric chair despite her attorney's pleas that she had a mental age of eight. Police found several help-wanted ads in the purse she left behind at the murder scene, including the ad her victim placed.

They arrested the "little slip of a thing." She was barely 100 pounds and a smidge over five feet tall.

Detectives wondered how Sykes would have the strength to thrust the knife into Freeda Wodlinger's heart. Attorney Michael Saxe, Freeda's brother, told reporters, "No one can convince me she did not have a man to help her in the murder."[13]

Autopsy records are still sealed, but the victim may not have been much larger than Sykes. Her newspaper headshot shows a thin, attractive face, and, in an era when men were usually larger than their wives, her husband Harry was just five feet, six inches tall and 150 pounds.[14]

Within three hours of Corrine Sykes's arrest, police had a confession.[15] Soon they had several from the rattled young woman whose attorney would later say had a mental age of 8. Corrine told police she took the $20-a-week job to rob the house.[16] She said she followed Wodlinger from room to room, holding a knife wrapped in a dust rag behind her back.[17] At one point, she said, she acted alone. At another, she pinned it all on Jaycee Kelly.[18] Police said she also told them, "After I stabbed her, I took the rings off her fingers. I sure like jewels."[19]

Sykes told detectives she gave Kelly a ring, the pearls, and a sable neck piece right after the heist. He denied it. Detectives looked hard at Kelly after they found Sykes's torn and bloody tan skirt and turquoise sweater in his apartment. The blood splatter in the Wodlingers' bathroom told a different story, though, and not one of his fingerprints was at the murder scene.

Kelly stuck to his story that he just employed Sykes as a waitress. He said he paid her $35 a week and $10 went to her mother because she was a widow.[20]

When a reporter visited Sykes's mother's neat red brick and white stone home at 1803 North 24th Street, Almena Sykes was blunt: "Corrine was so tender and mild, but she wasn't very smart, and she didn't use the brains the Lord gave her."[21]

Mrs. Sykes's comment percolated throughout North Philadelphia, the third-largest Black community in the country since the 1920s, when the Great Migration of African Americans from the South sextupled the city's Black population.[22]

African Americans and whites were given pause when word circulated that Sykes's grade school principal had recommended she be institutionalized, but there were no institutions that accepted Black children. Some questioned if Corrine Sykes, who spent four terms in one grade, really made the detailed four-page confession police said she had.

Even Rabbi Louis Wolsey, addressing mourners at Freeda Wodlinger's funeral, reminded the standing-room–only crowd, "How can we say our hands are guiltless so long as slums and ignorance are allowed to exist in the world? This was the work of an insane person who had no knowledge of the world."[23]

Freeda Wodlinger's brother was not as forgiving when he heard police had found the murder weapon encrusted with his sister's hair and blood, wrapped in a dust rag and tucked into the family's baby grand piano. The Wodlingers noticed the knife went missing on Sykes's first day on the job, he said, and they assumed it was mislaid. "But all this time, this beast had it in her possession and killed my sister with it," Saxe said.[24]

Following the slaying, fear seeped across Philadelphia's tonier neighborhoods, where live-in housemaids were in high demand in the days before automatic washers, clothes dryers, and dishwashers. The most desirable were women 20 to 25—around Corrine Sykes's age. They were old enough to know how to cook and clean and young enough to handle heavy lifting. As more reports of sticky-fingered servants surfaced, Mayor Barney Samuel called for stricter rules for employment agencies. That didn't work.[25]

Just as things were getting back to normal, Philadelphians woke up to this headline on May 9: "Crazed Servant Stabs Housewife." The newspapers noted the event unfolded six blocks from the Wodlinger house.

It was the true tale of 38-year-old Mrs. Rose Older, whose 224-pound maid became riled when she heard President Truman proclaim V-E Day on the radio. The maid said something about how he'd never be as good a president as Roosevelt. Then she switched her patter to the Wodlinger murder. She said when Corrine Sykes gets out of jail, "she's going to be the biggest person in this country." With that, she grabbed Mrs. Older, who had been cleaning the electric refrigerator, around the neck. The quick-thinking housewife bit the maid's left hand and broke loose. Her attacker grabbed a kitchen knife and stabbed her once in the head and twice in the neck. Mrs. Older tried to get away through the cellar, with the maid right on her heels. She tripped at the bottom of the steps, and the maid inflicted two more wounds.

Despite being half the size of her attacker, the housewife managed to make it to a side door and escape. She heard the maid screaming behind her, "I'm going to kill you." Mrs. Older got to the safety of a neighbor's house, where she gasped out her story and collapsed. Meanwhile, the maid returned to the Older home, retrieved her coat and hat, and was seen leaving by the front door.

The Olders had hired the murderous maid through an employment agency. She had excellent references. The press reported she had been a pleasant, friendly worker until she went mad.[26]

The *Inquirer* gave the story the same play as its report that the Russian army had found Hitler's body in the ruins of Berlin.

The Sykes case reverberated in Philadelphia's African American community, too, because domestic work was the solid support beam for Black neighborhoods. While unskilled men could be furloughed whenever the economy dipped, a well-to-do housewife would keep a good maid because it was too expensive and too time-consuming to train a replacement.[27]

While some African American professionals displaced in the Great Migration worked as servants in Philadelphia, most maid-matron relationships mirrored the one between Corrine Sykes and Freeda Wodlinger. Wodlinger was the well-traveled stay-at-home wife of a prosperous insurance man. Her brothers were center-city attorneys. She lived in a $6,800 home and spent her spare time doing charity work. Sykes was the maidservant who left school after fourth grade. Her late father, who left school after seventh grade, had come north in the Great Migration and landed a job in the City Reduction Plant, where workers extracted saleable grease and nutrients from food waste.[28] The two women had little in common. Their relationship was transactional.

Into all this stepped Philadelphia native Raymond Pace Alexander, the city's preeminent African American attorney. Alexander had worked as a bootblack, a paperboy, and a dockworker en route to earning degrees

Attorney Raymond Pace Alexander worked until the last hour to stop the execution of Corrine Sykes, but he was unsuccessful. He said she had a mental age of eight.

from Penn and Harvard Law. The *Philadelphia Tribune*, one of the city's Black newspapers, compared him to Abraham Lincoln.[29] Columnist Elijah Hodges called him a bronze Clarence Darrow.[30] Alexander's wife Sadie, who earned an Ivy League doctorate and an Ivy League law degree, was the first African American woman admitted to the Pennsylvania Bar.

Pace Alexander, as he was called, became a pivotal figure in the case. He hadn't planned it that way. Two days after the Wodlinger murder, Alexander sent a condolence note to fellow attorney Michael Saxe, the victim's brother. He said he was shocked and dismayed "any human being could have acted so cruelly towards another woman."[31]

Then, Sykes' family asked Alexander to defend her. At first he declined. He said his heart wouldn't be in it. Eventually, he agreed to serve as one of the 20-year-old's pair of court-appointed attorneys.

The courtroom was so packed for jury selection that Judge Vincent Carroll broke precedent to permit observers to stand along the courtroom's back wall. Jaycee Kelly wedged himself among them. That fact made the next day's papers, along with the news that 300 American planes were dropping the new "firebombs" on the city of Tokyo. There was also an advertisement for the sore throat rub the 10-year-old Dionne quintuplets favored.

From the get-go, Alexander tried to convince the all-white jury that Sykes had a mental age of eight and Kelly was pulling her strings. Sykes testified that Kelly threatened to kill her mother and her sisters if she didn't rob for him.

Judge Carroll interrupted Alexander's defense and overruled his objections. When Alexander got Kelly on the stand, the judge warned Kelly that he had been arrested as an accessory after the fact and advised him not to answer Alexander's questions.

Judge Carroll kept the pressure on Alexander in the courtroom, and, when the attorney returned to his office, hate mail from white citizens awaited him.

On March 14, Philadelphia children were happily playing outside as temperatures finally veered toward spring, but inside the courtroom, Corrine Sykes hung her head and closed her eyes as newly widowed Harry Wodlinger identified the blood-encrusted knife used to kill his wife.

Then a policeman read this stunner from Sykes's signed confession about the last time she saw her boss: "She was lying there, and she seemed to be grunting. I went into a room and took the pearls and the money, and also went to a drawer and took the fur piece."[32]

The next day, when the prosecutor asked point blank if she did it, Sykes's loud moans filled the courtroom and she started to shake. Then, her sister Florence, sitting in the front row, rose partially to her feet and shouted, "Girl, come on. Tell the truth."

When the prosecutor pressed again, Sykes said, "I don't know, sir." Then she collapsed.[33]

The prosecution painted Sykes as a woman smart enough to get a job that paid $20 a week and board, smart enough to deceive her employer, and smart enough to prepare to kill her victim by hiding the knife under a dust rag. Judge Carroll pointed out that Sykes had been convicted of burglary before she met Jaycee Kelly.

Alexander never asked for an acquittal. He asked the jury to consider the case of his client as a social problem and sentence her to life without parole. "Despite the terrible features of the crime, shocking as they are, if the only penalty is to strap that child to the electric chair, we have not advanced far from the Dark Ages," he said.[34]

The jury took five hours and one minute to return a guilty verdict punishable by death.[35]

Sykes stood at the bar, seemingly stunned. Then, without a sound, she fainted to the floor.

The odds of a young woman being sent to the electric chair seemed so slim before the trial began that one of the city's African American newspapers had run this headline to allay fears: "Death Penalty Unlikely for Maid in Murder Case."

Only one woman had been electrocuted in Pennsylvania history. In 1931, "Iron Irene" Schroeder went to the chair for slaying a state policeman while fleeing the scene of a grocery store holdup.

The 22-year-old waitress was also known as "the Blonde Tiger."

Six other women had been sentenced to die in the chair, but all eventually got off with life, even a woman who murdered her own baby.[36]

So, on sentencing day, when the usually passive Sykes heard Judge Carroll say the words "the application of the current of electricity shall continue until you are dead," she emitted a piercing scream and fell to the floor. Two court attendants picked her up and carried her, kicking and fighting, out of the courtroom.[37]

Alexander sought a new trial based on the prosecution withholding evidence that Jaycee Kelly burned Mrs. Wodlinger's fur piece as well as on prejudicial remarks allegedly made by Judge Carroll.

A common pleas judge brushed off Alexander's filing with, "If she had gotten her just desserts, she would have been tried in January and executed in February. No one but a cold-blooded murderess could have plotted and executed such a fiendish crime."

The Pennsylvania Supreme Court ruled Kelly's action did not prove he was involved in the slaying, and the justices ruled it was acceptable for the trial judge to inject his opinion.[38]

Alexander won four gubernatorial reprieves, but it was becoming evident he couldn't save his client's life.

Elijah Hodges, top columnist for an African American city newspaper, wrote that Alexander "covered himself with lasting glory" for his work on the case, but he had two strikes against him at the outset: "First, a colored woman accused of murdering a white woman. Second, the evidence against her."

"His masterful conduct of the case merits the gratitude of the whole race," the columnist wrote.[39]

Alexander made an eleventh-hour plea to the governor. The US Supreme Court refused to hear the case. He sent a heartfelt letter saying his client, with a mental age of eight, was released from prison with no support and she landed in a world she was incapable of negotiating.

That news landed on page three of the *Inquirer*, under a story about a Lawrence, New York, woman who collapsed and died on her way up the aisle on her wedding day and was buried in her wedding dress.[40] The Sykes case was still front-page news to the *Evening Bulletin*, but the item about Alexander's poignant plea was shoehorned between a news story on the Federal Bureau of Investigation arrest of three former servicemen who took A-bomb photos and a large photo of a smiling toddler who stood to inherit $10 million after the death of her mother.

Almena Sykes visited turreted Moyamensing Prison to pray with her daughter on Friday, October 11. She found Corrine in good spirits.

Mrs. Sykes didn't listen to the radio or read the papers on Sunday, October 13. She said she was afraid to see any news that the governor refused to stay Corrine's execution, scheduled for the next day.

Mrs. Sykes did implore Ruth Rolen, a reporter for the *Philadelphia Tribune*, to call the governor on Corrine's behalf. Rolen wrote a column explaining that she knew the last-minute call would be useless, but she made it to give solace to a sobbing mother. "She was still trying to save her child," Rolen wrote.[41]

Corrine left her cell at Moyamensing early Sunday for the six-hour ride west to rural Rockview Penitentiary, home of "Old Smokey," the state's electric chair. The sedan that carried her, with a prison matron, a guard, and two state policemen, blew a tire en route, so it was almost 3 p.m. when they drove up the long prison driveway. Corrine was taken to a special cell, where she asked to meet with the prison chaplain.

Her last meal was a chicken dinner prepared in the warden's own kitchen. She made no special requests.

She was spared the customary head shaving. As with Schroeder, officials removed the hair only from the small section in the back of her head where the electrodes would be placed.

About 11:30 p.m., an hour before she was scheduled to die, Sykes asked a matron to write a letter to her mother. In it, she promised to be brave. She also revealed whether she was guilty, but her mother said she would show the letter to no one except her Baptist pastor.[42]

Meanwhile, close friends and family members were heading to 1803 North 24th Street in the dark to gather for prayer at Almena Skyes's house as Corrine was led to the electric chair 220 miles to the west.

As they prayed in Philadelphia, Corrine walked the stretch that inmates at Rockview call "the last mile." She wore a gray flannel prison dress with a white pinstripe, bobby socks, and brown shoes. She had gained almost 10 pounds since her arrest, but she moved briskly. Chaplain C. F. Lauer led her into the small gray death room at 12:28 a.m.[43]

Taking her seat in the electric chair, Corrine seemed to pay little attention to the preparations for her electrocution, but she carefully scanned the faces of the six official witnesses and the four reporters assigned to cover her death.

She listened to the chaplain as he softly intoned the 23rd Psalm. Then she lowered her eyes and waited silently. She made no final statement. The only sign of nerves was her tightly clenched fists.[44]

She was strapped into the chair at 12:31 a.m. The 2,000-volt charge traveled through her body. The *Philadelphia Afro-American* reported that she jerked convulsively against the straps that held her, and Dr. R. E. Carrier examined her and ordered another contact. She was pronounced dead at 12:37 a.m.[45]

The headline in the *News Herald* in rural Franklin, Pennsylvania, was "Negress, 22, Is Electrocuted." The state capital's *Harrisburg Telegraph* put it on page 11: "Housemaid Pays Supreme Penalty in Knife Slaying."

The front page of the *Daily Item* in Sunbury, Pennsylvania, blared, "Negress, 22, Dies Calmly in Chair at State Prison: Philadelphia Domestic Convicted for Brutal Slaying of Employer Tight-Lipped at Death." The *Philadelphia Afro-American* headline was "Corrine Sykes Dies in Electric Chair, First Woman Executed in Fifteen Years."

The death certificate listed the cause of death as judicial execution.

The doorbell at Almena Sykes's home started ringing as soon as word came that the execution went off as scheduled. Mrs. Sykes, wearing a red flowered dress, thanked friends for stopping by in a steady, almost cheerful voice. She said she felt good because her daughter accepted God and went bravely.

"We all have to go one way or the other. The only difference is the time and place and how," she told people. "Death has been on the job a long time, and he hasn't missed out yet."

She told a reporter she felt very sorry for the Wodlingers: "I know how they must feel. But, if there is an empty chair at their home now, there is one at mine too now."

Her only resentment was reserved for Jaycee Kelly: "Corrine's father died six months before this thing happened, and I feel that, had he been alive, this would never have happened," she said. "Corrine was young. She put her faith in Kelly. He turned out not to be a man and let her down. But we all make mistakes. She just paid very dearly for hers."[46]

Florence Matthews, one of Mrs. Sykes's other daughters, was awaiting sentencing for aiding her husband in a jailbreak.

Mrs. Sykes arranged a private funeral service for Corrine that Thursday, but she did not attend. She said she wanted to "remember Corrine as I saw her alive." The sole close relative among the 40 mourners was Helen Allen, one of Corrine's sisters. About 400 people stood outside, according to a story in the *Baltimore Afro-American*.[47]

The next day's major city newspapers carried dozens of help-wanted ads for live-in maids. Most required excellent references.

Corrine Sykes's execution and Freeda Wodlinger's murder still divide Philadelphians. Many people believe a white man made a deathbed confession, but there are no newspaper reports to confirm that, according to a *Philadelphia Tribune* reporter who traced all the rumors for a 1950 story. [48]

A piece in the *Philadelphia Tribune*, one of the city's two African American papers, discussed the deathbed-confession reports in 1950: "During the fall, a report swept the city that a radio commentator announced a white man had confessed to the slaying of Mrs. Wodlinger, and Corrine had died an innocent girl."

The *Tribune* reporter said some people remembered hearing it and other people said someone else had told them about it. He checked with the most frequently named radio station. A spokesman said there was no mention of Sykes or Wodlinger at all.

The rumors swept the city again, but in a different guise, according to the *Tribune*: "This time the account of the confession of a man on his deathbed was supposed to have been printed in a daily newspaper in very small type. Again, there were those few who said they had actually read the article. And, again, there were numbers who had talked to someone who read it."

Again, the *Tribune* checked the newspapers and called the proper authorities, but no story turned up.

The reporter asked Raymond Pace Alexander if he had heard of a deathbed confession. Alexander called the report "silly."[49]

Chapter Three

Willie Sutton, the Making of a Folk Hero

One victim said watching one of Willie Sutton's robberies was like being at the movies, except the usher has a gun. The rail-thin elegant dresser elevated bank robbery to an art form with his clockwork precision and icy cool execution.[1]

Sutton arrived in Philadelphia as a public enemy in 1933, but he left as a folk hero in 1947.

Three daring prison breaks made Sutton famous. Two of them happened in Philadelphia.

He tunneled out of maximum-security Eastern State on Fairmount Avenue in broad daylight in 1945. Two years later, in a blinding snowstorm, he climbed the three-story-high stone wall surrounding the maximum security Holmesburg Prison on Torresdale Avenue.

The bank robberies that got him into prison were as carefully planned as the jailbreaks that got him out.

He entered one bank through the skylight. He robbed another disguised as a mailman. He posed as a Western Union messenger to pull off a daring $100,000 gem robbery at a well-trafficked jewelry store in broad daylight.

He always had a cigarette or a stick of chewing gum in his month. He carried a pistol or a Thompson submachine gun to heists, because he said you can't rob a bank on charm or personality,[2] but, at the end of his career, he told a reporter the guns were never loaded because he was afraid someone might get hurt.[3] He said he'd abort a job and leave the dough behind if a woman screamed or a baby cried.[4]

Sutton, a New Yorker, learned makeup tricks backstage at Broadway theaters while waiting for his chorus girl dates. He rented costumes from a theatrical supplier. He once sent himself a telegram so he'd have a fresh Western Union envelope for a ruse as a telegraph messenger.[5]

His most publicized robberies took place in the Depression-wracked 1930s, after millions of honest Americans lost their life savings in bank collapses and public sentiment against bankers was at an all-time high. His cavalier attitude and clever lines led reporters to dub him "the Babe Ruth of bank robbers."[6]

The quote that cinched Sutton's fame was actually a misquote. When asked why he robbed banks, he purportedly brilliantly responded, "Because that's where the money is." Sutton maintained the reporter made it up. He allowed that the quote did sound like something he'd say, but he was adamant that he never said it.

Sutton said he planned capers for the sheer thrill of it. He said he once robbed a bank when he had $30,000 in his pocket—the equivalent of $460,000 today.[7]

The FBI used several photos of Sutton to track him after his escapes. After one escape, Sutton underwent plastic surgery and wondered if he looked different enough. He and a friend visited a New York City post office to see how much the photo on the FBI's Most Wanted poster looked like him.
COURTESY OF FEDERAL BUREAU OF INVESTIGATION

"I was more alive when I was inside a bank, robbing it, than at any other time in my life," he wrote in one of his two autobiographies. "I enjoyed everything about it so much that one or two weeks later I'd be out looking for the next job."[8]

Next to holdups, Sutton said he'd rather read than do anything else. He read Adam Smith and Oscar Wilde, Herman Wouk's *The Caine Mutiny* and Bishop Fulton J. Sheen's *Peace of Soul*. He quoted Voltaire. He explored the theories of psychologists Sigmund Freud, Carl Jung, and Karl Menninger. Arthur Schopenhauer, a German philosopher who wrote of ways to overcome the painful human condition, was a favorite. He loved *The Wandering Jew* by Eugène Sue so much that when he turned the last of its 1,200 pages, he turned back to the first page and started over.[9]

Sutton was known as a master of disguise and a gentlemanly bandit. He was also, prison wardens discovered, an accomplished escape artist.

He landed in Sing Sing three times, and, just before Christmas 1932, he sawed his way out of an "escape-proof" cell there. His freedom was fleeting. Fifteen months later, he was back in cuffs following a machine-gun robbery at Philadelphia's ornate red-brick Corn Exchange Bank at Second and Chestnut Streets.

He was sentenced to 25 to 50 years in a cold plaster cell at Eastern State Penitentiary on Fairmount Avenue. In the next nine years, he would plan five escapes.

Eastern State Penitentiary was once the most famous and most expensive prison in the world. It had running water and central heat before the White House. Opened in 1829, it was part of a controversial movement to rehabilitate inmates through labor and solitary confinement. Up to 10,000 tourists a year came from around the world, either to view the building's innovative spokes-of-a-wheel design or to observe a new Quaker-rooted method of invoking penitence through solitary reflection. Charles Dickens, the Marquis de Lafayette, and Alexis de Tocqueville were among the visitors.

After his visit, Dickens knocked Eastern's "hopeless solitary confinement." He called it wrong and cruel.[10] Prisoners had little contact with guards, who delivered meals through small feed doors. They exercised in individual yards where they saw no one. On rare trips outside their cells, they wore heavy hoods so they could not communicate with others.

Solitary confinement was officially abandoned in 1913, but the administration remained unenlightened. One night the warden got drunk and shot up a cellblock.[11]

Prisoners' cells were originally designed to resemble chapels, with 20-inch-thick white masonry walls and high arched ceilings. They were, by the time Sutton arrived 105 years later, timeworn, clammy, and sometimes fetid.

When guards slid the heavy one-and-a-half-inch outer door over the bars of a cell, only one ray of sun could shine through the narrow slip of a skylight in the 10-foot-high ceiling. The floor was concrete. A spigot and a toilet occupied one corner. Sutton spent the entirety of World War II in lockup there, but not because he never tried to leave.

He attempted five escapes—swimming nude through sewers, hoisting himself through a skylight, tunneling 100 feet under the prison yard, and having friends attempt to bust him out on two occasions.

In 1941, Sutton put his prison art classes to use. He made a mold of his own face and hand and painted them in his likeness. With an assist from a prisoner who worked in the barber shop, he was able to add real brown hair, eyebrows, and eyelashes. He tested the dummy before the aborted escape, hiding in a corner of his cell while the night guard passed with his flashlight. The guard stopped momentarily, looked, and continued on his way. The escape was aborted, but the dummy was so realistic that guards later said Sutton missed his calling. He should have been a sculptor.

After Sutton was transferred out in 1945, a prison official secreted the head away for himself. Seventy-six years later, the man's grandson took his treasure on TV's *Antiques Roadshow*. Appraiser James Supp set the probable value at $2,500 to $3,500. He called the head a "masterpiece."[12]

Between D-Day and V-E Day, while other Americans were riveted by the spectacular events of World War II in Europe, Sutton and 11 other prisoners were secretly digging a 100-foot tunnel out of Eastern State Penitentiary.

Clarence "Kliney" Klinedinst, a prison scavenger who could have been a stunt double for a young Frank Sinatra, designed the tunnel and began digging it from his cell. Eventually, he and Sutton recruited 10 other prisoners who would slip behind the false panel Kliney had painted to match his cell walls, and they'd scrape away at the dirt with spoons and flattened cans. They filled their pockets with the excavated dirt and discreetly scattered it in the prison yard. They constructed a brightly lit, ventilated passageway under the 30-foot-high prison walls to the street.

Sutton once said if you gave Kliney two weeks, he could get you Ava Gardner, and, if you gave him a year, he could get you out of prison.[13]

The tunnel complete, the prisoners slipped into Kliney's cell through sawed bars on their way to breakfast on April 3, 1945. They removed the plaster panel and squeezed into the tunnel. The length was just 100 feet—a little less than the length of three yellow school buses—but there was a 12-foot drop because the prison wall extended 9 feet belowground. It looked like they were successful as they scrambled out of the hole just inches beyond the 10-foot-thick prison wall.

Sutton remembered seeing the blue skies as he climbed out of the opening, but, as luck would have it, their brazen daylight escape was quickly foiled. Two beat cops who happened to be walking to a corner police box from different directions that morning were thunderstruck to see prisoners suddenly emerging from a hole near the corner of 22nd Street and Fairmount Avenue.[14]

Sutton was halfway out of the hole when he saw them. The police were so stunned that they did not draw their guns until three prisoners were already on the run. Sutton, soaking wet and covered with mud, began running down on Fairmount Avenue. The police ignored the other men popping out of the hole like gophers and took out after him.[15]

Police cornered him in front of a factory after a helpful citizen shouted his whereabouts. Sutton was about to make a run for it when a prowl car on a routine patrol rounded the corner. He was caught in 180 seconds. "All I could think was, 'Oh shit, shit, shit, shit,'" he wrote later.[16]

For his months of work, Kliney won three hours of freedom. Only two escapees managed to break free, and both were recaptured within seven weeks.

Willie Sutton and his fellow escapees were wet and muddy when they were captured minutes after climbing out of the 100-foot tunnel they spent months digging. Sutton was captured in 180 seconds. Later, he wrote, "All I could think was, 'Oh shit, shit, shit, shit.'"

Angry guards filled the tunnel with ashes and covered the entrance with concrete.

Sutton, Kliney, and most of their crew were eventually transferred to Holmesburg Prison on Torresdale Avenue in Northeast Philadelphia. There, Sutton's legend was guaranteed when they pulled off the first successful escape since the prison walls were completed in 1894.[17]

On February 10, 1947, the convicts lashed two 20-foot ladders together with copper wire and rope made of mop strands. Entering the prison yard in the 3 a.m. darkness, they propped the ladders against the 35-foot-tall stone wall that ringed the prison. When a guard shined a searchlight on him, Sutton, wearing a guard's coat, hollered, "It's okay! It's all right. It's an emergency!"[18] The guards, whose views were obscured by heavy snow, did not immediately sound the alarm.

The escapees jumped into a milk truck and forced the driver to speed them away from the prison. On the way, they each grabbed a bottle of milk and toasted their escape. When the driver complained his boss would dock him for the missing milk, Sutton passed him a $5 bill.[19]

The *Philadelphia Inquirer* let readers know that all five of the convicts who broke out were veteran escapees. It dubbed them "troublesome, truculent badmen."[20] One was David Aiken, who had become Philadelphia's first car thief in 1913.[21]

FBI Director J. Edgar Hoover fumed over the headline-garnering escape and Sutton's swelling popularity.[22] Average Joes were rooting for him. Tabloid readers eagerly followed his exploits. When he appeared in newsreels, moviegoers applauded.

Even Sutton didn't understand his new status as a folk hero. "Hell, I was a professional thief. I wasn't trying to make the world better for anybody except myself," he wrote later.[23]

An incensed Hoover placed Sutton on the bureau's new Ten Most Wanted Fugitives list on March 20, 1950, along with a kidnapper, several murderers, a mail-train robber, a member of the Barker Gang, and a man who had stuffed his strangled wife's body into a steamer trunk.

Despite his picture hanging in every post office, Sutton hitchhiked back to his native Brooklyn and managed to live undetected around the corner from a police station there for five years.

He chose a Puerto Rican neighborhood where residents paid less attention to the standard English-language newspapers. One of the skills listed on his Wanted poster was fluent Spanish. He took classes in prison and practiced late into the night.

On St. Patrick's Day, 1949, Sutton stood on Fifth Avenue in Manhattan, watching the parade from the sidelines despite the manhunt.[24]

After he underwent plastic surgery to make his nose less recognizable, he and a friend went to the post office to view his Wanted poster and see how different he looked.[25]

The FBI posters were routinely mailed to police stations and post offices as directed, but, because Sutton was a meticulous dresser, his also went to clothing stores and tailor shops.[26]

He might have ordered his shirts under any of his favorite aliases: Richard Courtney, Lee Holland, or Richard Loring.

Arnold Schuster, a 23-year-old suit salesman, pored over the Wanted posters mailed to his father's clothing store, so, when he spotted Sutton on a downtown subway on February 18, 1952, he recognized him and trailed him. Schuster flagged down two police officers, the first step in pinching Sutton after his five years on the lam.[27]

Two officers interviewed Sutton briefly, but he convinced them his name was Charles Gordon, and he had a car registration to match. Thinking it was just a close shave, Sutton went back to installing a battery in his car while the officers returned to the station. When a suspicious detective heard the story, though, he instructed the pair to bring Mr. Gordon to the police station. When the officers returned, Sutton had a .32 automatic lying against his stomach in a holster, but he chose not to use it. At the police station, he kept up the Charles Gordon charade until the fingerprint man said, "That's Sutton." Without drama, he said, "You're right." Det. Louis Weiner told reporters that Sutton was the nicest crook he ever locked up.[28]

The police held a press conference, crowing about the officers involved in the arrest but forgetting Schuster, who fancied himself an amateur detective and wanted the rumored large award for nabbing Sutton.[29]

It turned out there was no reward, but the apologetic police quickly acknowledged Schuster's central role in the manhunt. It didn't turn out as he had hoped. After the new medium of television cast him as the hero who spotted Sutton, his family got so many threatening phone calls that they had to change their number.[30]

At 9:10 p.m. the next Saturday, when families at home were listening to the radio program *Gangbusters* report the capture of Willie Sutton, Schuster stepped off a crosstown bus and was shot to death on the sidewalk a few yards from his home. Police thought it was a gangland murder because the assailant shot him twice in the groin and drilled a bullet through each eye.[31]

Photographers captured a horrific scene—the impeccably dressed young tipster, wearing a suit and fine topcoat, sprawled on the cement with holes where his eyes were and his blood trickling down the sidewalk.[32]

Willie Sutton was grief stricken. He didn't like being associated with shooting people. He tried to add $10,000 of his savings to the ballooning reward pool for Schuster's killer, but police persuaded him it wouldn't look right. The case went cold for almost two decades.[33]

Police were baffled until gangster Joe Valachi's tell-all book about the Mob was published in 1968. In *The Valachi Papers* he said Mob boss Albert Anastasia saw Schuster accept kudos for the capture on television and said, "I can't stand squealers. Hit that guy."[34]

Anastasia had no connection to Sutton. After he had Schuster killed, Anastasia ordered a hit on the hitman to cover his tracks.

In Lucky Luciano's memoir years later, he implied Schuster's senseless slaying was one reason Anastasia himself was shot in a barber chair in 1957. "Anastasia was really off his rocker," Luciano said.[35]

With Sutton back in the headlines, Meyer Berger, the top human-interest-story writer at the *New York Times*, interviewed the robber's unsuspecting landlady. She told Berger that Sutton was "one nice gentleman" who brought her red roses at Thanksgiving and Christmas. Her only complaint: that one night when she reprimanded him for bringing a woman and a bottle of whiskey to his room.[36]

William Francis Sutton, who spent nearly half his adult life in the clink, was sentenced to 30 to 120 years at New York's Attica State Prison. While he became famous as Willie Sutton, the name law enforcement gave him, his friends there called him by the name he preferred—Bill.[37]

He served nearly 18 years before a judge commuted his sentence for good behavior and bad health on Christmas Eve, 1969. The 68-year-old stickup man, bent with age and ill with emphysema, looked up at the judge and said, "Thank you, Your Honor. God bless you." He cried as he walked out of the courtroom.[38]

Sutton withdrew $12 million from banks during his career, but he had to apply for welfare to pay his rent upon his release from Attica. He told reporters he wouldn't need the welfare checks for long, because he was writing a second book.[39]

He had authorized the best-selling *I, Willie Sutton*, penned by journalist Quentin Reynolds, in prison in the early 1950s, but he donated the proceeds to fight juvenile delinquency, because he was rattled to hear young boys considered him a hero.[40] He said he should never be a role model. "Crime is a sucker's game. I'm speaking as an expert," he said.[41]

In 1970, a bank hired Sutton to tout its new credit card in television ads. By then, he was recognized as the country's most successful bank robber. Major magazines like *Life* and *Reader's Digest* profiled him. Two major publishers offered him book deals.[42]

He penned a second book titled *Where the Money Was* in 1976. In it, he wrote, "I had heard many things about Philadelphia when I was a kid, none of them good."[43]

In 2005, 60 years after Willie Sutton saw the sky during his three minutes of freedom, archaeologists employed a robotic rover and ground-penetrating radar to find Kliney's tunnel and map it.[44]

While the legend of Sutton and Klinedinst still draws tourists to Eastern State, they weren't the prison's most audacious escapees.

The 1927 escape of murderer William Bishie and highway robber William Lynch was totally unexpected. When a phone in one of the prison's sentry towers went on the blink, Bishie and Lynch were dispatched to help.

The duo hit a tower guard with a lead pipe, hurled him off the tower, unfurled a long rope, and descended 40 feet to freedom. Before they exited, they deftly cut the wires to the prison's alarm system.

The guard, who landed on a tiny strip of wet grass, survived.

Bishie fled to Syracuse, New York. Despite his Wanted poster being on file at the police station there, he was hired as a traffic patrolman. He was recaptured in the fall of 1934 when a former friend tipped prison authorities to his whereabouts.[45]

CHAPTER FOUR

Self-Made Widows

A CHUBBY-FACED TAILOR MASTERMINDED THE LARGEST MASS MURDER plot in US history in Philadelphia in the 1930s. His partners in crime were unhappy housewives.

Love potions, hexes, the evil eye, and arsenic sprinkled on spaghetti were standard tools of the arsenic murder ring operating in the heart of South Philadelphia during the Great Depression.

When they ran out of arsenic, the killers resorted to bludgeoning with a sandbag, ill-fated fishing trips, and hit-and-run "accidents." They tried, albeit unsuccessfully, to buy live typhoid germs.

Their goal was to collect life insurance payouts. Police estimated the ring netted nearly $100,000—about $1.9 million today. One stupid move resulted in a dramatic reversal of fortune for the ring leaders in 1938.

When the case broke wide open, the usually quiet corridors of City Hall were filled with fortune-tellers, womanizing witch doctors, and a parade of self-made widows in black dresses.

Every day the newspapers would report a new unimaginable twist or turn in the case. A suspect chewed glass. The judge ordered 70 bodies exhumed. A male suspect took a swing at the jury forewoman. A fortune-teller rose from her seat and began scratching like a cat.

An ample-necked widow tried to hang herself with a small hand-kerchief. An exhumed body had been stuffed with wood shavings. Three suspects were so afraid of getting the evil eye that they cowered from each other in the hallways of City Hall.

When the arsenic murder ring trials opened, the corridors of Philadelphia's ornate City Hall filled with witches, fortune-tellers, and self-made widows in black dresses.
BEYOND MY KEN, WIKIMEDIA COMMONS

And, when detectives arrested a filling station attendant's wife for slowly poisoning her first husband, her rattled second husband told detectives, "I don't know whether I should get a doctor or a lawyer first."

One suspect carried all his worldly possessions into court daily, in a large brown paper bag tucked under his armpit. The prosecution's star witness was on leave from Sing Sing, where he was serving a life sentence for slaying his sweetheart. One suspect matter-of-factly explained that he "cleaned house" for people, meaning he banished the evil spirits residing in their bodies.

The ring's code for killing a man was "We're going to send him to California."

Before it was all over, 23 suspects would be convicted, 15 would serve life sentences, and two cousins would go to the electric chair, one sullen and resigned and the other desperately trying to stand up.[1]

It was the largest murder case in Philadelphia history, so vast that it strained the city's justice system.

When the victim count hit 56, police set up a mammoth, professional sports–size scoreboard to keep track of it all. The *Inquirer* took a photo with an adult woman standing in front of it. It towered over her.[2]

The ring's unravelling began in 1938 with a single counterfeit $10 bill and a dogged detective.

It ran unfettered for six years, though, fattening the wallets of the four ring leaders—Morris "the Rabbi" Bolber, Carina "Witch Woman" Favato, and wily cousins Paul and Herman Petrillo.

Bolber, who described himself as "sort of a psychiatrist," set up a voodooist practice on Seventh Street in 1931. He handed out 2,000 handbills one day and got his first case the next—a young woman who believed her mother-in-law was returning from the dead in the middle of the night to scratch her.[3]

He boasted that 2,000 Philadelphians sought his prescriptions for love, power, money, health, and happiness. He said he could stop a trolley car midblock with his powers.[4]

Bolber, who claimed to have studied under an ancient Chinese sorceress, dispensed love potions, magic charms, and sometimes death powder.[5]

He muttered magic chants over old socks. He told believers to hang fish on their clotheslines in the moonlight or cremate dead birds in their rowhouse furnaces. To stop one man from beating his wife, he set strands from the hubby's hairbrush afire at midnight.[6]

One lawyer called Bolber the fastest talker he had ever met. Bolber called himself the ring's "finger man"—meaning he fingered likely prospects for murder.[7]

Paul Petrillo, a short, bald, nearsighted 47-year-old tailor who combed his salt-and-pepper hair straight back, claimed he could talk with the devil himself.[8]

One woman who had an affair with Paul Petrillo said he was her "demon lover." She believed he could summon God and devils.
SPECIAL COLLECTIONS RESEARCH CENTER, TEMPLE UNIVERSITY LIBRARIES, PHILADELPHIA, PA

Petrillo was a self-professed *fattucchiere*, or male witch. He sold luck charms and magic potions and life insurance policies in his Passyunk Avenue tailor shop. The dapper father of seven was considered the brains of the ring. Despite his marital status and his paunch, he was also considered the ring's Romeo.[9]

Disillusioned housewives flocked to Carina Favato for magic charms to turn their husbands into successful and faithful men. Unbeknownst to them, she slipped small doses of poison in their drinks as she counseled them, just enough to make them ill. Then she would win their confidence by pretending to heal them with witchcraft.[10]

The squat 45-year-old spiritualist threw a party the day her heavily insured stepson died and bought a car after her husband succumbed.[11]

Her English was limited, but her confidence wasn't. When a news photographer tried to snap her photo, she swung a large leather pocketbook in his direction.[12]

Carina "Witch Woman" Favato, one of the arsenic ring leaders, sold housewives charms to turn their husbands into faithful and successful men.
She threw a party the day her heavily insured stepson died.
SPECIAL COLLECTIONS RESEARCH CENTER, TEMPLE UNIVERSITY LIBRARIES, PHILADELPHIA, PA

Even after Herman Petrillo was sentenced to death, he told people he would beat the murder rap and become a Philadelphia detective. He tried to stop the guards whose job it was to strap him into the electric chair.
SPECIAL COLLECTIONS RESEARCH CENTER, TEMPLE UNIVERSITY LIBRARIES, PHILADELPHIA, PA

Herman Petrillo, a slight 40-year-old barber from suburban Langhorne, had a side business as a counterfeiter. He often flashed a big roll of bogus bills. The married father of five wore stylish suits fitted to his five-foot, five-inch frame. He also had a way with the ladies. He was known as the "smoothie" of the ring.[13]

He was the one who passed the counterfeit $10 bill that tipped authorities to the ring's existence.

The role of chance was paramount in the capture of the four key players.

If Herman Petrillo had not used that bogus bill to buy a bag of potato chips that day in May 1938, the early morning of Monday, October 20, 1941, would have unfurled much differently for him. Prison guards probably wouldn't have had to force him back down into Pennsylvania's electric chair while he screamed, whimpered, and struggled to stand.

He did buy the chips at a Frankford taproom that day, though, and, that afternoon, the barkeep took the day's receipts to the bank. The teller eyed one bill skeptically and said, "You've been gypped. It's counterfeit." He asked where the barkeep got it.

Only one customer stood out when the bartender replayed the day in his mind. A short, dark, bald man in a black-and-white checkered suit grabbed a bag of chips and peeled the $10 off a fat roll of bills before he took off in a big maroon sedan.[14]

The description and the counterfeit bill landed on the desk of William Landvoight at the US Secret Service office in Philadelphia. Landvoight recognized the bill as one of the bogus notes flooding Philadelphia that spring. He assigned an agent to find the man in the maroon sedan.[15]

By chance, about the same time that agent was birddogging Petrillo, about 40 miles to the south, George Myer was being released from jail. Myer hoped to open an upholstery cleaning business on the up-and-up, but he needed a $25 loan to do it. Someone steered him to Herman Petrillo.[16]

Unbeknownst to Myer, Petrillo was part of a six-year-old network of killers-for-profit that had its own doctors, druggists, undertakers, insurance agents, and even a matchmaking service for new arsenic widows.

Its ranks included a soothsayer, a chicken store operator, a mother of five, a moon-faced witch doctor, a University of Pennsylvania veterinary student, a John Hancock Life Insurance agent, an obstetrician who had lost his savings in the 1929 stock market crash, and a woman with two live husbands and three dead ones.

Myer was floored when Petrillo offered him 100 times the amount he requested free and clear, but there was a grim hitch. He showed Myer a heavy 18-inch lead pipe.

Petrillo said he would give Myer $600 in cash or $2,500 in counterfeit bills if he would bludgeon Ferdinand Alfonsi with the pipe and then push the 38-year-old father of two down a flight of stairs. It had to look like an accident, he said, so the victim's buxom 27-year-old wife could collect on a double indemnity insurance policy.[17]

Myer, trying to stay on the right side of the law, went straight to Philadelphia police. They laughed. They suggested he had an overactive imagination.[18]

He visited the Treasury Department's Philadelphia office next. They were skeptical about the murder angle, but they jumped on the counterfeiting information. They asked Myer to introduce their undercover agent to Petrillo.

Convinced the agent was a professional assassin from New York, Petrillo offered him the same deal he had offered Myer. The treasury agent agreed to do the job if Petrillo paid him $2,500 in counterfeit cash.[19]

Then, suddenly, the intended victim was rushed to the city's National Stomach Hospital with an ailment that resembled pneumonia. He wasn't expected to live.

He survived long enough for treasury agents to slip into his hospital room and inquire about life insurance. Alfonsi told them he had no insurance. His friend Herman Petrillo did introduce him to an agent, and he signed some applications, but he received a letter saying he had been rejected. His wife, Stella, read it to him because he couldn't read English.[20]

He had no clue his wife held several policies on his life. They totaled $8,250—more than $150,000 today.[21]

Arsenic poisoning is such an easy way to murder that it's sometimes dubbed "inheritance powder." It's not an easy way to die, though. It disrupts the cell's production of adenosine triphosphate, the molecule that transports energy through the body so it can perform basic tasks.[22]

Victims suffer convulsions, hair loss, muscle cramps, intestinal agony, problems swallowing, excessive sweating, severe joint pain, and impaired nerve function that produces a pins-and-needles sensation in the hands and feet.

While Alfonsi's joints and muscles were seizing up, Herman Petrillo was bellyaching to the undercover agent about long he was taking to die: "We loaded him down with arsenic and he still lives. We can't understand it. The ------ must have nine lives, because we gave him enough arsenic to kill six men."[23]

By the time Ferdinand Alfonsi died, detectives discovered that Stella Alfonsi and Herman Petrillo had been having an affair. They had all the evidence they needed to charge the two with murder. It might have ended there, but chance intervened again.

An insurance investigator happened to spot Petrillo's picture in the paper. He instantly recognized him as the man he had met at Carina Favato's home after the sudden death of her seemingly healthy and heavily insured 17-year-old stepson.

By luck, the investigator was friendly with Det. Lt. Samuel Riccardi, a city homicide detective. He told Riccardi that Favato had insured her stepson for a whopping $13,200 although the boy earned only $6 a week as a baker's helper.[24]

Riccardi, who spoke Italian well enough to serve as an interpreter in a pinch, began putting the pieces together in his mind. He remembered Favato from a case involving witchcraft. He once caught the case of a homeless man who had been killed for insurance in her neighborhood. And he learned three men Favato nursed had died in quick succession.

On a hunch, he asked the district attorney to exhume the stepson's body. Like Myer at the Philadelphia Police Department, Riccardi was laughed out of the DA's office.[25]

After learning that Favato had applied for 18 insurance policies on her stepson, Riccardi tried again. Again, guffaws.[26]

He tried a third time. After another gust of sarcastic laughter, he was given a choice. If he insisted on being pig-headed, he was told, he could sign an affidavit to petition the court for exhumation. Of course, if he were wrong, the Favato family might sue, and he'd be such a laughing-stock he'd probably have to resign from the police department.[27]

He signed the affidavit.

The boy's stomach and liver were loaded with arsenic.[28]

The autopsy was an eye opener. An assistant district attorney realized it was the tip of something big. It would not be easy to prove that a murder-for-profit ring rooted in the Old World *malocchio*, or evil eye, could thrive in the third largest city in the country in the era of radio, instant coffee, and skyscrapers, but Vincent McDevitt was reasonably certain he could do it.

The assistant DA was as indefatigable as Riccardi. He read every poison case that had resulted in an acquittal since 1905. He found they all had two things in common: police didn't protect the exhumed corpses from contamination, and prosecutors didn't prove that less than one-eighth of a teaspoon of arsenic can kill an average-size adult.[29]

McDevitt's team followed strict procedures, and they reexamined dozens of old suicides, suspicious falls, and hit-and-runs. Their zeal created different problems. They ran so many tests that they swamped the city coroner's office, at least until J. Edgar Hoover, director of the FBI, offered his lab to handle the overload.[30]

The broad sweep of the arsenic ring was becoming more apparent. Police traced cases over state lines to Delaware, Connecticut, New York, and New Jersey. Some were reported on the West Coast.

Referring to the dark French folktale about a wealthy man who marries six women and kills them all, Riccardi said that, if all he had heard was true, the arsenic widows case would "put the Bluebeard killings in France in the piker class."[31]

The grand jury returned 28 indictments on May 19, 1939—the largest number in city court history.[32]

That big news was overshadowed by the standing room–only arraignment of Mrs. Rose Carina that day. Headline writers dubbed the thrice-widowed suspect "the kiss of death" and "the rose of death." She had been nabbed by FBI agents that week after spending two months on the run, working incognito in a Lakewood, New Jersey, underwear factory.

Every seat in the courtroom was taken, and the throng of spectators outside was so dense that Carina was nearly separated from the detectives escorting her. Philadelphians wanted to see the woman police said used her charms to woo victims for the ring.

She had been married five times but only two of her spouses survived—the two who refused to buy life insurance.

Her legend had grown with every newspaper mention. One acquaintance described her as "buxom." Her fifth husband told reporters he found her "irresistible." Police called her a "professional widow." Her old neighbors called her "a marvelous cook."

Carina's big brown eyes fell on the impressive crowd outside the courtroom and she said, "My goodness. I must be an awfully important woman! This is some reception!"

Reporters on the lookout for a siren instead observed a short, stout matron enter the courtroom, staring out at them through thick-lensed glasses set on a prominent nose. Her face was heavily made up. She was dressed entirely in black, save the artificial white gardenia on her shape-

Rose Carina was married five times, but only two of her husbands survived—the two who refused to buy life insurance. Reporters, who had been told Carina was irresistable, were sorely disappointed when she appeared in court.
SPECIAL COLLECTIONS RESEARCH CENTER, TEMPLE UNIVERSITY LIBRARIES, PHILADELPHIA, PA

less coat. As the arraignment began, she fidgeted in her seat and bit the nails on her chubby fingers.

One disappointed correspondent described her as the "no-longer-blooming Rose of Death."

That may have been premature. She drove up to court with her latest boyfriend, a Lakewood barber. They had started living together while she was on the run. He knew her as Mary Jonas.[33]

Newspaper subscribers were intrigued to read that soothsayers and love potions and black magic still existed in the city that boasted the sleek new 36-story Philadelphia Saving Fund Society Building, the second tallest air-conditioned high-rise in the country, the one with the 26-foot-high red neon rooftop letters visible for 20 miles at night.[34]

Although you could walk from the bank tower to South Philadelphia in fewer than 40 minutes, the 10-square-mile neighborhood to the south had more connections to 19th-century Italy than it did to center city in 1938. Almost a century before it was home to IKEA, Citizens Bank Park, and Lincoln Financial Field, the peninsula bordered by South Street, the Schuylkill River, and the Delaware would become home to families who had known each other for generations in America and in Italy. Immigrants settled on the same blocks where their *paesani* lived—people from their villages in Italy. Their bankers, lawyers, doctors, priests, undertakers, and fortune-tellers were *paesani*, too.[35]

When the Depression lingered from 1929 to 1941, they shared the same dire prospects too, because South Philadelphia had the highest unemployment in the city. Some blamed the evil eye—bad luck given to you intentionally or unintentionally by someone else.[36]

Believers were on constant watch for small signs they linked to *malocchio*—recurrent hiccups, several people yawning in unison, a person whose eyes were flecked with another color.[37]

Many wore charms shaped like devil's horns or phallic symbols to distract the evil eye. They paid witches to cast spells to keep them safe and help their families prosper. That's how the arsenic murder ring found its victim pool.[38]

They set themselves up as witch doctors and faith healers to gain the trust of hundreds of superstitious immigrants. They tricked some into buying life insurance. To scare others into it, they staged seances and demonstrated the evil eye. They offered disenchanted wives illegal abortions, and then blackmailed them into insuring their husbands.[39]

They bought small policies from different companies, so no physicals were required and no alarms were set off.

Some spouses were duped. Paul Petrillo told Rose Carilli the white powder he gave her would make her husband stop drinking. It did. It killed him.

Dominick Cassetti said two witches forced him to sprinkle magic powder on his wife's spaghetti.

Dora Sherman paid Morris Bolber $500 to cure her paralyzed grandson, but she wound up in jail after her husband died of a heart attack.[40]

Herman Petrillo was the first to go to trial. He was charged with the arsenic murder of Ferdinand Alfonsi, the 38-year-old who had lingered in pain for seven weeks.

Petrillo usually moved with a swagger, but he twisted his hands nervously as his jurors were selected. When Judge Harry McDevitt asked jurors if they could apply the death penalty if he were convicted, Petrillo winced, possibly because, outside the courtroom, Philadelphians called Judge McDevitt "Hanging Harry."[41]

Petrillo, who fancied himself a ladies' man, probably considered himself lucky that his future would hinge on a jury of seven women and five men. The forewoman was a fortyish homemaker from Germantown. The other jurors were a nurse, a clerk, a secretary, an unemployed man, a bar owner, a vacuum cleaner salesman, an ice cream worker, and four additional homemakers.

Petrillo's 19-year-old son, Clement, dressed in a suit and tie, topcoat, and fedora to attend the jury selection, was exiting the courtroom when he spotted homicide detective Anthony Franchetti in the corridor. Clement Petrillo lunged at him. The detective fought back. It took two guards to separate them. They sped the boy out of City Hall. He was not arrested.[42]

Prosecutors had 60 witnesses available to take the stand on the first day of testimony if needed—doctors, pharmacists, convicts, scientists, widows, neighbors, life insurance salesmen, and a witch.

Although it was St. Patrick's Day, Petrillo was in no mood to celebrate. He sat silently listening to a 27-year-old shirttail cousin identify him as one of the heads of an "insurance murder ring." Thin and bespectacled John Cacopardo said Petrillo told him their method of murder was foolproof. They used an undetectable powder.[43]

Two medical men shocked spectators when they testified that Petrillo had asked them to sell him live typhoid fever germs.

Dr. Henry D'Alonzo said Petrillo asked for typhoid germs, and, when he countered with, "What the hell do you want them for?" Petrillo just said there was $200 or $300 in it for the doctor if he got them.

Benjamin Winokur, a pharmacist, said Petrillo didn't stop when he told him he wouldn't get him typhoid germs. He asked about hydrocyanic acid, the chemical used in gas chamber executions. He said he wanted it for a hair preparation.[44]

Nobody on that opening day could predict that Herman Petrillo would be singing his head off to detectives within six weeks, spilling every detail of the operation, but he would still die in the electric chair at 12:32 a.m. on October 29, 1941.

Petrillo smiled and sneered his way through the first week of testimony. He seemed amused by all the attention, one court watcher said. But, when the trial resumed the next Monday, his temper started showing.

When an insurance salesman's testimony irked Petrillo, the barber sprang from his seat screaming, "You're a liar! That's a lie!" He sank back into his chair, but he glowered at the insurance man.

Two days later, it was Petrillo's turn to convince the jurors he was not lying. From the witness stand, he denied trying to buy typhoid germs. He denied that he offered an undercover treasury agent $2,500 to kill Alfonsi. He denied everything in the prosecution's skillfully stacked case. None of it was true from start to finish, according to him.[45]

Before he was permitted to leave the stand, the judge asked him why he had put checkmarks near arsenical formulas in a drug catalog found at his home. He said he didn't make checkmarks, and he only had the catalog because he was perfecting a hair formula he called "New Life."[46]

The prosecutor closed his case by asking jurors to recommend the death penalty: "Give him a taste of the suffering he caused those unfortunates we had to dig from their graves," he said.

The jury stayed out for only four hours and 15 minutes, and they spent nearly a third of that time eating dinner.[47]

When they returned at 9:30 p.m., Petrillo seemed renewed. His manner suggested he was confident he would be acquitted, almost that he was enjoying himself. He probably didn't notice that jury forewoman Margaret Skeen's face was almost dead white.[48]

Her voice was firm but low when she stood and announced: "We find the defendant guilty of murder in the first degree."

And then, in almost a whisper, the homemaker said, "We recommend death in the electric chair."

Before the last words had left her mouth, Petrillo sprung from his chair and rushed toward the jury box, his face twitching. Snarling at the forewoman, he began cursing: "You ---------!" He took a swing at her. She shrunk back. It took four husky guards to restrain him.

They whisked him away as he struggled ferociously, grumbling more curses. His feet barely touched the floor as the four men hurried him out of the courtroom. They just flung him, arms and legs sprawling, through the swinging doors.

The scene left the packed courtroom gasping.[49]

In the row behind Herman Petrillo's empty chair, tears streamed down Paul Petrillo's face. Recent widows Stella Alfonsi, Carina Favato, and Susie di Martino sat stunned. The district attorney had not yet announced which of them would be tried next.

"The evidence presented so far only scratched the surface," Judge McDevitt told the jury. "Scores and scores of victims perished at the hands of his group of assassins who were on a mad quest for money."[50]

Detective Riccardi stood to announce that his squad had picks and shovels and affidavits ready to exhume 70 bodies the next day.

He said to expect "wholesale arrests." Warrants were being issued to round up suspects before they fled.

The story made the papers in St. Louis, Tampa, Boston, Racine, Alexandria, Los Angeles, and burgs in between. The next issue of *Official Detective Stories* featured the case on its cover. Advertisements for the 15-cent magazine promised "the inside truth written right from the police records."

All the publicity brought hundreds of unsigned letters flooding into the murder squad from as far away as Chicago, and the anonymous tips inside them led to at least 25 additional arrests.[51]

What went on inside Philadelphia's sculpture-bedecked City Hall would rivet readers across the country for the rest of the year. The block-wide building had its own story—it is the largest freestanding masonry building in the world. And, although the suspects and jurors at the arsenic ring trials probably never would have suspected it, the turn-of-the-century building they visited daily was designed to be the world's tallest building. It never gained that title because the Eiffel Tower and the Washington Monument both surpassed it during its 30-year construction period.[52]

Carina Favato came there on April 18 to face charges that she murdered her 17-year-old stepson, Philip Ingrao, for $13,200 in life insurance.

Favato, whom newspapers called "a Lucrezia Borgia," showed up in court looking nothing like the oft-widowed Renaissance beauty who was also handy with poison. Her gray-streaked hair combed untidily, Favato looked bewildered in the same faded black dress and shabby black coat she had worn for her arraignment.

She did make it clear, through a court-supplied interpreter, that her first name was not "Corina," as had been reported. It was "Carina," which means "dear" in Italian, she said.[53]

Favato sat with her hands folded in her lap as her lawyer chose the jurors who would decide her future. She showed little interest in the panel—a clerk, a mechanic, a housewife, a bartender, a carpenter, a paper hanger, a music teacher, an electric inspector, an insurance agent, an unemployed woman, and two unemployed men.[54]

Even when the interpreter explained that the judge was asking jurors if they would apply the death penalty if she were convicted, Favato showed no emotion. Maybe she already had an inkling they would never vote on her fate.

The four other defendants sat in the spectator gallery, listening as insurance agents from a half dozen companies took turns in the witness box. Herman Petrillo occasionally sneered. Once he shook his head no. Paul Petrillo smiled when one witness referred to him as "the professor."[55]

Favato had applied for 18 life insurance policies on the dead 17-year-old, the agents said.

Home Life agent Joseph Millici said he arrived at Favato's home 45 minutes after the boy's death, and he attended the wake and burial, but he saw no evidence of grief. "I never saw Mrs. Favato cry during any of those times. There was no distress or sorrow," he testified.[56]

Witnesses related bizarre tales of witchcraft and magic water and dead men's bones, but Favato didn't react. She sat stony-faced as witnesses told how she threw a party the day her stepson died and built a recreation room in her basement soon after.

It was the testimony of a 37-year-old widow that caused the case to fork abruptly. Susie di Martino, widow of arsenic victim Giuseppe di Martino, spoke in low tones. Favato probably saw all the jurors lean forward in unison to catch her every word, bending over so far that their bodies formed the letter V.

The wispy widow said her husband's doctor wanted him to go to the hospital, but Favato told them not to go. Her husband died the next day.

She said she knew there were three policies on her husband's life, but she did not know about a fourth policy worth $1,979 until Mrs. Favato asked her to sign the insurance check. She never got the money, she said.[57]

The evidence against her was piling high by the time Favato suddenly rose from her chair and blurted out, "All right. If you want me to talk, I will talk." Spectators were stunned. There was a moment of tense silence, then pandemonium. The guards restored order.

Her lawyer quickly entered guilty pleas in all three murders she was indicted for—those of Ingrao; his father, Charles; and Giuseppe di Martino. Favato was called before the judge. With her attorney and her interpreter beside her, she pronounced the word "guilty" in Italian.

As she turned to walk back to her seat, she let out an audible sigh, and a look of relief spread across her face. But, later that day, she told detectives she feared others involved in the ring would take revenge on her by harming her son, Joseph Pontorelli.[58]

Her confession was the biggest news in Philadelphia, but April 21 was an interesting news day around the world.

In Los Angeles, Al Capone was denied early release from prison on tax evasion charges, and orchestra leader Herbie Kay sued screen star Dorothy Lamour for divorce. In Washington, DC, Philadelphia manufacturer Robert Yarnell warned a congressional committee that secret police in Germany were persecuting Jews there. In London, Princess Elizabeth turned 13. She began her birthday with a pre-breakfast walk with her eight-year-old sister, Margaret Rose. Her favorite present was a pair of long silk stockings from her mother. The birthday girl also received a movie camera from her uncle, the former King Edward VIII, who had abdicated the crown to marry Wallis Warfield Simpson, an American divorcee.[59]

It turned out Carina Favato's maternal instinct was correct. Her son Joseph had already received a threatening letter and a phone call before police could dash him from his home to a secret address in the Northeast. The female on the other end of the line threatened to have him killed unless he told his mother to "keep her mouth shut."[60]

By that time, Favato was closeted in a room at City Hall, where detectives with their shirtsleeves rolled up were questioning her. Knowing his mother might avoid the electric chair if she helped detectives, Joseph Pontorelli arrived at City Hall flanked by two police officers. He urged his mother to talk freely despite the threats against his life. As detectives grilled his mother, the stocky 24-year-old with the pencil-thin moustache paced back and forth, chain-smoking cigarettes.[61]

In eight hours of questioning, Favato implicated one woman in six murders, and she gave detectives enough evidence to hang a dozen men.

She told police some wives knew the white powder she prescribed was poison. Others thought it was a strong love potion that was potentially fatal. When their husbands died, they kept mum about the powder for fear they would be indicted as accomplices. A few faithful wives wanted proof the powder was harmless before they would give it to their husbands. For them, she said, she gulped teaspoons of flour instead of the powder she sent home with them.[62]

Detectives took suspects on outings to bars and restaurants to keep them talking freely. They talked so much that detectives brought in a string of new suspects—more widows, a 250-pound strongman who knew Al Capone, a gum-chewing, beret-wearing veterinary student, and a respected obstetrician who had lost his investments in the stock market crash.[63]

Police also identified three people marked for death and saved them in the nick of time.

Herman Petrillo, separated from all the action, grew restless inside his cell at Moyamensing Prison. What he did in the last days of April was a tipping point for the case, but it didn't change the grim trajectory of his own future one speck.

Whether he just wanted a few days out, or he thought he'd avoid the evil eye if he came clean, or he secretly hoped buddying up to detectives would help him avoid the electric chair, Petrillo started singing to the homicide squad on April 27.

He said he wanted to make a clean breast of everything and give police every assistance possible. His timing was off. Carina Favato had started talking a week earlier, spilling so many specifics that the stenographer carried a stack of notebooks out of the interview room.[64]

Detectives said Petrillo almost cheerfully implicated himself in 32 murders. He admitted selling arsenic. He gave up the names of the ring's executioners. And, when detectives took him out for a restaurant meal and a long ride through Fairmount Park, he began to boast about his other illegal activities.[65]

The next two years would be a roller coaster for Herman Petrillo. The state supreme court did reverse his conviction, but he was convicted for a second murder. He was headed to the electric chair in two years, but he didn't believe that in April 1939.

He returned to his cell boasting that he had friends on the detective squad. He talked incessantly about how he would "beat the chair on this rap." He even spoke of his plan to become a county detective.[66]

He wasn't the only one who was imagining things in lockup.

Carina Favato was acting so jumpy in jail that guards thought she was feigning insanity to save herself from the electric chair. She jabbered incoherently. She cursed other prisoners. She screamed that witches were running around her cell.

She attempted suicide twice in the same day. First, she tried to hang herself with a small handkerchief knotted tightly around her broad neck. Then, she used a safety pin to puncture her arms and scratch her wrists until blood dripped from them.[67]

Whenever the arsenic suspects were questioned together, each seemed panicky that one of the others would give him the evil eye. They'd cry out, "Don't you look at me that way. Don't you give me the eye!" Bolber, whose brown eyes had darker spots in them, was most often accused of giving it.[68]

The nationwide publicity the case generated led to a reunion between a mother and a son she had not seen in 18 years. Grace Mancino of Buffalo, New York, was taken aback when she spotted a story about the arsenic deaths of her own ex-husband and 17-year-old son. She and Charles Ingrao were divorced when their two sons were young, and he had led her to believe her boys were dead.

When she saw her ex's photo in the paper, Mancino contacted Philadelphia police, hoping at least one of her long-lost sons might still be alive. Police put her in touch with her 18-year-old son, Michael, who had left Philadelphia right after his brother's death to work with the Civilian Conservation Corps (CCC) in Carlsbad, New Mexico.[69]

By random chance, Detective Franchetti of the city homicide squad was a volunteer with Big Brothers in Philadelphia. He was the one who helped Michael enroll in the CCC, a national relief program that gave three million young, unmarried men work in rural settings during the Depression.

Mancino had no money to travel to New Mexico to see her son Michael, but he hoped to visit her in Buffalo as soon as he finished his enlistment with the CCC. "She's crazy to see me and I'm crazy to see her too," he said. "You know how it is when a fellow learns about his mother, and he's never seen her. It's great to know I have a real mother. When I do get to go see her, I'll never leave her again."[70]

A few days later, city police got a call from another Buffalo resident. Mary Angalone was reading an arsenic ring story when her eyes fell upon a photo of Josephine Romualdo, whom she recognized as her father's Philadelphia landlady. Fearing the worst, she asked police to check on 59-year-old John Falcone.

It turned out Falcone had moved out of Mrs. Romualdo's boarding-house a week earlier, and he had never taken a meal there. "What? Me get poisoned?" he said. "Not me. I'm my own cook. Tell my daughter I'm all right."[71]

A parade of widows and witnesses were questioned daily in the murder squad room on the first floor of City Hall. No one was expecting a suicide attempt when arsenic widow Camilla "Millie" Giacobbe voluntarily appeared for questioning on May 8, 1939.

All morning, Giacobbe denied she was involved in the 1932 arsenic murder of her hatmaker husband, Antonio. Then, at lunchtime, she asked permission to return to her Passyunk Avenue apartment to bathe, dress, and gather papers that would prove her innocence.

Det. Aldo Candelore and stenographer Janet McDaniel accompanied her to her apartment near Paul Petrillo's tailor shop, an area police nicknamed "Arsenic Alley" because of the large number of ring members living there.

When they arrived at the apartment, Giacobbe asked Candelore to go to the cellar to light the hot water heater. McDaniel and Giacobbe climbed to the second floor. The *Inquirer's* next-day story about what happened minutes later described McDaniel as "pretty as the dickens" and said Candelore "could get a job in any man's circus bending horse-shoes with his heavy fighter's hands."

Unbeknownst to the detective and the stenographer, the suspect already had tucked a suicide note in her pocketbook.

Slightly built McDaniel, who was also a widow, helped the 195-pound suspect with her bath and was giving her an alcohol rub when, suddenly, Giacobbe jumped up and darted into her bedroom, slamming the door behind her.

McDaniel heard the sound of a drawer opening and a click. Recognizing it as the snap of a pistol misfiring, the 100-pound single mother of two whipped open the door. She leapt on Giacobbe, grasping her arm and dislodging the muzzle of the .32-caliber revolver that the woman had trained on her own head.

Candelore, who was still downstairs, heard the shot and dashed upstairs, taking the steps several at a time. He disarmed Giacobbe before she could get off the other shots, but she became violently ill. She had also gulped poison.[72]

McDaniel rushed her to the hospital. Giacobbe lived to testify against Paul Petrillo. That sworn statement made big headlines, even in a modern-day witchcraft trial.

Giacobbe swore the tailor-turned-witchman was her "demon lover"—and she made it clear "demon" was no misnomer. She said he literally could command God and devils. He put a jinx on her, she said, so she acted under his spell.[73]

So many ring members were talking that police were able to pick up 75 new suspects, including a doctor, an insurance agent, a typewriter salesman, a warehouse worker, several additional widows, and Carina Favato's boyfriend.[74]

The detectives' success highlighted a few shortages. City council had not passed a budget in six months, so vendors were supplying services to the city on the cuff, including food for the dozens of suspects questioned at City Hall. The city was behind in its rent payments, its telephone bill, even in awarding $25,000 in prize money to the winning Mummers who had marched on New Year's Day.[75]

On June 7, an anteroom of Judge Harry McDevitt's courtroom was burglarized. Lawyers suspected it was an attempt to destroy evidence in the arsenic case. Police pointed out that a robber could drill through the floor straight to the city treasurer's office one floor below. A pawned typewriter quickly led to the thief. The police and the lawyers guessed wrong. John Alexander, 30, said he was out of work and hungry, so he just robbed the first place he came to.[76]

Paul Petrillo went on trial for the murder of Luigi La Vecchio in September 1939, the first of six murder charges against him.

A victim's pretty 25-year-old daughter jumped out at Petrillo, fists flailing, as he walked up the courtroom aisle. Shouting, "You killed my father," she got in several blows before guards could peel her off the short, stooped-shouldered tailor. The incident landed in the headlines as "Petrillo Attacked by Arsenic Orphan."[77]

The most talked-about moment of the trial was the silent evil-eye duel between Paul Petrillo and Morris Bolber. Bolber, sitting on the witness stand, swiftly unnerved Petrillo with an attempt to put the evil eye on him. Petrillo, visibly upset, opened the first and fourth fingers of his hand with the other three fingers closed, and pointed the hand at Bolber, trying to ward off the eye.[78]

One widow shocked court watchers when she testified she saw Petrillo kill her husband. After more than 100 witnesses had testified against him, Petrillo returned from a lunch break on September 28 and flipped his plea to guilty. Whatever he was expecting, he was still sentenced to death.[79]

Philadelphia detectives were beginning to wonder if the shirttail relative who testified against him wasn't telling the truth when he said he was serving a life sentence for a murder his Uncle Paul had committed. Police in New York never picked up on it, though, and John Cacopardo remained imprisoned for another 13 years. His Uncle Paul didn't live that long.[80]

Within two years, the *fattucchiere* who had so many sexual assignations that police called him the Passyunk Avenue Casanova would die alone except for an assigned priest.

One of the last letters he wrote would go to his eldest son, Vincent, who had already changed his surname to Petril. Still, the tailor's last morning would be better than his cousin Herman's.[81]

Stella Alfonsi's trial opened on Monday, October 23, 1939. It was a glum morning for city football fans. NBC had broadcast the first televised NFL game in history the previous afternoon. The Brooklyn team routed the Philadelphia Eagles 23–14 at Ebbets Field.[82]

Alfonsi, the youngest of the alleged arsenic widows, wore a black dress and a matching turban for the first day of her murder trial. Reporters, who often used the adjective "comely" to describe her, noted every detail of her appearance: "Although she has been in prison for a year, Mrs. Alfonsi gave no evidence of that fact when she appeared for her trial," one wrote. "She was smartly dressed, completely in black, with a black turban on her head, with black pumps on her feet and a black purse in her hand. She also displayed a new wave in her black hair. She appeared perfectly at ease."

Whenever a woman was being examined as a prospective juror, Alfonsi silently shook her head "no." Only two made it onto the panel—a maid and a housewife.[83]

The mother of two flinched when the prosecutor called her a Lucrezia Borgia, the same label newspapers had applied to Carina Favato in the spring. She shouted "liar" at one detective as he testified. Prosecutors said she and Herman Petrillo killed her husband so they could marry, but she maintained her husband had been poisoned by some unknown person.[84] The case went to the jury on the first anniversary of her husband's death at the National Stomach Hospital.

As the jurors walked out to deliberate, Alfonsi's hysterical mother screamed, "Give my child a break! She's not guilty!"[85]

Alfonsi had three advantages the other widows didn't: she had never talked to the police, the insurance policies lapsed while her husband lingered in the hospital, and her court-assigned attorney was Raymond Pace Alexander, the Harvard Law graduate destined to become Philadelphia's first black judge.

The odds seemed in Alfonsi's favor. Up until then, the only woman ever to die in Pennsylvania's electric chair was Irene Schroeder, executed in 1931 for the fatal shooting of a state trooper during a grocery store holdup in rural Butler. Juries had already recommended the death penalty for arsenic widows Grace Giovanetti and Josephine Romualdo, though.[86]

When the jury foreman mouthed the words "not guilty" on October 28, Alfonsi fell back into her chair. As a murmur of surprise spread around the courtroom, the dark-haired widow nodded at the jurors as if to thank them.[87]

When Alfonsi was finally freed on November 4, her mother, Christiana Leberto, said they were looking forward to a family dinner, but not until they went to church to thank the Blessed Mother for the acquittal.[88]

Cameramen snapped the 30-year-old receiving kisses from her 12-year-old sons, Ralph and Leopold. Ralph had run away from his grandmother's home in Bristol, Pennsylvania, five times, trying to get to Philadelphia to see his mother in jail.[89]

Alfonsi told reporters she wished the world would remember her only as a woman who had an unfortunate experience.[90]

Rose Carina, the stout fugitive whose looks had disappointed male reporters in May, had already been convicted of one arsenic murder when she faced a jury for another in December. She should have known things were going to break her way the second time, because, when she broke down in tears as her lawyer made his final plea, a 74-year-old juror cried in unison.

When the not guilty verdict came in, Carina cried, "Oh, God bless them all." Then she collapsed.[91]

The prison grapevine at Moyamensing carried the good news to the women inmates before Carina was returned to jail. When she walked into the cellblock to serve her time on her prior conviction, the women banged their tin cups against the bars and chanted, "We want Alexander! We want Alexander!"[92]

The weirdest moment of the trials was Salvatore Sortino's testimony that he paid a member of the ring $50 to learn how to hatch a tiny devil under his armpit. The burly 36-year-old carried an egg in his armpit for nine days, hoping to hatch a little devil. On the ninth day, he waited in a cellar for the devil to appear, but none did. To add to his disappointment, he was sentenced to a life term for drowning Ralph Caruso for the ring in 1934.[93]

Susie di Martino, charged with killing her husband, Giuseppe, was one of the saddest cases among the arsenic widows. She became ill in jail. Carina Favato was a voluntary nurse in her home for the three days leading up to her husband's death, so some speculated that the widow, too, may have been suffering from arsenic poisoning. While other widows profited from their husband's deaths, di Martino lost her purse containing $1,100 in insurance money somewhere in Germantown before her arrest. Her lawyer said she walked over every street she might have been on multiple times, almost day and night for six weeks, but was unable to find the purse or the cash. She was sentenced to 3 to 20 years at the

Morris Bolber received a life sentence, which he served at Eastern State Penitentiary on Fairmount Avenue.

Industrial School for Women in Muncy, a women's prison in the mountains east of Williamsport.[94]

The arsenic murder case lasted two and half years. Detectives investigated nearly 100 deaths and said victims could have numbered in the thousands. Twenty-one murders were proven in court. The investigation resulted in 23 convictions, 15 life sentences, several 2-to-20-year terms, and two executions.[95]

All four ring leaders were convicted of murder. Carina Favato and Morris Bolber received life sentences in return for supplying detectives with an unabridged who's who of the murder operation. The Petrillo cousins talked too late to save themselves.

Paul Petrillo, who once held 60 insurance policies on people marked for murder, traded his life for his 1932 victim Luigi LaVecchio's on the early morning of March 31, 1941.

He took his last meal of the usual Sunday prison fare at 4 p.m. and then took a long nap. He was awakened at 11:50 p.m. to take the 30-step walk to the electric chair. His only words were, "It's all right with me. I have nothing to fear."[96]

Looking pale from months in prison and with his eyes still half-closed in sleep, Petrillo shuffled into the execution chamber and calmly took his seat in the electric chair. He never glanced at the official witnesses. Once a self-professed practitioner of the black arts, in his last moments he repeated the prayers of Rev. F. P. McCreesh, the prison's Catholic chaplain.

The executioner threw the switch at 12:31 a.m. After four shots of 2,000-volt current, Dr. J. G. Weixel declared Petrillo dead at 12:34.[97]

His brother claimed his body for burial at Holy Cross Cemetery in Yeadon. His grave is about six miles from his old tailor shop on Passyunk Avenue, where customers could buy a suit, a magic charm, or a life insurance policy.

His cousin Herman, who always bragged he'd beat the chair, followed in his cousin's footsteps 202 days later.

For 18 months, Herman Petrillo tried, by every means possible, to get his sentence commuted to life. He even appealed to President Franklin D. Roosevelt.[98]

He did live three years longer than his victim, Ferdinand Alfonsi, who succumbed at the National Stomach Hospital in October 1938 after seven weeks of intense pain.

Petrillo spent about four hours of his last day on earth whispering through the bars with Willie Jones, a killer whose cell adjoined his.[99]

He wrote letters to his wife and children and to Warden Stanley Ashe. He ate the regular prison fare, but sparingly. He spent some time in frenzied prayer. Witnesses said it sounded like he was talking gibberish. He died pleading for mercy.[100]

When guards came for Petrillo, Jones started singing: "Holy, Holy, Holy! Lord God Almighty! Early in the morning our song shall rise to Thee . . ."

Reverend McCreesh, the Catholic chaplain, recited prayers as he led the way to the death chamber. Guards had to hold Petrillo upright for the short walk.

With Jones's soulful voice still audible in the background, Petrillo protested his innocence as he was strapped into the chair. He made several attempts to rise from it.

As guards were adjusting the lethal contacts, Petrillo stretched out his arms, looked in the direction of the official witnesses, and said, in broken English, "You wouldn't want to witness the death of an innocent man! Give me a chance to prove my innocence!"

The guards pushed him down, but he tried to rise again. He started to say, "I want to see the governor," but, when the head contact and mask were slipped over his face, his words disintegrated into a scream. By then, Jones had segued to singing "No Rest for the Weary."

Executioner James Lee Wilson pulled the switch at 12:30 a.m. Two thousand volts of electricity shot through Petrillo's body. Three minutes later, Dr. Weixel and Dr. Otto Ranik declared him dead. Jones kept singing in his cell.[101]

Prison superintendent Dr. J. W. Claudy told reporters Petrillo had expressed fears for the futures of his five children.[102]

Petrillo's sister Dolores came from Philadelphia to pick up his body. Three days earlier, he had made her the beneficiary of his $660 life insurance policy. His previous beneficiary was his wife, Margherita.[103]

The Petrillos were the only members of the arsenic murder ring who were doomed to the electric chair, but most of the convicted ring members sat out World War II in prison. Fifteen served life sentences, and many others were jailed for years.

Carina Favato served her life sentence in a fieldstone cottage at Muncy. Several arsenic widows were jailed there, spending their days bent over sewing machines or working the 325-acre farm that surrounded the prison.

Favato died of a stroke at Williamsport Hospital on July 21, 1952 and was buried in Muncy Cemetery. She was 57.[104]

If it were 20 years earlier, she might have been placing an egg under the arm of one of her disciples in South Philadelphia. She told them chickens lay smaller eggs called devil's eggs in June and July, and, if you place one under someone's arm then, it will put an evil spirit inside him.

World War II was already underway before Morris Bolber was sentenced for his part in the ring. Although he broke out in a smile when he heard the judge say he would serve life instead of death in the electric chair, he never gave up hope he would get out of prison.

Bolber, who bragged to police that he personally knew of 70 individuals killed by the ring, applied for a commutation twice. The one-time witch doctor had returned to his Jewish faith and wanted to move to Israel. The closest he got was Eastern State's small but well-appointed synagogue.

Bolber was writing a book about himself in prison. He called it *The Book of Moses*.

His third appeal was pending when he died of heart disease in 1954 at age 67. A relative claimed his body for burial in Mt. Jacob Cemetery in Glenolden, a western suburb of Philadelphia.[105]

In 1945, fugitive Josephine Sadita gave herself up, the last of the ring members to be brought to justice. She said she had been plagued by her conscience since she jumped bail on a murder charge in 1939. The mother of five was on the run throughout the war.

Sadita's luck turned. The assistant district attorney could no longer locate the witnesses he needed to try her for murder. She was charged only with practicing medicine without a license and obtaining money

Morris Bolber, who gave up witchcraft and returned to Judaism in prison, petitioned to be released so he could live out his years in Israel, but the closest he got was the synagogue at Eastern State.

under false pretenses. She wept quietly in court as she was sentenced to an indeterminate term at Muncy.[106]

Jerry Cacopardo, the young Sing Sing inmate who testified against his uncle Paul, steadfastly maintained he was serving time for a murder Paul committed. When a letter turned up that showed he had been the fall guy for his uncle, a judge vacated his sentence in 1952, 16 years after he had been jailed. Given his freedom, he attended seminary and eventually became pastor of large Presbyterian churches in New Jersey and Florida. In 1961, E. P. Dutton published Cacopardo's story, *Show Me a Miracle: The True Story of a Man Who Went from Prison to Pulpit*.[107]

When Cacopardo delivered book talks, he often told his listeners he sometimes feared his Uncle Paul would "send him to California."

Det. Sam Riccardi was transferred out of the homicide unit before the arsenic case was finished. Higher-ups said it was by his own request. Rumors of a shakeup in the city detective bureau were denied. Riccardi's last police assignment before his death in 1973 was as skipper of the Motor Harbor Patrol, a police boat that patrols both sides of the Delaware River.[108]

Willie Jones, the killer whose soulful tunes set the tone for Herman Petrillo's walk to the death chamber, got three reprieves from the chamber himself. The 26-year-old laborer became a cause célèbre for anti-death penalty advocates. The American League to Abolish Capital Punishment supported Jones through three trips to the state board of pardons and an appeal to the Pennsylvania Supreme Court. Members handed out fliers displaying photos of him with the caption, "This is Willie Jones. He is not guilty. We the people will kill this boy for a crime he did not commit."[109]

Jones's tireless attorney, Albert B. Desaldri, put an overwhelming 13 witnesses on the stand in his exhaustive appeal to the state supreme court. In barely articulate English, Desaldri said, "He was arrested by white men, tried and convicted by white men."[110] In the end, though, Jones took the 30-step path to the death chamber in the early morning of Monday, November 24, 1941. He paid with his own life for the holdup slaying of Frank Akerson, a meatpacking plant foreman. It was a busy day at Rockview. Jones was pronounced dead at 12:34 a.m. Another condemned man was led to the chair at 12:37 a.m.[111]

The reign of the Philadelphia arsenic ring outrivaled the weirdest fiction, proclaimed a headline in the tiny *Daily Item* in Sunbury, Pennsylvania.

The certificate of death for arsenic victim Raymond Mandiuk at the state Bureau of Vital Statistics illustrates that. The principal cause of death is listed as "arsenical poisoning." Under other contributory causes of death, the coroner wrote, "Agnes Mandiuk, Morris Bolber, David Brandt."[112]

Janet Hayes McDaniel, the stenographer who jumped on Millie Giacobbe's back to thwart her suicide attempt, eventually became a police officer. She was the first woman promoted to detective in Philadelphia.[113]

The arsenic murder ring made headlines across the country in 1939 with its sex, greed, arsenic, magic charms, fortune-tellers, voodoo priests, and methodical murder, but it was largely forgotten by the late 1950s, except in the homes where it happened.

On October 20, 1957, 16 years to the day after Herman Petrillo begged for his life in the death chamber, *Inquirer* reporter Frank H. Weir wrote: "Sometimes, the whole malignant plot seems as remote as a decayed civilization, and then, a name in the news, the death of an elderly convict or a proceeding before the State Board of Pardons will recall it like a half-forgotten nightmare. For years to come, isolated incidents will remind Philadelphians of the macabre events that shocked the nation."[114]

Chapter Five

The Six Philadelphia Brothers Fictionalized on *Boardwalk Empire*

THE MURDEROUS D'ALESSIO BROTHERS IN HBO's *BOARDWALK EMPIRE* are based on a real-life band of six brothers from South Philadelphia.

Newspapers crowned them the most feared family of gangsters in Philadelphia history. Leo, Pius, Willie, Lucian, Teofilo, and Ignatius Lanzetta made headlines from palm-fringed Miami to star-studded Los Angeles.[1] Each brother was known for something. Leo was the leader. Pius's nickname was "the Brain." Ignatius was the dapper dresser. Teo was the baby. Lucian was a hothead. Willie was the quiet one.[2]

Reporters loved to point out that three of them were named after popes, but the similarities stopped there.[3]

Police called them murderers, white slavers, bootleggers, and numbers writers, but no Lanzetta ever was convicted of a crime that carried more than a 10-year sentence.[4]

The six were arrested more than 100 times, but the charges rarely stuck. Teo was arrested five times in one week. He was picked up twice in the same day. Willie had 22 arrests on his record but only four convictions. Lanzettas were held as suspects or material witnesses in 15 murder cases.[5]

Smart-alecky Pius made a habit of walking into police stations and saying, "I hear you're looking for me. Well, here I am."[6]

Once, after a holdup, he popped into a precinct and announced he had nothing to do with the heist, but he knew where the getaway car was. Police found it where he said it would be.[7]

Pius, the quintessential tough guy, never punched back, even with a particular detective who made a habit of hitting him in the mouth with the back of the hand. Blood rushing to his lips, he always kept his cool.[8]

As the Lanzetta mythology swelled, national newspapers described them as suave, dark-complexioned, flashy dressers who sometimes made women swoon. They favored gabardine suits and blue and purple shirt-and-tie combinations. Catholic newspapers added that Pius often carried rosary beads in his pocket.[9]

A nationally famous actor got lucky when he visited one of the Lanzettas' gambling palaces while he was playing in Philadelphia. He walked out $11,000 ahead—albeit briefly. Police said Lanzetta henchmen kidnapped the actor, took his winnings, and held him captive in a taxicab for hours. The star was too frightened to testify against them, police said.[10]

While Police Inspector John Driscoll ranked the brothers "public enemies number one," his men had little luck pinning a major case on them.[11]

Pius, Lucian, and Ignatius did short prison stints, but they were out more than they were in. Prosecution witnesses almost always got cold feet. That was especially true after a *New York Daily News* reporter wrote that any key witness against a Lanzetta could expect "almost certain termination" before his day in court.[12]

Frustrated police began arresting the brothers for vagrancy and suspicious character. When Willie was hauled into court on one vagrancy charge, the magistrate dismissed the case and told the defendant he was the best-dressed vagrant ever to appear in his court.[13]

One *Inquirer* reporter said the Lanzettas won in court so often that it was getting monotonous. Each scrape with the law added to their wise-guy legend.[14]

Pius emerged as a coldly cruel quipster who said things like, "It's too bad a man hasn't two lives because, in the underworld, there are things that merit death. Sometimes the only way you can make a guy understand is to kill him, but you hate to do it. If you could just stand him up and shoot him and say, 'Now, don't do it again,' wouldn't it be swell."[15]

Pius Lanzetta lived only nine days past his 37th birthday. On New Year's Eve, 1936, Pius was shot down inside an Eighth Street sandwich shop as he reached for a bottle of soda he would never get to drink.

SPECIAL COLLECTIONS RESEARCH CENTER, TEMPLE UNIVERSITY LIBRARIES, PHILADELPHIA, PA

Philadelphia police couldn't stop the Lanzettas, but rival gangsters did—in grisly style.

Leo was the first to die. Five masked men shot him as he left his saloon on a hot high-summer night in 1925. Families who had been trying to get cool on their front stoops scrambled for cover.[16]

On New Year's Eve, 1936, a cloud of gun smoke suddenly surrounded Pius as he was putting a straw in his soda pop at a South Philadelphia sandwich shop.

Willie's killers tied his burlap-wrapped body to a car running board in broad daylight, motored out to the Main Line, and heaved the corpse over the fieldstone wall of a socialite's stately home.

The Lanzettas' bloody reign over South Philadelphia straddled two distinct eras—the Roaring '20s with its flappers, big spenders, and speakeasies, and the Great Depression of the 1930s. The brothers adapted.

Like their father, a liquor dealer who emigrated from Italy, they had an entrepreneurial streak.[17]

Children pose for a news photographer outside the South Philadelphia store where Pius Lanzetta and two others were shot to death in a gruesome gangland slaying.

They got their start by supplying bottles, corks, fake labels, and counterfeit revenue stamps to established bootleggers. It was the criminal equivalent of a swimmer sticking a toe in the water to gauge the temperature.[18]

It didn't take long for one of them to spot an opportunity—a way to sell booze without trucking it in from Canada, sailing it into Atlantic City, or hiring chemists to convert industrial alcohol. Their plan relied on their understanding of Philadelphia's immigrant neighborhoods with their thousands of rows of houses complete with basements and back alleys.

The Lanzettas organized an "alky cooking" empire. They gave rowhouse residents home stills and all the corn, sugar, and other ingredients they needed to produce saleable liquor right in their cellars. Soon, thousands of microdistilleries were supplying all the homemade hooch the brothers could sell.[19]

Philadelphians everywhere winked at Prohibition. It was an "open town." A swank rooftop bar operated openly at the midtown corner of Broad and Locust. More than 10,000 speakeasy operators were arrested in 1935, but only 43 even paid a fine. Police officers gleaned $2 million a year in payoffs for looking the other way—the equivalent of $29 million today.[20]

So much money was up for grabs that gangsters began murdering their rivals. It started on Catherine Street when drive-by shooters downed Joseph Bruno with 14 bullets on August 18, 1925. The 26-year-old bootlegger lived just long enough to refuse to tell police the name of his killer. He did make them a deathbed promise: "I'll get the man."[21]

Bruno's murder set off a lurid chain reaction.

The next night, Ignatius Lanzetta was grazed by a drive-by shooter.

That Saturday night, a long black touring car pulled up in front of Leo Lanzetta's Bainbridge Street bar. As Leo and his kid brother Lucian strolled out the door shortly before 8 p.m., five masked men jumped from the car, all with their hands in their right-hand coat pockets. An instant later, each man fired one shot. As the touring car sped away, Leo lay in a pool of his own blood with two shots to the head, two to his right side, and one in his neck. Seventeen-year-old Lucian, who had been standing shoulder to shoulder with him, was unharmed.[22]

The Lanzettas were on edge after Leo's death at age 30. Whenever the city got too chancy, they packed up their mother and took up temporary residence in Tampa, Florida, or Dearborn, Michigan.

Once, when they wanted to return to Philadelphia after an absence, Pius put out feelers. When a reporter said the cops were promising "a hell of a beating" to anything that looked like a Lanzetta, they opted to stay in Tampa.[23]

A one-chance-in-a-million shooting incident outside a South Street pool room led Pius to flee to Michigan briefly in the spring of 1927. Two city detectives were searching for robbers who had stolen $33,000 from the Belmont Trust Company. They saw Pius leaving the pool parlor and mistook him for one of the bandits. For his part, he mistook the detectives for rival gangsters out to get him.

Pius fired three shots at one of them and winged the other. When the men kept chasing him after he shot back, it suddenly dawned on him that his pursuers were police.

Pius darted into the pool room, ran up to the third floor, climbed out a window to the roof, hopped down to a lower roof, and finally leapt down to Warnock Street, where he made his escape. He started down an alley, but he spotted detectives loading witnesses into a police wagon. He turned the other way and began plotting a hasty departure for Dearborn.[24]

With Prohibition ending on December 5, 1933, the brothers schemed to expand beyond their nightclub and two palatial gambling dens. They segued to numbers writing, the best-paying racket after bootlegging ended. As always, they dipped their toes in the water first.

In June 1932, they declared themselves in on Camden's numbers business. They forced two African American numbers bankers to quit and turn their play over to them. Powerful bookmaker Al Silverberg told the Lanzettas to get out of town, but they ignored him.[25]

The Lanzettas chose the wrong enemies. Silverberg was already wanted for one murder. Pius's iffy partnership with numbers writer Nig Rosen in Philadelphia was fraying, and Rosen had the backing of Dutch Schultz and other New York racketeers. Plus, some thugs still blamed

Pius for the drive-by shooting deaths of John "Big Nose" Avena six months earlier and Joe Zanghi in 1927.

Pius no longer seemed so indomitable, especially on the day in September 1936 when Ignatius was sentenced to 5 to 10 years in prison under New Jersey's gangster law. It was the longest sentence ever doled out to a Lanzetta.

Ignatius appeared unmoved in the courtroom, but the usually stoic Pius leaned forward as if he had not heard the judge correctly. Then he pillowed his forehead on his arms and collapsed forward onto the back of the chair in front of him.[26]

The sentence would be overturned by the Pennsylvania US Supreme Court two years later, but Pius would not live to see that. He would live only nine days past his 37th birthday.

In the dying hours of 1936—at the same time 15,000 Mummers around the city were taking three prancing steps forward, three weaving steps back, and then a whirl with their umbrellas, practicing their patented shuffle to parade down Broad Street in the 36th annual Mummers Parade the next morning—Pius Lanzetta's right hand reached for a bottle of pop he would never get to drink.[27]

It happened shortly before 4 p.m. in a small sandwich shop at 726 South Eighth Street. The place was owned by retired prizefighter Joe Grimm, a local celebrity. Grimm's moniker was "Iron Man" because he always got up after a punch.[28]

Grimm's wife, Carrie, was getting a penny's worth of candy for a child when she saw the three men enter. Witnesses described them as swarthy and tight-lipped. They walked by so swiftly that Mrs. Grimm didn't see their guns. When she asked them what they wanted, one shoved her aside and said, "We don't want nothing."[29]

They moved as fast as their intended victim. Lanzetta himself was so fleet disposing of court charges that he had earned the moniker "Pius In-And-Out" Lanzetta."[30]

Not suspecting he was about to be attacked, Pius put a straw into his bottle and began bending his backside into a rickety wood chair. Suddenly, he found himself in the ultimate tight spot. Bullets flew around the small alcove. Slugs tore holes in his left hand, his left shoulder, his cheek, his throat, and his heart. One blast tore off the crown of his head. When the smoke cleared, his lifeless body was sprawled across the table under a portrait of the prizefighter who always came up for more.[31]

Two unlucky bystanders—one sitting at a nearby table and one waiting at a counter—were cut down in the spray of bullets.

As the last hours of 1936 unfolded, tens of thousands of Philadelphians gathered around City Hall to welcome the new year. A mile and a half away, the mood was somber as detectives interviewed the Grimms and other witnesses to the gruesome triple slaying. Carrie Grimm said it all happened so fast, but she did notice one man button his shotgun under his coat as he left.

Teo Lanzetta's holiday was spent identifying his big brother's body.[32]

The next day an editorial writer at the *Morning Post* in Camden opined, "A sawed-off shotgun in the hands of an underworld gunman did something yesterday that police have vainly tried to do for 15 years."[33]

Only 18 people turned out to mourn the leader of the most publicized band of criminal brothers in the East, but a 200-man police guard circled the tiny nest of mourners. The *Inquirer* said police were there to ensure the surviving brothers did not develop cases of "acute lead poisoning," as Pius and Leo had.[34]

Pius's mother and sister, heavily veiled in black, and Willie, Lucian, and Teo, with their hats pulled down over their eyes, gathered around the rose-and-carnation-covered mahogany casket that carried their loved one's cremated remains. Ignatius, who was incarcerated, could not join them.

The cortege of four funeral cars and a hearse sped from the funeral home to Chelten Hills Cemetery at 50 miles per hour, following a red police escort car. Once they arrived, the service took fewer than five minutes.[35]

While the Lanzettas were mourning Pius's demise, Pius's former partner, Nig Rosen, was celebrating it with friends in South Jersey. Their revelry came to an abrupt halt when police arrested them under a law that forbids congregation of two or more men who each have three or more criminal convictions.[36]

After she lost Pius, Michaelena Lanzetta begged the rest of her brood to come to Dearborn with her and get honest jobs. Teo was serving three years at Leavenworth on narcotics charges, but Lucian and Ignatius moved to Michigan to join her.

Willie had been holed up in Tampa, living an almost hermitlike existence after a gunman broke into his home and opened fire with a machine gun. He opted to return to Philadelphia instead of Dearborn. His mother, a deeply religious woman, lit a candle for him.[37]

Once a member of the most feared family of gangsters in city history, at age 38 Willie had no money except whatever he could bum from acquaintances. He was trained as a shoemaker, but he set his sights on becoming a numbers kingpin again.

Willie Lanzetta's killers waited several hours for his body to go into rigor mortis, and then they crammed it into a potato sack, tied the sack to the running board of a car, and drove it to the Main Line, where they dropped it over a fieldstone wall.

Police believed he got tied up with a Camden mob on the outs with Rosen's powerful 69th Street Mob in Philadelphia. Detectives said Willie had an annoying habit of not knowing when he had been cut out of a deal.

Eight days before he lost his life, he received a warning that something would happen to him if he didn't change his ways.[38] Instead of watching his step, Willie accompanied his old bodyguard, Fats Del Rossi, to an Upper Darby apartment.

Whether they planned to make peace or shake down Rosen's men, Willie's plan went haywire when the men they were meeting told Del Rossi to beat it and he did.

Police think Willie tried to fight his way out of the apartment, because his corpse had a black eye. Someone turned the radio on full blast. Then Willie's protests were stopped by a small-caliber bullet behind his right ear.[39]

The tidy and patient killers swathed Willie's head wound in towels to avoid blood dripping inside the apartment. Then someone pushed Willie's knees to his chest. They waited for rigor mortis to stiffen the body in that shape. They pulled two large burlap bags marked "potatoes" over it and used thin wire to sew the bags shut. Then they casually toted them downstairs and tied them to the running board of their car for a road trip. After motoring to an isolated corner of tony Lower Merion Township, they pulled over in front of Mrs. Thomas Ashton's stately home and hurriedly heaved the bags over her low fieldstone wall.[40]

Twenty-one-year-old Charles Williams was delivering groceries for McQuillan's Meat Market in Narberth when he jumped the wall the next day. When the lanky deliveryman unexpectedly landed beside the curious sacks, he pulled out his pen knife and cut into one end. Willie's bloody head popped out. Williams kept his own head and quickly called out to a postman, who agreed to stand guard on the body parts until Williams could run a quarter mile to a service station to summon the police.[41]

Even city police who came out to view the corpse didn't recognize Willie because his face was caked with blood. He was still fully clothed in the garb he wore to the meeting—a shirt, a green gabardine suit, purple ribbed socks, and tan shoes.[42]

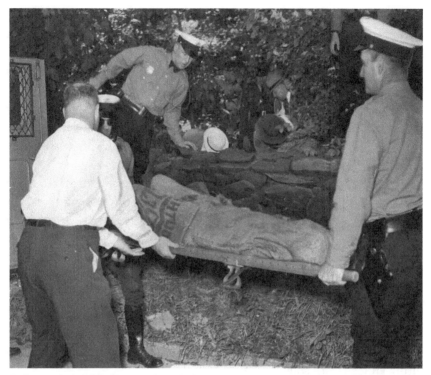

Police retrieve Willie Lanzetta's body from the front yard of a socialite's stately home in 1939. A meat delivery boy taking a shortcut stumbled over a potato sack and used his pen knife to see what was inside.
SPECIAL COLLECTIONS RESEARCH CENTER, TEMPLE UNIVERSITY LIBRARIES, PHILADELPHIA, PA

Fingerprints identified the body as William Lanzetta, with a police record of 22 arrests and four convictions. Capt. William Shaffer of the Lower Merion Police thought Willie's killers were part of Rosen's 69th Street Mob, which had vowed years earlier to blast every Lanzetta henchman out of Philadelphia.

The *Inquirer* headline was "Unity of Lanzettas Shattered Only by Their Foes' Bullets."[43]

Willie's body was headed for an unmarked grave in the city's potter's field, a triangular plot at Luzerne Street and Whitaker Avenue in North Philadelphia. In the nick of time, his impoverished relatives passed the hat to scrape together $30 for a cremation service.[44]

His brothers did not attend his funeral. Teo was still serving time at Leavenworth. Ignatius and Lucian did not want to run the risk of returning to Philadelphia.[45]

A single funeral car carried his weeping mother, Michaelena, and his pretty 27-year-old wife, Bessie.

The young widow told reporters her husband had lost all his money in bank failures and was stone broke when he was killed. It was a humiliating end for a man who had once been part of Philadelphia's first family of crime.[46]

As the Wilmington, Delaware, paper wrote two days after the funeral, "Willie Lanzetta always wanted a sendoff like the big shots, but all he got was a $30 cremation. A jar of ashes was all that remained of him."[47]

No arrests were made then, but in 1940 police speculated that hired hitmen who had killed a string of mobsters in the 1930s were probably responsible for Pius's and Willie's deaths.

The speculation centered on a Detroit gunman, a Los Angeles contract killer, and "Pittsburgh Phil" Strauss, a triggerman whose fees were very reasonable because, police said, he would rather kill a man than drink an ice cream soda.[48]

After 1940, the Lanzetta name all but disappeared from Philadelphia headlines. The three surviving brothers were all starting over in other places.

Lucian joined the US Army six months before Pearl Harbor and served through most of World War II. After the hostilities overseas, he returned to Dearborn, where he worked in the building and construction trades.[49]

Teo was imprisoned on drug trafficking charges for most of the war years.

Ignatius got a job at the Ford Motor Company in Dearborn, where he rose to foreman.[50]

CHAPTER SIX

The Prison Where
Al Capone Was a File Clerk

AL CAPONE GOT HIS FIRST TASTE OF PRISON IN PHILADELPHIA.[1] IT started with a one-in-a-million chance event—or a meticulously planned hoax.

Lt. Jack Creedon and Det. James "Shooey" Malone were driving down Market Street on Friday night, May 17, 1929, when they suddenly spotted the man accused of orchestrating the St. Valentine's Day Massacre. Al Capone seemed out of place in Philadelphia, but his features were clear under the brilliantly lit marquee of the Stanley Theatre.[2]

Malone had seen Capone at a prizefight in Miami. He nudged Creedon and said, "That's Scarface Capone." Creedon nodded.[3]

But, before they could catch up, Capone and his bodyguard slipped into the theater's massive pink travertine marble lobby. The lawmen figured there might be trouble if they approached the gangsters inside one of the city's largest motion picture palaces on a Friday night, so they waited outside. The theater manager agreed to help steer Capone in their direction. Not taking any chances, they called in 20 traffic policemen to cover all the exits of the 3,000-seat theater.

An hour and 20 minutes later, Capone strolled out into the blinding marquee light, slightly in front of his bodyguard. Malone walked over, pulled back his coat to reveal his badge, and told the two they were under arrest.

Al Capone's first prison term was served in Philadelphia.
FEDERAL BUREAU OF INVESTIGATION

Creedon noticed Capone had his right hand in his coat pocket, so he clutched the arm and pulled it out. He explored the pocket and found a blunt-nosed .38. The barrel had been sawed off so the gun would fit easily in the palm of a hand.

Malone grabbed Slippery Frankie Rio, the bodyguard, who had a gun in a belt at his waist.

Rio carried a small roll of bills—but they were all ones. Capone had $25 on him—but he was wearing a $50,000 diamond pinkie ring.

Neither man said a word at first, then Capone blurted out, "What's the idea of picking us up? We're only passing through your town. We're not even stopping here. We'll be out of your town within the next hour."

Malone described Capone's attitude as one of "good-natured disdain."[4]

It may or may not have occurred to Capone that his good friend Max "Boo Boo" Hoff of West Philadelphia had specifically warned him a week earlier not to wear a gun when he changed trains in Philadelphia.

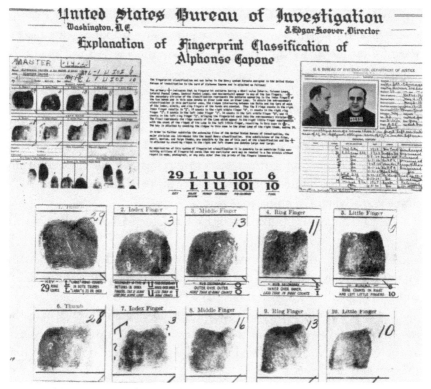

Al Capone's fingerprint card verified his identity in the days before the FBI's Next Generation Identification system, which performs more than 300,000 computerized fingerprint searches a day.
FEDERAL BUREAU OF INVESTIGATION

Nobody said much on the four-block trek to City Hall. Malone thought Capone regarded it as a joke and figured he'd be sprung once he got there. "He'd done that so many times in Chicago and other places he thought he could do it anywhere," Malone said.[5]

Magistrate Edward Carey made it clear Philadelphia was different, saying, "Mr. Capone, authorities in other cities are afraid of you. We are not afraid of you in Philadelphia."

Up until that point, Capone had stood before the bench, holding his white fedora in his hands, listening respectfully and speaking in low tones, but he instantly shot back, "And I am not afraid of you!"[6]

As he walked out of City Hall to the waiting police car that would whisk him to Moyamensing Prison for processing, Capone spotted Lieutenant Creedon and snapped, "Well, you are the ------ I can thank for this extended vacation."[7]

When he was interviewed by Lemuel Schofield, the city's affable young director of public safety with a paunch as large as his, Capone told Schofield he wanted to retire. Puffing on a fat cigar, Capone unloaded. He hadn't had peace of mind for years, he said. He was tired of checking into hotels under assumed names to thwart his enemies. "Three of my friends have been bumped off in the last two weeks," he told Schofield. "I never know when I'm going to get it."[8]

He said he hadn't been able to leave his home without his bodyguard, Rio, for the past two years.

"You fear death every moment, and, worse than death, you fear the rats of the game who would run around and tell the police if you didn't constantly satisfy them with money and favors," he said.

He told Schofield he was returning from Atlantic City, where the most powerful bootleggers in the country had spent a week sequestered at the President Hotel. He said they all signed on the dotted line that there would be a truce.

"I have a wife and an 11-year-old boy I idolize in Palm Island, Florida. If I could go there and forget it all, I would be the happiest man in the world," Capone said during the extended heart-to-heart.

He said he would give everything to be able to quit the rackets right then, the tremendous profits notwithstanding.

Capone proudly told Schofield had never spent any time in prison. "Not a minute," he said.[9]

All the while, Schofield knew the judge would likely impose a stiff prison sentence, but Capone had no idea. The next morning's breakfast of baloney, dry bread, and coffee might have foreshadowed what was in store for him on May 17.[10]

Capone's lawyers offered to pay up to $100,000 and guarantee that Capone would never enter Pennsylvania again in exchange for having the case discharged. Instead, the judge imposed the stiffest sentence the law allowed—one year in jail with a possibility of two months off for good behavior. When Capone heard the judge's sentence, his face turned dark red.[11]

Soon, he was handcuffed to two detectives. Within hours, he would be Prisoner No. 90725 at Holmesburg Prison. The news made headlines coast to coast.[12]

"Sentencing of Al Capone Gives Gangland Laugh" was the headline residents of the tiny coal town of Shamokin, Pennsylvania, saw when they opened the *Shamokin News-Dispatch* at the breakfast table. It was not a laugh for Capone, who had been thrown for a loop.[13]

In the aftermath of the St. Valentine's Day Massacre, Capone was as well-known as Babe Ruth or Henry Ford or Charles Lindbergh or Rin Tin Tin.[14]

His operations reportedly grossed $105 million a year, although he meted out a third of that for muscle and payoffs.[15]

His offhand quips were widely quoted, among them "When I sell liquor, it's bootlegging. When my patrons serve it on a silver tray on Lake Shore Drive, it's hospitality."[16]

The lightning-quick arrest and conviction of the king of American bootleggers stunned the nation.

The *Brooklyn Daily Eagle*, Al's hometown paper, echoed papers across the country: "The matter of getting Scarface Al Capone into jail was almost too easy."[17]

Columnists questioned whether Capone might have sought lockup with his trusty bodyguard rather than returning to Chicago to face the consequences of the most brutal massacre in gangland history.

The *Chicago Tribune* went further. It reported that Capone knew Malone and Creedon well and had even hosted them at his Miami mansion. The writer speculated it was a setup that backfired when the judge inexplicably imposed a stiff one-year sentence.[18]

Although prisoners usually traveled by the vanload, authorities were taking no chances after rumors surfaced that Capone's enemies were gunning for him in Philadelphia, too. When Capone and Rio were transferred to Holmesburg Prison to begin serving their sentences the next day, the duo and their police escorts had a van to themselves. Five more detectives followed in a second van, guns out.[19]

Ten guards and detectives made a thick circle around Capone as he exited the van and was led into Holmesburg. His good cheer left him as he glanced around the grim jailhouse. His only comment was, "Not much like home here."[20]

He said nothing else, but his face betrayed his displeasure when he was handed prison denims in return for his custom-tailored suit designed with room for a concealed shoulder holster.[21]

Capone, who, until that morning, expected the people around him to dress well, speak with cultured accents, and address him as "sir," was ordered to shower. Then his already close-cropped hair got an even shorter regulation prison cut. He was ordered to remove his 11.5-carat diamond ring. The sparkler, with a large center stone flanked by two sets of smaller stones in the shape of swords, went into the prison safe.[22]

Newspapers reported his every move in prison: "Capone Gains Eleven Pounds." "Max Hoff Visits Capone." "Capone Reads *Life of Napoleon*." "Capone Doesn't Go to Church on Sunday."[23]

Meanwhile, the two men who achieved some fame as Scarface's captors were chafing at the persistent speculation that Capone wanted to be caught so he'd be safely locked away 750 miles east of Chicago. "It's enough to make anybody want to quit being a copper," said Malone, who took down Capone and Rio with Creedon. "We take a chance and pinch two of the most dangerous characters in the racket. They have guns on them, and they know how to use them. Then, everybody hollers frame up."[24]

After the original flurry of speculation, calmer heads did wonder why a man with millions at his disposal would choose a year in prison far from his family over some other self-imposed exile such as visiting long-lost relatives in Campania, the stunning coastal region at the top of Italy's boot.

Four days in, the *Philadelphia Inquirer* headline was "Scarface Gloomy Amid Jail Routine." When he wasn't pacing up and down, Inmate 90725 was being treated like any other new prisoner. He was given a thorough physical, with the prison doctor rapping his hairy chest with heavy fingers. His blood was extracted for testing.[25]

Officials said he seemed like a lost soul. He spoke only when spoken to, and, even then, he answered in monosyllables. He was a long way from where he was a week before, on the Atlantic City boardwalk, laughing and posing with faces from the front pages, larger than life in his custom suits in Easter egg colors.[26]

Capone's Bertillon card, the oversize file cards prisons used to keep "the measurement of a man," said Alphonse Capone, 30, was five-foot-nine and seven-eighths inches, 242 pounds, with a stocky build, hazel eyes, black hair, and a medium-dark complexion. The list of his scars and marks ran over the two allotted lines. One of the aliases listed on his card was Scarface.
COLLECTION OF EASTERN STATE PENITENTIARY HISTORIC SITE

Meanwhile, the judge who jailed Capone received nearly 50 letters and postal cards chewing him out, including one with a hand-drawn skull and crossbones. When one letter threatened to send a "Chinese pineapple," or hand grenade, to the office, the judge's clerk quit for the day.[27]

On August 9, Capone was quietly transferred to Eastern State Penitentiary, the foreboding century-old behemoth on Fairmount Avenue, a crumbling Gothic Revival edifice on 11 acres, all of it ringed by a 30-foot-high stone wall. Lest any "enforced guests" attempt to tunnel out, the wall continued for more than three yards belowground.

Eastern State was built to inspire penitence in 1821. Inmates were left alone in their cells to contemplate their wrongdoing. They received meals through a feed door. When they left their cells, their faces were

More than 2,000 people lined up 10 deep on the wide sidewalks outside Eastern State to witness Capone's release from prison, but the warden pulled a fast one.
COLLECTION OF EASTERN STATE PENITENTIARY HISTORIC SITE, GIFT OF ALAN J. LEFEBVRE

covered with hoods, so they never saw other prisoners. It was a Quaker experiment in rehabilitation that failed miserably. By the time Al Capone arrived 108 years later, prisoners were allowed radios, Victrolas, and artwork in their cells.

The official reason for Capone's transfer was overcrowding at Holmesburg, where inmates were housed three to a cell. At Eastern State, he would be known as Number 5527C.

The number system replaced names for all official tracking at the prison. An ornate brass plaque in the central hallway honored former prisoners who went on to serve in World War I, and one who died in service overseas. The prisoners, though, are unnamed, listed only by their inmate number: "Died for his country: B6686."[28]

Most of the men there were incarcerated for serious crimes—robbery, burglaries, murder, and, in another era, horse thievery.

Capone's Bertillon card, the oversized file cards prisons used to keep "the measurement of a man," said Alphonse Capone, 30, was five-foot-nine and seven-eighths inches, 242 pounds, with a stocky build, hazel eyes, black hair and a medium-dark complexion. The list of his scars and marks ran over the two allotted lines, but most of the space was taken to describe the two whitish cuts on the left side of his face that earned him one of the aliases listed on the card: Scarface.

His other aliases were listed as Alphonse Capone and Al Brown. They did not include the childhood nickname his best friends still used for him: Snorky. He was euphemistically listed as a paper and leather cutter.[29]

Capone was the second member of his family to take up residence in Philadelphia. His younger brother Matty was enrolled at Villanova College in one of the fashionable suburbs that ringed the city.[30]

Eastern State's concrete corridors were lined with pipes. Small skylights and the occasional corridor door were the prisoners' only glimpse of the sky. Some sections became so hot in the summertime that prisoners used their water spigots to flood their cement-floored cells. But Capone was assigned one of the four airy cells on "Park Avenue," a circular wing considered the prison's prime real estate.

Capone and an embezzler shared a cell on the airy corridor prisoners dubbed "Park Avenue." The cells were slightly larger than in the rest of the prison. The re-created cell is on display at Eastern State Penitentiary Historic Site.
COLLECTION OF EASTERN STATE PENITENTIARY HISTORIC SITE

His cell was outfitted with many of the comforts of home. He made instant friends by spending more than $1,000 on crafts made by prisoners—figurines, ship models, inlaid boxes, and cigarette cases. In an interview with a local newsman, he described his new digs as "very comfortable."[31]

He and his cellmate, "Bill" Coleman, an embezzler who worked as the prison statistician, enjoyed waltzes from a cabinet radio, Victrola music, and the soft glow of a desk lamp. In addition to the standard toilet and spigot, the cell had sufficient room for a polished desk, two cots, a French dresser, and a table topped with a vase of gladioli. Prisoner-made flowered rugs covered the cement floor. Framed artwork dotted the walls. A smoking stand in the form of a butler in blackface held a single ashtray.[32]

Still, Capone's was not the most impressive of the 1,800 cells. Some inmates kept canaries. A few tried to train rats as pets. One had an organ in his cell.[33]

Capone got a plum job as a file clerk.

He subscribed to magazines, made long-distance calls, and gave interviews to the press. When he met with Frank Nitti, Jake Guzik, or his family members, he did it in the warden's office.[34]

He closely followed newspaper stories about himself, and guards noticed he'd become intensely angry whenever a reporter referred to him as a killer.

Capone, who had pitched for a semi-pro baseball team in Brooklyn two decades earlier, played again at Eastern State.[35]

The deputy warden described him as "meek" and "orderly."[36]

Shortly after Capone arrived at Eastern State, Dr. Herbert M. Goddard performed a minor operation on his sinuses in the small prison operating room. Two weeks later, he removed Capone's tonsils, which had been bothering him for years.

Ten months later, when Capone was released, Dr. Goddard told reporters, "I can't believe all they say of him. In my seven years' experience, I have never seen a prisoner so kind, cheery and accommodating. He does his work—that of a file clerk—faithfully and with a high degree of intelligence. He has brains. He would have made good anywhere, at anything.

"I cannot estimate the amount of money he has given away. Of course, we cannot inquire where he gets it. He is in the racket. He admits it. But you can't tell me he's all bad," the doctor said.[37]

Capone gave $25,000 to $30,000 to less fortunate prisoners and their families while he was jailed. His prison behavior was good enough to knock two months off his sentence.[38]

He and Rio were scheduled for release on St. Patrick's Day, 1930. In an unusual step, the warden, Herbert "Hardboiled" Smith, secretly drove to Harrisburg to get the governor's signature on their release papers.

A circus atmosphere prevailed in Philadelphia on March 17. As a *Chicago Tribune* columnist put it, "There's so much noise in the street, on the front page, over the radio, everywhere, you'd think it was a presidential election, but it isn't. It's just Al Capone being let out of jail."[39]

That morning, the sidewalks facing the prison were 10 deep with 2,000 men, women, and children awaiting a glimpse of Scarface Al

Capone. News photographers set up their tripods in the street and atop box trucks. Uniformed police, suit-clad detectives, and reporters milled around for hours. All assumed the warden was waiting for release papers to arrive from Harrisburg.[40]

Lewis Edwards, 33, a former inmate who was involved in a sensational 1923 jailbreak, drove up in a big automobile. Edwards had been recaptured in Honolulu years earlier and served out his sentence. He was a favorite of the warden. The crowd watched as the gates opened for him.

When a portly, dark-skinned man drove out of the prison, the crowd swarmed his car. He insisted he was not Capone, to no avail, until someone noticed that his face bore no scars.

Occassionally, the crowd spirit would be revived when a guard opened one of the heavy iron doors to the prison, but they all simply took peeks at the crowd and pulled the doors shut.

Detectives Creedon and Malone, who had captured Capone at the movie theater, rode up to the gate on other business.[41]

In Chicago, patrolmen tramping through the snow in front of the Capone home on South Prairie Avenue knew a butcher's boy had delivered two 18-pound turkeys to the tidy red brick house, so they assumed a welcome-home dinner was on tap, but they had not yet spotted the guest of honor.[42]

Then, shortly after dark in Philadelphia, Hardboiled Smith appeared before the crush of waiting reporters to announce that Capone had been secretly transferred to Graterford Prison more than 24 hours earlier and released from Graterford that morning.

"We certainly stuck it in your eye," the warden said. "The big guy went out of here yesterday at dusk in a brown automobile to Graterford Prison. Try to find out where they've gone."[43]

"We gave everybody a good jerking around. Pretty slick if you asked me. Capone has been out of here since yesterday, and nobody got wise to it," he said.

Smith looked shocked when men and women booed and hissed him. One angry reporter shouted, "How much did you get for this, warden?"

"You get the hell out of here and stay out," was all he could muster as he slammed the prison gate in their faces. The crowd shouted and hurled rocks at the iron-studded prison door. A boy's band from the neighborhood added to the racket, playing, "Hail, Hail, the Gang's All Here" over and over.

Police Capt. Gus Beppel and his men had been standing outside the prison from late Sunday afternoon until 8 p.m. Monday night. When Beppel saw two patrolmen he knew come on the scene, he shouted, "What do you think of that! Twenty-four hours on this job and then Smith comes along and says, 'What are you hanging around here for? They've gone hours ago.' That's what he said to me!"

Dr. Goddard, the surgeon who thought Capone was a model prisoner, came out to calm the crowd at one point as a member of the Pennsylvania State Board of Prison Inspectors. Smith was with him.

"This statement will explain everything," Dr. Goddard said. "We feel that our action in this case was justified . . ."

Reporters interupped him. "Where is Capone now?"

"Wouldn't you like to know," Smith shouted, further inflaming the crowd. "Al is well away from here by now. He's safely out of the city."

"What's all the special consideration for a gangster?" a reporter grumbled. "Does the fact that he is reputed to be worth millions have anything to do with it?"

"It does not," Smith insisted. "While he was here he was treated the same as everybody else. We believe his life might be in danger, and we took precautions. That's all."[44]

Criticism of the warden didn't end on the sidewalk in front of the prison. It continued at civic meetings and business luncheons for weeks. The president of the United Business Men's Association demanded the warden explain the favoritism. And when Charles P. Taft, son of the late president, visited the city, he made a point of mentioning that the consideration shown Capone was "perfectly ridiculous."[45]

Immediately after the warden's announcement, reporters who had been keeping vigil veered off in all directions. Official word was that Capone and Rio had a plane waiting for them at Central Airport in Camden. Rumors spread that the duo hopped the Broadway Limited to Chicago, but reporters who searched the train when it stopped in Pittsburgh couldn't spot them. Newsmen checked every westbound train out of Philadelphia.[46]

Capone might have slipped past them because he had lost 20 pounds eating prison food, and he had taken to wearing gold-rimmed spectacles to combat eye strain from the whitish walls of his prison cell.[47]

A *Pittsburgh Press* reporter summed it up: "Nobody knew when he would arrive or how he would come, but everybody was expecting him momentarily, some by land and some by air."[48]

A Ford Trimotor plane sitting at Central Airport in Camden could ferry 14 passengers to Chicago in eight and a half hours, but it only played the role of decoy, engaged at its usual rate of $50 an hour waiting time and $200 an hour in flight. Gilbert Waller, the pilot, eventually told reporters that Jake Guzik and Ralph "Bottles" Capone had hired him, and they paid in advance. He added that he was satisfied to wait forever at the charter rate.[49]

While papers had Capone feasting at home in Chicago, sunning himself in Florida, and hiding out in Indiana and six other states, he actually spent his first night of freedom in West Philadelphia.

He stayed at a friend's house, went to bed by 10 p.m., and woke early to a sumptuous breakfast before boarding a different private plane that took off for Chicago around 5 a.m.[50]

While officials in Miami and Chicago preemptively warned Capone he wasn't welcome back, the Rapid City Chamber of Commerce in South Dakota's Black Hills sent him a letter inviting him to make his home there. It quoted a verse from the Scriptures admonishing those who criticize the crimes of others. And, in Monticello, Iowa, Capone got 50 write-in votes for mayor.[51]

While Capone was jailed in Philadelphia, a *Chicago Tribune* rewrite man named Fred Pasley pieced together a quickie biography of the 31-year-old bootlegger. *Al Capone: The Biography of a Self-Made Man* was released on January 1, 1930—almost 11 weeks before Capone was.[52]

On March 24, a smiling Alphonse "Scarface" Capone appeared on the cover of *Time* magazine with a fresh flower in the lapel of his three-piece suit.

By then, he was back in his Lexington Hotel office in Chicago, sitting behind his mahogany desk with the gold-encrusted ink stand and the French phone that looked too dainty for his blunt, hairy fingers.

Pictures of George Washington and Chicago mayor "Big Bill" Thompson looked down at him as he granted an interview to a *Chicago Tribune* reporter. It would be headlined "Capone's Story: By Himself."[53]

Al Capone lived another 16 years, but by the time he died at his $40,000 waterfront villa on Miami's Biscayne Bay, his brain was riddled by syphilis.

He suffered a stroke on January 21, 1946 and succumbed to pneumonia four days later. At his death, he was broke.

He and his wife, Mae, and their son were living on handouts from his family members. He owed the federal government money, and his lawyer said his ethereal white mansion on the bay was "mortgaged to the hilt."[54]

Albert Francis Capone Jr., the son the beer baron once said he idolized, changed his name to Albert Francis in 1966. He had just been arrested on a traffic violation and had been convicted of petty larceny the previous year, and he said the incidents were played up in the press because of his surname.[55]

By then, the idolization of his father as king of American gangsters was already underway.

Eventually, Harvard Business School students would analyze his entrepreneurial strategies.[56]

There are more than three dozen books about him, including a graphic novel and a Newbery Honor children's book.

And 75 years after his death, Capone's Dinner and Show in touristy Kissimmee, Florida, would sell souvenir T-shirts with his face and this caption: "The beatings will continue until morale improves."

More than 314,000 visitors tour Eastern State Penitentiary each year, where Capone's cell is a major attraction.[57]

In 1986, nearly 30 million viewers tuned in to see Geraldo Rivera open a safe believed to be used by Capone when his offices were located in the Lexington Hotel. Entertainment exec Sheldon Cooper, who greenlighted the project, said he knew it would draw an international audience. "You go to Europe and say 'Al Capone,' and they make a pistol with their finger," he said.[58]

And, if Capone could walk into a movie palace or flick on a television today, he might see himself on the screen. At least 17 actors have portrayed him, including Rod Steiger, Titus Welliver, F. Murray Abraham, William Devane, William Forsythe, Jon Bernthal, Ray Sharkey, Eric Roberts, Robert De Niro, Ben Gazzara, Jason Robards Jr., Neville Brand, Isaac Keoughan, Michael Kotsohilis, Tom Hardy, Cameron Gharaee, and Stephen Graham.[59]

Chapter Seven

The Most Sensational Robbery in Philadelphia History

HORACE WALKER WAS STEPPING OFF A TROLLEY WHEN HE SPOTTED four men pushing a blue Buick sedan in front of the Olney Bank and Trust branch on Mascher Street. He started across the street to lend a hand. As he got closer, he saw the men had black stockings pulled down over their faces. Seconds later, he was caught in a fusillade of bullets.[1]

The 26-year-old druggist had unwittingly walked into the middle of the most sensational bank robbery in Philadelphia history.

The Olney Bank and Trust Robbery of 1926 also would have been the most lucrative bank heist in city history—if it had worked.

For a few brief moments, the young bandits had $80,000 in their hands—almost $1.2 million today.[2]

Any savvy bettor would have predicted the robbers would prevail. They were professional holdup artists who had planned the caper for weeks and timed it to a T. They outfitted themselves with high-caliber weapons and plenty of reserve ammunition. They successfully exploited a weak link in the bank's cash transfer routine. They knew that 60-year-old bank messenger William Miller would have at least $80,000 with him when he stopped at the Mascher Street branch at 9:45 a.m. on Tuesday, May 4, 1926.[3]

What they didn't count on was the extraordinary pluck of the ordinary people of Philadelphia.

When the bank car rolled up at 9:45 on the dot, Miller and Patrolman Joseph Kaelin were seated in the back. The satchel wedged between them was filled with $80,417 in cash. William Lee, a policeman's brother, was the driver. Officer Kaelin, 35, was often assigned to bank jobs because of his reputation as a crack shot.[4]

Miller popped in and out of the branch quickly. As Kaelin bent over to push the car door open for him, a big Buick roared up out of nowhere. It zigged and zagged to block their exit.

Five muscular men in their 20s swarmed out of the Buick, shouting profanities. One was less than five feet tall. One was nearly six feet. Their faces were distorted under tight silk-stocking masks.

Kaelin went for his revolver, but he was unable to coax it from its holster in the cramped backseat. Desperate, he took a swing at one of the stockinged faces. A second later, he heard a shotgun blast. Slumping to the floor of the car, the last thing he saw was an arm grabbing the $80,000.[5]

At that moment, it appeared the robbers were successful. Officer Kaelin lay semi-conscious, blood spilling from the back of his head. The Buick couldn't be traced to them because it was stolen. The thieves had been watching the street for three weeks, so they knew the beat cop assigned to Mascher Street would have already pulled the police box and passed by. It seemed like they were scot-free.

Then Officer Anthony Pizzo came into the picture. The beat cop was running a few minutes late that morning. He had spent some time helping schoolchildren cross a busy intersection. Just as he was about to turn onto Mascher Street, he heard gunfire. He drew his weapon, cautiously rounded the corner, and opened fire just as one of the bandits heaved the satchel into the Buick. The robbers returned fire with revolvers and sawed-off shotguns.[6]

When a bullet whirred past his ear, Pizzo took cover behind a slim metal pole and kept shooting. One witness said it was the most courageous thing he'd ever seen because the patrolman's head and most of his body were exposed. One of Pizzo's bullets shattered the Buick's commutator, blocking the flow of electricity to the engine. The car jerked to a stop. The driver, cursing, flung his door open and ran off.[7]

Pizzo sprinted to the car and leapt into it, trying to place the other three men under arrest. As they bolted from the car, he followed, emptying his gun as he ran. As he closed in on them, one dropped the loot. The patrolman turned to a boy standing in the street and instructed him to get the satchel back to the bank. One of the robbers cursed Pizzo and yelled, "We'll get you for this!"[8]

Officer Kaelin, now lying in the street and still bleeding from the back of his head, propped himself up on one elbow and fired at the fleeing robbers.[9]

Then, one of Pizzo's bullets made contact with the left calf of lanky, light-haired Harry Bentley, the largest of his four targets. The bullet didn't bring down the athletic 23-year-old. Mrs. Elsie McElroy, who watched it all from the window of her home at 118 West Wyoming Avenue, saw Bentley limp off in the direction of the others.

Joseph Curry, the 28-year-old ringleader, spotted a horse-drawn green-and-white milk truck with the driver out delivering. Tall and thin, Curry leapt into the driver's seat while the other gunmen scrambled into the back of the wagon to build a protective barrier of wood-and-wire milk bottle cases.

Curry, who wore his black hair parted down the middle, grabbed the reins and beat the horse until it was galloping down Rising Sun Avenue as fast as an automobile.[10]

Until a few minutes earlier, Pizzo had been looking forward to an afternoon of light duty at the circus. Suddenly, he was in a lopsided battle with four bandits.

But then, miraculously, his fellow officers and the people of Philadelphia put their thumbs on the scale.

That made for one of the most unpredictable days in Philadelphia Police Department history.

Instead of running from a hail of bullets, men and women ran into the streets to offer any help they could. Those who had cars invited police officers and armed strangers to jump in. Citizens armed themselves with handguns and rifles and knives, and, in one less successful instance, a broom.

Hundreds of housewives called the Philadelphia Police. They all heard gunshots—but on different streets. One woman said she believed someone might be robbing a horse-drawn milk wagon.

Howard Jayne and Charles McCready were laying a new piece of gas pipe on Rising Sun Avenue when they heard somebody fire a high-caliber pistol. They decided to see if they could help.

George Stark, a mechanic, had been trying to sell a touring car when the shooting started. He made a split-second decision to jump behind the wheel and join the pursuit.

Fred Loskamp, a garage owner who was inside the bank when the bandits struck outside, heard the shots and ran out. He saw Officer Pizzo firing a pistol from behind a narrow pole. He looked in the other direction and saw a stocking-faced man hoist a satchel into an automobile.

Instead of backing up into the safety of the bank, Loskamp ran to a nearby butcher shop and asked if anyone had a gun he could borrow. Failing there, he raced into the street and shouted that he needed a gun. A woman tossed him an automatic pistol and an ammo clip from her second-story window. He caught the pistol but not the clip. As he turned to pick it up, one of the robbers took a shot at him, but missed.[11]

Loskamp returned fire, but he missed, too.

In his peripheral vision, he could see that Officer Pizzo was pursuing the man.

Loskamp ducked up Palethorp Street, where he jumped on the running board of the touring car driven by George Stark. Stark had already picked up David Rittenhouse, a night watchman, and Walter Miller, a poultry salesman. They decided to tail the milk truck.

Meanwhile, William Miller, the bank messenger, spotted the boy with the $80,000 satchel walking toward the bank. Flashing his credentials, he instructed the boy to hand him the bag. The boy refused. They walked to the branch side by side.

McCready and Jayne, the gas company men, announced they were going to join the chase. Horace Walker, the druggist who stepped off the trolley, retrieved a sawed-off shotgun from the floor of the abandoned Buick and handed it to McCready as he and Jayne sped off.

With Jayne driving and McCready literally riding shotgun, the gas men spotted one of the bandits at a corner. Luckily, Frankie "Tenderloin" Doris had slipped on the sidewalk. McCready dove from the truck, tackled Doris, and wrested the gun from his grip. An ice truck driver arrived on the scene in the nick of time, wielding an ice axe.[12]

At 4606 Rising Sun Avenue, Officer Harry Cooper had just given his infant son, Harry Jr., a bottle. He had a cigarette and a second cup of coffee in front of him when he heard a sound his wife thought was just a car backfiring.

"That's no backfire," he said. "That's shooting. I've got to see what it is." Running out the door dressed in his uniform and an old brown sweater to ward off the temperatures that had dropped from 82 to 42 overnight, he told her, "Don't worry. Be back in a minute."

All Sadie Cooper could see as she watched the father of her five children run toward the noise was someone in a milk wagon firing bullets and hurling glass bottles into the street.[13]

Officer Cooper was running, weapon in hand, when Jayne came by, driving the gas company truck. Jayne told him to jump in. Cooper hopped on the truck's running board and began firing at the milk truck.

Volley after volley was exchanged between the milk truck and the two vehicles in pursuit. When Loskamp and Stark got about 30 feet behind the milk truck, they saw Jayne and Officer Cooper directly in front of them, closing in on it.

Officer Cooper, who had slipped into the passenger seat, still had his weapon trained on the truck. Loskamp saw two bandits shooting out of the back of the wagon and lobbing milk bottles into the street, hoping to puncture Jayne's tires.

Cooper held his fire to avoid hitting bystanders, but he steadied himself for a clear shot at the horse, hoping to bring the bandits to a stop. Suddenly, Joseph Curry, one of the bandits, bent out of the milk truck. He and Cooper fired almost in concert. Seconds later, Jayne felt the officer crumple beside him. He knew he had to steer toward the hospital.[14]

Stark, coming up from behind, boldly maneuvered the milk truck to the curb at Eighth and Erie. The gunmen leapt out, escaping down alleys and side streets.[15]

In the excitement, Curry's mask came nearly off, so Loskamp and Stark memorized his face.

Stark searched the milk truck and discovered a .38-caliber pistol. He went after the bandits with it.

Meanwhile, Officer Pizzo saw two men running toward Greenmount Cemetery. One of them jumped down a railroad embankment. Pizzo followed him so closely that he almost fell over him on the way down. The robber, panting and exhausted, fired at Pizzo, but he missed. He raised his pistol for a second shot but Pizzo, who had his own pistol, shouted, "Drop it." William Juliano, dog-tired, gave up.

Mrs. Elsie Baker and her husband, Fred, were drinking coffee in their West Percy Street kitchen when they heard their front door open. "It must be the laundryman," Mrs. Baker said. Instead, Harry Bentley and Joseph Curry, huffing and puffing, hustled through their kitchen and out their back door. The Bakers ran in the other direction.[16]

From her rear window, Mary Kreitter saw two men leaving the Bakers' house with guns drawn. Believing they had killed her neighbors, she boldly braced her broom across the alleyway to block their exit, but one of the men just pushed her aside.[17]

Stark was talking to a knot of excited bystanders on Erie Avenue, all of them on the lookout for four men in overcoats, when a man wearing a red sweater elbowed his way into the crowd. "Where're they at? Where're they at?" he asked. "Which way did they go?" Stark, the only member of the group who had been in on the chase, thought he recognized the man, but not the sweater.

"Why, you're one of them yourself," Stark said. "You're the one who was shooting from the wagon." Curry, wily enough to know the jig was up, reached for his gun.

Before he could draw it, Loskamp ran up behind him. In a jaw-dropping move, the garage owner jammed the automatic pistol he had borrowed from the woman on Rising Sun Avenue into Curry's neck and shouted, "Drop that gun, or I'll blow your head off."[18]

Meanwhile, Stark, leaving the block in his touring car, now with a shattered windshield and a bullet-ridden roof, gave Patrolman Eugene Biehler a lift. When they got near the corner of Fifth and Bristol,

Stark spotted Harry Bentley, the tall bandit Pizzo had shot in the calf. Unarmed and hobbling, he was arrested without a fight.[19]

Four thieves were headed to jail, outdone by ordinary Philadelphians and beat cops working in concert.

By the end of the month, all four gunmen would be sentenced to death for the murder of Officer Cooper.

Harry Cooper could have kissed his wife and infant son goodbye that morning and headed for the circus, where he was assigned for special duty that day. He could have ignored the gun battle.

Four days later, hundreds of Philadelphians climbed up the same steps he ran down on his way to his death. Mayor W. Freeland Kendrick was among them. They came to pay their respects to the hero policeman. They filed past his casket. On the breast of his dark blue serge suit lay a wreath from his five children, bearing the inscription "Our Daddy." The small room was filled with floral tributes, including a broken police shield set in roses displaying his badge number, 1584. Outside, 125 uniformed policemen and a detail of mounted police stood guard.[20]

Under a new law, all four bandits were tried for Officer Cooper's murder because it occurred during the commission of a felony they all took part in.

Curry, the triggerman, was tried first, a scant seven days after the robbery.

Charles Edwin Fox, the city's thin, spectacled district attorney, explained the rush to judgment to reporters: "We do not believe in railroading, but we do believe in expediting cases like this. We believe prompt action is a deterrent to crimes of this kind, if there is any deterrent."[21]

It was heralded as the first trial in US history to introduce film as evidence. Prosecutors reconstructed the robbery on film, with uniformed officers portraying the patrolmen involved and detectives playing Doris, Curry, Bentley, and Juliano.[22]

The arrested men hired two of Philadelphia's best defense attorneys—Louis E. McCabe and the legendary C. Stuart "Chippy" Patterson Jr.

Chippy Patterson and Joseph Curry got along so well that reporters were taken aback to hear them make puns and trade jokes in the courtroom. Although Curry grew up poor and Patterson's father was dean of the University of Pennsylvania Law School, when Curry addressed the famed attorney, he routinely shortened his nickname to "Chip."

One reporter said Curry acted more like a courtroom spectator than a man on trial for his life—often turning to smile at his wife and mother in the rear of the courtroom and occasionally flashing a grin at a juror.[23]

Only four of Patterson's hundreds of murder clients were executed—until 1926. All four bandits were sentenced to die in the electric chair.[24]

A fifth bandit escaped the chair. The meticulously planned caper included a backup driver. The fifth man, an experienced wheelman, waited in a stolen green touring car parked a block from the bank. His role was to run interference for the men in the blue Buick. If police gave chase, he'd get in the way. If the getaway car foundered, he was the backup.

He was all set to tail the Buick until he saw Officer Pizzo coming around the corner. He drove through the melee but never stopped, even when Frankie Doris spotted him and called out to the others.[25]

The newspapers speculated he would turn up dead for abandoning his partners, but that seemed unlikely, because none of the four ever gave up his name.

On Monday, March 7, almost 44 weeks after they bolted from the disabled Buick on Mascher Street, the bandits were pacing their small, windowless cells on death row at the State Correctional Institution at Rockview in rural western Pennsylvania. Their prison pants were already sliced from ankle to knee to make it easy to put the electrical contacts in place just after midnight.[26]

They were allowed no last visits from family or friends, but Juliano's father might have been shocked anyway to see his son without his thick dark curls. All the prisoners' heads had been shaved four days earlier to allow quick positioning of electrical conduits when they took their seats in the chair.[27]

Five of the condemned men's family members showed up at the prison gate the day before the execution, wishing the warden might relent, but they were turned away. The guards did relay Gert Doris's message to her husband: Be brave, do not tell anything, and walk to the chair with a smile on your face.[28]

Their five-hour trip on winding rural roads wasn't entirely wasted. They contacted a local funeral director to make arrangements for their loved ones' bodies.

The four condemned men smoked incessantly on their last night on earth. Their cell floors were littered with cigarette butts.

They would all face the same fate shortly, but they made much different use of their last 24 hours.

Frankie Doris was on the edge of collapse. "Why didn't my friends help me?" he asked anyone who would listen. "They didn't even come to see me. Why didn't they help me out of this jam?" He let out a long stream of profanity against individual gang members whom he said "threw me down." Before he left his cell, he wrote his name and his execution date on one wall.[29]

William Juliano was fatalistic: "I guess we were meant to die this way," he said. "It seems that every time we had a chance for a reprieve some big crime was committed in Philadelphia, and public sentiment

Philadelphians turned out to honor Officer Harry Cooper, who died in the chase, but they turned out again for the funeral of Joseph Curry, left, one of the men who went to the electric chair for killing the patrolman.
SPECIAL COLLECTIONS RESEARCH CENTER, TEMPLE UNIVERSITY LIBRARIES, PHILADEL-PHIA, PA

said thumbs down." Guards said Juliano was awake all night. At some point before he left his cell, he covered part of the wall with a crude heart with his name and his execution date.[30]

Joseph Curry, 28, spent his last day discussing his assets with his lawyer, Chippy Patterson, to ensure his wife, Aggie, and mother would be able to live comfortably. That night, Curry wrote letters to his loved ones. He wrote nothing on his wall.[31]

Harry Bentley took up a different legal matter with Patterson. He signed a detailed statement that Patterson said would exonerate at least one man serving a prison term. Like Curry, Bentley spent the evening writing to family members. He also wrote on his wall: "This is no man's land."

Because there were no windows in the cells and no way to tell time, several times during the last 24 hours, Bentley asked the guards, "How much longer?"[32]

That night, the condemned men, none of whom would live beyond his 20s, were asked if they had any last wishes.

Curry, still playing it as if he were unfazed by his death sentence, requested roller skates.

Bentley asked to hear a song called "It's That Old Pal of Mine." He said it reminded him of his father. An inmate who knew it was fetched to sing. Even the guards were touched hearing the ballad waft through the corridor of the death house.[33]

Six newsmen and six other witnesses took their places in the chilly death chamber before 7 a.m. The yellowish-gray room was devoid of decoration, save six black signs with gilt letters spelling out "silence."

To get to their concrete benches, official witnesses had to squeeze past the large roped-off electric chair. The chair was topped by a large ventilator hood identical to the vents that remove smoke from restaurant grills. The concrete floor was bare, except for a worn and faded green rug directly under the chair. The six window shades were drawn, and all the lights in the room were extinguished, except the one concealed in the ventilator hood. It bathed the electric chair in bright light.[34]

Meanwhile, convicts in the prison yard saw newsmen lined up against the fence, waiting for word from the witnesses, and shouted,

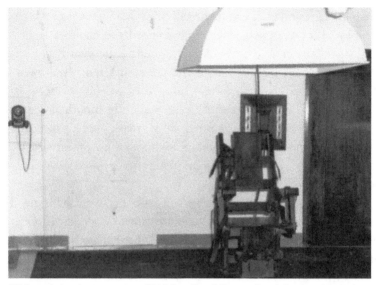

All four defendants went to "Old Smokey," Pennsylvania's electric chair, shown above. In 1927, the chair stood behind a small green door in a small room on the death row corridor at the State Correctional Institution at Rockview in Benner Township, near State College.
PENNSYLVANIA DEPARTMENT OF CORRECTIONS

"You guys come here to see the shocks?" "Shocks" is prison jargon for electrocution.[35]

Curry was the first to walk down the narrow, darkened corridor to the small green door that led to the electric chair. The previous day he told his attorney that he had made his peace with God. He said his sole regret was shooting Officer Cooper. He said he did not even know he killed him until he was taken to the station house after his arrest. He said with three cars chasing the milk wagon, it was "unavoidable."[36]

For the witnesses, the first hint that the executions were about to start was the faint sound of a voice raised in prayer in the corridor. A guard opened the green door and prison chaplain Rev. B. A. O'Hanlon entered, wearing a white surplice over a black cassock, with a red sash draped over his shoulders.

Chanting a prayer in Latin, the tall priest led Curry into the chamber by the hand. He stopped when they reached the chair. A tight-lipped Curry kissed the cross he was clutching before the guards grabbed him by his gaunt arms, placed him in the chair, and quickly drew a heavy leather belt across his torso to rein him in. As attendants began attaching sponges and electric conduits, Curry silently mouthed prayers. He continued as they pulled a grotesque brown mask over his face and head. As the executioner pulled the voltage switch, an uncomfortable buzzing noise commenced. Father O'Hanlon instinctively raised his voice as if to cover it.[37]

Curry's fingers suddenly convulsed into his hands, his head shot back, and his thin body might have come out of the chair if not for the heavy strap. A tuft of smoke floated upward from his head mask to the ventilator. Then the buzzing ended. The doctor pronounced Curry dead at 7:05 a.m.

The attendants began the process of removing Curry's corpse from the chair. One dabbed at the rug under his feet with a cloth, mopping up the water from the wet sponges that formed the contact points on his calves.[38]

When the mask was removed, witnesses said Curry's eyes were closed, but his lips still seemed to be formed in prayer. A guard rolled up a white enamel cart. Attendants grabbed the corpse by the shoulders and feet and flung it to the cart. The remains were whisked through the door to an adjoining room, where they were placed directly on the concrete floor.

Seconds later, witnesses heard Father O'Hanlon's voice coming up the corridor again. This time he led Bentley. Although the prisoner was not a Catholic, the others convinced him to accept spiritual guidance in his last minutes. He handed the cross back to the priest without kissing it.

Witnesses were shocked to see Bentley seat himself in the death chair. Almost instantly, the mask was over his head and face. When the buzzing started, Father O'Hanlon's voice rose again, but this time the buzzing grew louder as his voice did. A full eight minutes elapsed before the doctor pronounced Bentley dead at 7:14.[39]

Attendants quickly followed the same procedure, hurling the body on the metal stretcher. Just two minutes elapsed before Father O'Hanlon reappeared at the green door with Juliano, who was clutching a cross.

Juliano kissed the cross and turned toward the chair. He stared straight ahead as the attendants rushed to strap him in. Gaunt and less than five feet tall, he appeared frail in the high-backed, long-armed electric chair. His face was emotionless as they pulled the mask over his head.

When the executioner pulled the switch, witnesses noticed a wisp of smoke rise from the prisoner's small left foot. The execution was halted while attendants removed the heavy chest strap so the doctor could examine him. Witnesses noticed Juliano's chest was red.

When the switch was pulled a second time, the smoke grew thicker, and the buzzing sound was more distinct, as if flesh were being seared. The execution was halted again while the doctor used his stethoscope.

When the current was released for the third time, smoke billowed up. The power was cut for a third time, and the doctor stepped forward to examine Juliano. At 7:24 a.m., he turned to the witnesses and repeated for the third time that morning, "Gentleman, I pronounce this man dead." This time witnesses smelled burnt flesh.[40]

Attendants moved quickly to remove the small body, but, as soon as it was rolled out of the range of the ventilator, a nauseating odor filled the room. The attendant quickly rolled the cart into the adjacent room. The body was flung on the cement floor so quickly that Juliano's right leg rested on Bentley's right thigh.[41]

As soon as the corpse was out of sight, Father O'Hanlon brought Frankie Doris through the green door. When Doris wasn't bowing his head in prayer, his already lifeless eyes were fixed on the far wall.

When the voltage was applied, smoke rose from the crown of Doris's head, but it was sucked into the ventilator hood. A tuft of smoke rose from his left wrist. By the time the doctor pronounced him dead at 7:32 a.m., the odor of burnt flesh filled every part of the room.

The witnesses were asked to leave. As they did, they had to pass close to Doris's corpse, still in the electric chair with the grotesque head mask in place.[42]

In moments, the four bodies would be shifted from the cement floor to wicker caskets.[43]

Chippy Patterson had sought a pardon or a reprieve to the last second, but, for once, he was unsuccessful. His friends said he took the executions hard. When he visited Curry on the day before the execution, he recited snatches of the poem "Invictus" for him, thinking it might help him face his fate: "My head is bloody, but unbowed."

Patterson died in 1933, but his friends told his biographer that his physical deterioration began with his failure to save Curry and the others from the electric chair.[44]

The next day's papers carried all the dire details from Rockview's death row. One columnist speculated that the fifth Olney bandit may have been sipping coffee somewhere in the city while poring over the news of his friends' judicial executions.

The post-mortem exams of the condemned men showed that Curry, who always acted cool, died with painful acute appendicitis. He had complained about a pain in his side the previous night, but Juliano told him, "You'll forget all about it in the morning."[45]

Curry probably never imagined that, in two days, his funeral would draw thousands of spectators. The crowd waiting to see his casket carried out of his home, at 2715 Jasper Street, was so immense that 50 uniformed police were assigned to maintain order.[46]

Stories of the bandits' sad ends appeared on the front pages of papers across Pennsylvania. If they were written as cautionary tales, they didn't work.

Four days later and just over 150 miles to the west, a gang of thieves committed the first-ever armored car robbery on a rural road near Pittsburgh.[47]

CHAPTER EIGHT

Philly During Prohibition: Wet as the Atlantic Ocean

WHISKEY NEVER STOPPED FLOWING IN PHILADELPHIA DURING PROHI-bition. Alcohol was served at candy stores, cigar stores, and drugstores. Two men wearing hollow copper vests served as human speakeasies downtown. A 14-year-old boy in a Boy Scout uniform was caught dispensing liquor from his knapsack. The number of spots serving alcohol inexplicably climbed after the law went into effect. Philadelphia was soaking wet. A national magazine called it wet as the Atlantic Ocean.[1]

For Philadelphians, Prohibition was markedly ill-timed. The city was pining to enjoy life again after three straight years of unfathomable loss. On nearly every red brick block, residents were absorbing the deaths of 1,400 Philadelphians in the Great War and more than 10 times that in the Great Influenza of 1918.

Even before the United States entered the war, 27 Philadelphians lost their lives when a German U-boat torpedoed the *Lusitania*. Among the lost were eight members of the Crompton family of Chestnut Hill, who all perished despite the young father's attempt to buckle belts around his infant son and other five children to keep them afloat with him.[2]

Then 60,000 city boys left for World War I and 1,400 never returned.[3] Just weeks later, 12,000 Philadelphians succumbed within 35 days as influenza slammed the city. Bodies were stacked like firewood in funeral directors' yards. Coffins were auctioned to the highest bidders. Priests collected corpses off front porches. The final death toll was 17,500.[4]

The city was ready to forget, and distractions abounded. Philadelphians became early adopters of the automobile. Local boys returning from the European war drove motorized vehicles there and dreamed of having cars and trucks of their own. Self-starters, which Cadillac first installed in 1912, were becoming standard, making driving easier. The new cars had closed cabs, so they were useful in any weather. Homebuilders were incorporating auto garages into the rowhouses they built in the Cobbs Creek section of the city, at least 20 years ahead of the rest of the country. By the war's end in 1918, 7,000 trucks and 100,000 autos roamed city streets. Cars were so popular that the city's Automotive Row of tire stores and parts makers and auto showrooms stretched almost four miles down Broad Street, the city's broadest north-south street and the longest straight urban boulevard in the country.[5]

Market Street bisected Broad with a lineup of department stores to fuel city dwellers' dreams—Lits, Gimbels, Wanamaker's, Frank & Seder, N. Snellenburg & Co., and Strawbridge & Clothier.

Elsewhere in the city, proposals were afoot for a massive new library and a Greek Revival art museum. City fathers were planning a world's fair for the newly opened Fairmount Parkway. And widow Maria Nacchio and her eight children were twisting some of the first Philadelphia soft pretzels in their South Philadelphia bakery.[6]

Philadelphians were ready to toast to a brighter future, even if their alcoholic drinks were in teacups. The old arbiters of morality and decorum were slipping. The popularity of fiery anti-booze preacher Billy Sunday was fading, and once-powerful dance censor Marguerite Walz was running into family problems.

Sunday, once a star left fielder for the Phillies, chucked baseball to serve God as a celebrity preacher. He was so popular that women pushed and shoved their way into his revivals between 1914 and 1916. His sermons made headlines in major newspapers like the *Boston Globe*. For a while, he put whiskey in its place with his most-quoted line: "Whiskey and beer are all right in their place, but their place is in hell."[7]

But, by the early 1920s, Sunday's crowds were thinning with competition from other forms of entertainment—cars and dances and silent films.

Walz, a local dance teacher, landed in the pages of the *Ladies' Home Journal* after she convinced Philadelphia mayor J. Hampton Moore to appoint her the city's "dance censor" in 1921. Miss Walz instructed a crew of nearly 75 police officers how to crack down on cheek-to-cheek dancing, abdominal contact, and any form of shimmying. Her reign ended the next year after her brother George "Chubby" Walz was arrested for murder in New Jersey.[8]

When Prohibition was ushered in on January 17, 1920, circumstances suddenly favored a string of young, entrepreneurial sons of immigrants with mostly grade-school educations—Sam Lazar, Mickey Duffy, Charles Schwartz, and Max Hoff. Their bootlegging schemes brought together cops, chemists, big banks, small taprooms, international shippers, and the Reading Railroad. If they had been on the other side of the law, people would have used a newly voguish word to describe them. They'd be "go-getters."

Max "Boo Boo" Hoff stood five-foot-two and favored big bow ties, straw boater hats, and conservative suits with a .25-caliber Colt revolver in each hip pocket. At least once, he used one of them on a friend. The district attorney who could never quite nab him crowned him "king of the bootleggers."[9]

Max "Boo Boo" Hoff's defense attorney was a sitting US congressman.
COURTESY OF PARRY DESMOND

Damon Runyon and Westbrook Pegler wrote about Hoff. Al Capone counted him as a friend. Hoff sued heavyweight champion Gene Tunney. He attended a convention with Meyer Lansky and Lucky Luciano. A two-time winner of the Congressional Medal of Honor tried in vain to bring him down. His defense attorney was a sitting US congressman.

The line about him around the city was, "Whatever Boo Boo wants, well, that's what Boo Boo gets."[10]

When Hoff went to New York City in 1933 to watch 250,000 workers march up Fifth Avenue in support of the National Recovery Administration, he wasn't just one of the swarm of 1.5 million spectators watching from the sidelines. James Thurber noted his visit in the vaunted *New Yorker* magazine. Labeling him Philadelphia's public enemy number one, Thurber also revealed that Hoff was a serious slingshot enthusiast.

In reality, Hoff did tap his mark in about nine out of ten salvos. Using a simple rubber band and heavyweight tinfoil he bought at a florist shop, he usually aimed at the lower part of the body.

According to Thurber's humorous recounting, the bootlegger zapped a woman from a car window 50 feet away. She whirled around and slapped the man walking right behind her. To hear Thurber tell it, Hoff pinged one off a cop in Times Square from eight feet away. [11]

Hoff got his nickname growing up in South Philadelphia when his mother, in her heavy Russian-Jewish accent, would call his brother Lou for dinner. "Lou Lou" sounded like "Boo Boo" to their Irish and Italian playmates. They started calling Lou "Boo Boo," and his younger brother Max became "Little Boo Boo."[12]

The name stuck, even when his liquor empire covered more territory than Al Capone's Chicago operation, stretching as far as St. Louis and St. Paul.

Hoff quit school after eighth grade and worked in a cigar store for $12 a week. The owner quickly offered him a 25 percent raise because his personality attracted so many customers, but Hoff, who had a bustling nervous energy, turned it down. He wanted to be his own boss. He opened a pool room and a political club that was a front for high-stakes gambling. He became a prizefight promoter and a millionaire before he was 28.[13]

A Nashville newspaper said Hoff's boxing career began when he helped a fighter named Frankie Clark get some matches for free. The fighter's friends, according to the story, wanted Hoff to manage them, too, and so a business was born. However it began, Hoff grew the largest stable of boxers on the East Coast. He booked fights at venues like New York's Madison Square Garden. He was a head shorter than any of his boxers, which made for some eye-catching publicity photos.[14]

His height aside, boxers did what Hoff wanted. Newspapers called him a "fistic mogul." As lightweight Harry Blitman put it, "When the little man said come, you came."[15]

In 1928 Hoff filed legal papers in Wilmington, Delaware, making Max Hoff, Inc. the first stable of boxers to be incorporated in the US. He was savvy enough to snag sports-page headlines and smart enough to stay out of the news headlines as his bootlegging empire grew so large that he had 175 phones installed in his downtown office in the 1930s.[16]

Hoff was blessed with some of the best geography in the country for liquor production and distribution. The Delaware Valley was home to colleges and chemical companies where scientists knew how to make cocktail fixings out of the cheap industrial alcohol used in perfumes and photo paper and hair oils.

Hoff's three legal alcohol plants were the first step in reformulating industrial alcohol so it could be repackaged as 80-proof booze. The volume of industrial alcohol delivered to Philadelphia doubled during Prohibition. About 500 gallons of hair oil ingredients were shipped to one nearby village of just 50 residents.

Booze from other countries also flowed through the city's international port, on freight trains and in false-bottom coal trucks.

The Seventh Street Gang, homegrown hoods from Philadelphia, supplied the local muscle.[17]

LeRoy Helms met the gang close up when he was the 14-year-old pitcher for a firehouse baseball team outside Downingtown, not far from the white porticoed mansion that served as Hoff's hideaway in the early 1930s. When Boo Boo Hoff called the fire station to invite the team to his place for an afternoon game, the players decided to accept, but they agreed it would be best to let Hoff's team win.

The firehouse team was still agape at the 40-room mansion and the manicured lawn when Hoff's first player stepped up to the mound wearing a shoulder holster with a pistol inside. They noticed most of the opposing team was armed.[18]

Armed or not, Helms said Hoff's players were skilled competitors who obviously enjoyed the game. Afterwards, players were invited inside for food and drinks. Although Helms attended several impressive corporate dinners as an adult, he said he had never seen a better spread than Hoff put out in the middle of the Great Depression. As the visitors were leaving, Hoff invited them to take food home for their families.

Hoff, who neither drank nor smoked himself, warned the younger boys not to go anywhere near the beer, but he said the older boys were welcome to have a couple.[19]

It takes trusted relationships to make and ship 1.5 million gallons of illegal alcohol a year while under the watch of police and federal agents, and Hoff built a chain of them stretching from his European suppliers to the men who unloaded his railroad cars in St. Louis. Successful bootleggers like Hoff, who was netting $5 million a year, collaborate. The most successful forge unbreakable alliances. Whether his associates were faithful or fearful or financially rewarded, Hoff induced loyalty, even from one man he shot three times.[20]

Harry Krengel, an old friend of Hoff's, was sitting in a car, talking with Hoff, when he was shot in both legs in May 1940. Police were certain Hoff, who drove Krengel to the hospital, was the shooter. They had a motive in mind—a $20,000 loan Krengel failed to repay even though Hoff had fallen on hard times after Prohibition. Krengel refused to press charges. He said he didn't see any gun in the car, and he didn't know who had shot him.[21]

John Summers, who ran the small bar at Hoff's posh gambling house on Locust Street, admired his boss. "He was one of the finest fellas you ever met. You'd never have thought he was a racketeer or anything like that," said Summers, whose job was to serve illegal liquor, pay off city police every Saturday afternoon, and push all the liquor and roulette tables up into the fake walls when City Hall phoned in a 30-minute warning of an upcoming police raid.[22]

Historians estimate Hoff's wealth grew to $10 million by the early 1930s—about $153 million today. He kept a luxurious apartment in

West Philadelphia and a home in Cobbs Creek. He entertained friends at three nightclubs, several gambling venues, and his ornate-columned mansion near Downingtown. He often rented hotel ballrooms to fete visiting celebrity pals like singer Al Jolson.[23]

Hoff owned Franklin Mortgage and Investment Company, and his relationship with the prestigious Union National Bank was cozy enough to get the bank president fired.

Hoff's defense attorney was Benjamin Golder, a sitting US congressman.[24]

He routinely gave Christmas presents to thousands of people. One year he gave away more than $100,000 in gifts, much of it to police officers and city officials. He told a friend the money wasn't important to him. "All I want is to leave enough to support my wife and sons comfortably," he said.[25]

His generosity to police and city officials was so blatant that it often made the news. Under the headline "Prominent Quaker City Fans to See Fight," the *Inquirer* reported that Hoff would be in charge of a special train to run from Philadelphia to Jersey City, New Jersey, for the 1924 Harry Wills–Angel Firpo fight, and Judge Eugene Bonniwell and Magistrate Frank X. O'Connor would be on it.[26]

The man hired to topple bootleggers like Hoff arrived in Philadelphia with the new year of 1924. He was so widely admired that Will Rogers lauded him in his newspaper column, Lowell Thomas wanted to write his biography, and *Time* magazine put him on its cover. Like the new heads of police in New York, Chicago, and Los Angeles, he was a military man.

Short, wiry and erect, Brig. Gen. Smedley Butler had the distinction of being one of a handful of soldiers in history to win two Congressional Medals of Honor.

Mayor W. Freeland Kendrick appointed him. Kendrick, whom the *Inquirer* called the city's best-dressed citizen, was considered to have the widest circle of friends and acquaintances of any politician in Pennsylvania. The tall, back-slapping former insurance man knew thousands of people by their first names. He belonged to 50 fraternal organizations, and he was the former Imperial Potentate of the Shriners of North America, the highest honor any Shriner can be afforded.[27]

Kendrick, who ran on a law-and-order platform, gave Butler carte blanche to clean up police corruption and crack down on bootleggers. It was a tall order. Police counted 8,000 places to buy whiskey in the city limits, and other estimates were double that. Some speakeasies required secret passwords to enter; others featured underground escape tunnels. Rents for promising downtown corners quadrupled once Prohibition began.[28]

The new director of public safety was sworn in wearing his marine uniform, but afterwards he quickly switched to a uniform of his own making—blue with gold trim and a cape lined in bright red, each piece tailored to his needle-straight, five-foot, four-inch frame.[29]

Within days, Butler closed 973 saloons. He realigned police districts to thwart bribes in a city so crooked that police bribed other police to get on elite enforcement units where the payoffs were bigger.[30] He suspended eight police lieutenants for neglect of duty.

In his first year on the job, Butler closed 2,566 speakeasies. The total for the previous year was 220.[31]

Costumes and floats poking fun at Butler's police crackdown were suddenly banned from the 1924 Mummer's Parade, ruffling some feathers among the marchers.

His job was to take down the operations of men like Boo Boo Hoff, a bootlegger so cagey that he kept $10 million in 14 separate bank accounts under pseudonyms. It turned out Hoff wasn't nearly as big a headache for Butler as the man who hired him.[32]

The general, who led the country in arrests for intoxication in his first year, was too diligent for Mayor Kendrick, who knew exactly how much Prohibition his constituents wanted. Kendrick's vision for the city didn't include giant floodlights, police raids of private parties, or alcohol checkpoints on city streets.

After Butler's raiders repeatedly found young girls plied with liquor in private party rooms at the tony Ritz-Carlton hotel, he had no doubt the mayor would agree he should padlock the place. He was so sure he didn't ask. He went straight to the newspapers.

"We have in our possession conclusive evidence of drinking orgies in virtually all of the hotels," Butler told reporters. "The evidence centers around so-called parties in which extremely young girls, some of them only 16 and 17, have been given cocktails and other concoctions. Any place that connives in providing liquor for minors—mere children—is going to be punished."

Butler formed a squad of handsome, young undercover officers in formal dress who would crash private hotel parties and report violations of the liquor laws. He called them his fish-and-soup squad.

The Philadelphia Hotelmen's Association, representing the city's $45 million hotel industry, pushed back.[33]

Mayor Kendrick, planning the upcoming Sesquicentennial Exposition, a world's fair celebrating the 150th anniversary of the signing of the Declaration of Independence, was unwilling to alienate hoteliers by padlocking any luxury hotel.[34]

To boot, Kendrick nixed Butler's plan to revoke the dancing license of the glittery Bellevue-Stratford Hotel. The Bellevue, a clubhouse for the Philadelphia establishment, had hosted five US presidents. Society pages called the 1,090-room hotel the grande dame of Broad Street. Charity balls and society weddings there were lit by fixtures designed by Thomas Edison. Its ballroom was four times as large as the East Room of the White House.[35]

Kendrick said hotel business was vital to the city. Butler demanded there be no distinction between a hotel patronized by the rich and a corner saloon frequented by the poor. Their scrape made all the papers. Readers in places as far-flung as Utah, North Carolina, California, Wisconsin, and Texas were following the back-and-forth between the mayor and the general.

While they tiffed, Hoff kept his liquor businesses on keel and kept booking fighters for big matches in New Orleans, New York, and Newark.

After the mayor dashed his plans, Butler came to the epiphany that his hiring was a political move by Kendrick, who never imagined he would approach the job with such vigor.

Just before Christmas 1925, the mayor came to his own epiphany—that Butler would never go quietly. He abruptly told a group of surprised newsmen, "I had the courage to bring Butler here, and I have the courage to fire him."[36]

Just short of two years on the job, Butler was out. Before he left, he accused the mayor of lacking the moral courage to permit impartial law enforcement. He passed reporters proof that Kendrick had told him that it would be best to "lay off the big places."[37]

As he left office, Butler played off a quote from Civil War general William Tecumseh Sherman, who said, "War is hell." Butler turned it on Philadelphia: "Sherman was right about war, but he was never head of police in Philadelphia."[38]

Boo Boo Hoff's business went on unabated. When celebrities like Groucho Marx or John Barrymore played in Philadelphia, they could always get a drink during intermission. Theatergoers said the second act was always better than the first.

Sometimes, Hoff's betting, boxing, and bootlegging businesses crisscrossed. John Summers, who worked in Hoff's Locust Street gambling spot, remembered the afternoon of September 23, 1926, hours before the first Tunney-Dempsey heavyweight championship fight in Philadelphia. Hoff's place took in thousands of dollars in bets that morning, and all the big money was on Dempsey. About 3 p.m. the bettors returned.

"Boy, you'd have thought hell broke loose," Summers said. "Everybody was running around like chickens with their heads off. They all switched their bets to Tunney. They found out something and, sure enough, it turned out for them. But how they ever got the news, I don't know."[39]

The *New York Times* had been writing about the fight since July. The *New York Daily News* devoted 10 pages to it that morning; the *Philadelphia Inquirer*, 12. Millionaires Andrew Mellon and Vincent Astor were among the 130,000 fans who sat through 10 rounds in drenching rain. Twenty million more tuned in on radio.

Packs of batteries supplied the most incandescent light ever trained on a boxing arena, and 37 bright, cone-shaped beams were fixed above the ring. When retired lightweight champ Battling Nelson first saw it, he sat with his mouth agape at the spectacle of it for five solid minutes.[40]

The bettors who switched their wagers at 3 p.m. were correct. Tunney outboxed Dempsey from the first bell to the last.

Boo Boo Hoff sued Tunney for what he said happened minutes before Tunney walked out into the rain that night. Hoff said he lent Tunney's manager, Billy Gibson, $20,000 in the dressing room right before the fight, and Tunney and Gibson agreed the loan would be forgiven if Tunney lost but, if Tunney won, Hoff would get 20 percent of his earnings as long as he was heavyweight champion.

Hoff produced a written contract with two signatures—Gibson's and Eugene Joseph Tunney's. The hitch was that Tunney's legal name was James Joseph Tunney. For decades, fans puzzled whether Hoff lied or Tunney pulled a fast one.

A few days before their famed "long count" rematch at Soldier Field in Chicago the next year, newspapers published an open letter from Dempsey to Tunney, asking him to explain the $20,000 contract with Hoff. In the letter, published under headlines like "Dempsey Claims Fight Was Fixed," Dempsey told Tunney he knew Tunney beat him on the level, but he'd like Tunney to explain why Hoff was so sure Tunney would win that he'd forgive a $20,000 debt if he lost.[41]

"Before I got into Philadelphia on fight night, I was tipped off there's something phony about this fight," Dempsey wrote. Tunney refused to explain, and boxing officials defended Hoff.[42]

The long count rematch ended Dempsey's boxing career, but his good-natured acceptance of the outcome endeared him to fans. When his shocked wife saw his bloody, battered face and asked how it had happened, he said, "Honey, I forgot to duck."

His self-effacing quip was widely quoted for decades. It was the first thing President Ronald Reagan said to his wife, Nancy, when she rushed to the hospital to see him after he was shot by John Hinckley Jr. in 1981.

Dempsey retired after the long count fight. In 1935, he opened a restaurant across the street from New York's Madison Square Garden. Dempsey's became famous for its cheesecake. The cakes were shipped all over the world, including several each year to French president Charles De Gaulle.[43]

Max Hoff's name will always be an asterisk in the first Dempsey-Tunney championship fight.

The seven months beginning in August 1928 were bad for Boo Boo Hoff, but they were worse for about 164 Philadelphia police officers.

Two high-profile shootings and rising deaths from poison hootch tipped political will in favor of a special grand jury on bribery and bootlegging.[44] A main target was Hoff, but, after seven months of testimony, the district attorney still couldn't prove his guilt.

The probe resulted in the suspension or arrest of more than 160 police officers. It proved police were on the take to the tune of $2 million a year.[45] When officers were asked to explain their beach houses and high bank balances, they said they made extra money by betting on the right horse, being lucky at craps, being lucky at poker, raising thoroughbred dogs for sale, building bird cages for the retail trade, and lending money to people who later remembered them in their wills.[46]

Hundreds of police and public officials, including former Director of Public Safety George W. Elliott, received Christmas turkeys with large gift tags saying, "Merry Christmas from Boo Boo and the boys." It was rumored that many of the turkeys were stuffed with money.[47]

Edward Goldberg, proprietor of the store that would become the I. Goldberg chain, testified he sold machine guns, sawed-off shotguns, and bulletproof vests to Hoff.[48]

Louis Elfman, Hoff's former chauffeur, showed up to testify with his face battered. He testified that a Chicago boxer had beat him that week, then took him to Hoff's office, where the boxer warned him not to squeal on his good friend Max Hoff.[49]

Elfman and Goldberg made headlines, but, in the end, the district attorney couldn't pin anything on Hoff because his name seldom appeared on any paperwork. He operated businesses through trusted agents and dummy corporations that were tough to unravel.

Before the grand jury finished its work, Hoff's wife, Helen, died. News reports said she died of a chronic malady made worse by worry over the inquiry.[50]

The grand jury investigation ended on March 28, 1929. When it began, audiences packed into the courtroom, but, in the end, people walked out before the conclusion of the report was read. The murders were unsolved, and Hoff was untouched.

Two dirigible stories probably caught more newspaper readers' attention on the front pages the next day. A sudden gust above Lakehurst Naval Air Station tore an army blimp from the control of a 100-man landing crew and blew it a quarter of a mile, twisting its frame, ripping its fabric to tatters, and scattering its valuable helium gas to the winds. Meanwhile, the dirigible *Los Angeles* had given up its search for four persons lost in an amphibian plane after searching from Norfolk, Virginia, to the Fenwick Shoals Lighthouse off the Delaware shore.[51]

Hoff's Midas touch vanished after the grand jury and the repeal of Prohibition. His finances never recovered, but he lived another 12 years, remarried, fathered a second son, and always managed to keep a step or two ahead of the law.

When Al Capone was sentenced to a year at Eastern State Penitentiary for carrying an unlicensed, concealed .38-caliber revolver in a Philadelphia movie theater in the spring of 1929, records show Hoff visited him at least once.

Capone had come to Philadelphia on a seashore train and was killing time, waiting for a train back to Chicago, when he ducked into a Market Street movie theater. Two detectives arrested him as he walked out under the bright marquee lights.[52]

Just a few days earlier, Capone and Hoff had been laughing and joking on the Atlantic City boardwalk, Capone rolling down it in a sedan chair. They attended the Atlantic City Conference, along with Lucky Luciano, Nucky Johnson, Meyer Lansky, Dutch Schultz, Jake Guzik, Waxey Gordon, Frank Costello, and Johnny Torio. It was one of the first organized crime conventions.

It started awkwardly when the Jewish and Italian mobsters arrived at the exclusive Breakers Hotel on the Boardwalk, where Nucky Johnson, who was Irish American, had booked the rooms. The Breakers was restricted to white Anglo-Saxon guests. Once the hotel management realized who was checking in, some delegates were refused rooms. Johnson quickly ordered limousines to usher them to other hotels.[53]

The mobsters discussed their common business problems—violence, competition, and, most important, how to continue to make money when Prohibition ended.

Hoff, who spent millions on himself and others during Prohibition, saw his fortune wane after the law was revoked in 1933. By 1940, money was so important to him that his friend Harry Krengel may have been shot over an unpaid debt.[54]

The only joint he operated after Prohibition was the Village Barn, a jukebox restaurant near the University of Pennsylvania campus that served nothing stronger than soda pop.[55]

The law never defeated him, but cash flow and tax problems did.

Hoff, whose fortune was once estimated as high as $10 million, left a $500 estate when he died in his bed in his plainly furnished home at 4723 Larchwood Avenue on April 27, 1941. He left no will.[56]

His one hope—to leave enough money to support his wife and sons comfortably—was not fulfilled.

The *New York Daily News* headline was "Boo Boo Hoff, Prohibition Millionaire, Dies Broke."

The reporter summed up Hoff's life in boxing parlance: "The final bell rang today for Max Boo Boo Hoff, 48, onetime multimillionaire and muscle man of the Prohibition era, who gained national prominence for a mysterious connection with the Dempsey-Tunney championship prize fight."[57]

Chapter Nine

H. H. Holmes Meets the Hangman Here

Serial Killer H. H. Holmes built a booby-trapped hotel that lured tourists to their deaths during the 1893 Chicago World's Fair. He was never charged with any of their deaths, but he was hanged for murder three years later. That happened almost 800 miles away at 1400 East Passyunk Avenue in South Philadelphia.

What occurred inside a hallway at Moyamensing Prison on the gray morning of May 7, 1896, still ranks as one of the most bizarre hangings in city history. As one detective put it, it is a true story that outrivals fiction.

Holmes's hanging offense was the 1894 chloroform murder of his business partner, Benjamin F. Pitezel, in Philadelphia's commercial district. By the time a relentless sleuth tripped him up months later, the charming blue-eyed druggist was wanted in other parts of the country for bigamy, horse thievery, land swindles, insurance scams, and the murders of two women and three children.

H. H. Holmes gained fame in Chicago, but he was hanged in Philadelphia in one of the most bizarre executions in city history.
WIKIMEDIA COMMONS

He had pulled off far more elaborate schemes than the one that unhorsed him. He was married to three women at the same time. He worked his way through medical school pulling insurance scams. Even his name wasn't authentic. He was born Herman Webster Mudgett.

The Pitezel murder was a relatively simple insurance scheme. Holmes and Pitezel were in it together at the beginning.

They agreed to insure Pitezel's life for $10,000, buy a corpse from a medical school, burn and disfigure it, pass it off as Pitezel, and collect their payout. Pitezel planned to take his cut and return to the family he sorely missed in St. Louis.[1]

Holmes had another agenda that did not require a medical school cadaver. Rather than faking Pitezel's death, he would kill his partner. It might have worked, too, but Holmes got greedy.

Because he and Pitezel owned some land jointly, Holmes elected to kill the entire family his partner so missed—the widow and children, ranging from an infant to a 16-year-old.

If he could get all the heirs out of the picture, Holmes could take the whole pot for himself. Instead, in 14 months, he found himself pitching pennies in a damp prison cell, killing time while he waited to hear whether a jury would find him guilty.

They did. He was sentenced to die. His jig was up.[2]

It all began to unravel for him a year earlier on Tuesday, September 4, when a carpenter named Eugene Smith happened upon Pitezel's body. Smith originally thought he had discovered the body of Mr. B. F. Perry, because that is who Pitezel was masquerading as when Smith had met him one month earlier.[3]

Smith had been passing along Callowhill Street one day in August when he noticed a large muslin banner stretched across a red brick storefront. Red and black letters spelled out "B. F. Perry: Patents Bought and Sold." Smith inquired if Mr. Perry might be able to help him patent a saw set he had invented—a tool used to set the teeth on a handsaw.[4]

"Mr. Perry" suggested Smith bring him a model of his invention, which he did. On one of his visits, Smith noticed a fit, mustachioed man with vivid blue eyes and thick crescent eyebrows enter the building and climb straight upstairs to the second floor. He later identified the man as Holmes.[5]

When Smith had no news of his patent by the first week of September, he returned to 1316 Callowhill to inquire. He found the door unlocked, but the office empty. He gave a holler upstairs. He took a seat for several minutes. Finally, he thought it best to return the next morning.

Again, the office door was unlocked, but there was still no sign of life. He shouted for Perry. He decided to check upstairs. That's when he saw a sight that chilled his blood. A man's decomposing body lay across the floor, burned and disfigured and close enough to the window that the last of the summer sun beat down on it. The stench fouled the air. The face was too putrid to say for certain, but the victim had the same size and coloring as Mr. Perry, and some of the clothing was identical to pieces Perry had worn.

The corpse was removed to the city morgue, which was located directly behind the office building. When the lungs and stomach were sliced open, both emitted the peculiar sweet smell of chloroform.[6]

After the body was buried in the city's potter's field, a letter that should have raised a red flag arrived at the office of Fidelity Mutual Life Insurance Company. J. D. Howe, an attorney hired by Holmes, claimed B. F. Perry was actually B. F. Pitezel of St. Louis, one of Fidelity Mutual's insureds. His business partner would be in touch.[7]

When Holmes came to Philadelphia to collect the insurance money, he brought Pitezel's daughter Alice to identify the remains. Of course, Alice's mother probably told her the disinterred body she was identifying was actually a cadaver Holmes had purchased from a New York City doctor, doubled over into a suitcase and toted to 1316 Callowhill. She likely had no idea she was staring at her father, who was no longer in on the scheme.

The first act of the conspiracy went off without a hitch, at least for Holmes. Several weeks later, it got bumpier.[8]

Marion C. Hespeth, a notorious train robber jailed in St. Louis, contacted the police out of the blue. He said a former cellmate who had pulled off some lucrative insurance scams in the past had asked him to find a lawyer who could help him and his accomplice swindle a Philadelphia insurance firm. He promised Hespeth $500 for his help. Hespeth recommended J. D. Howe. Holmes didn't pay up, so Hespeth was spilling the names to the police—Howe, Holmes, and Pitezel.[9]

The insurance company hired the famed Pinkerton Detective Agency to get to the bottom of it, and the City of Philadelphia assigned one its top investigators. Meanwhile, Holmes's legend as a consummate con man was mushrooming. He sold horses he didn't own. He peddled bogus cures. One man paid him $2,000 for a machine Holmes said could turn water into gas. And Holmes conned Mrs. Pitezel into giving him two of her other children for safekeeping—Howard, age eight, and Nellie, age nine.

While detectives were on his trail in 1894, unbeknownst to them, Holmes was moving people around the country as if they were chess pieces. Like a puppet master, he shuffled his clueless third wife, two women in Chicago, three of Pitezel's five offspring, and Mrs. Pitezel and the remaining two children. His plan was to kill all the Pitezel family members, but he couldn't do it all at once.

He told the Widow Pitezel a litany of lies about the whereabouts of her family. He said her husband was hiding in South America. At one juncture, he told her that her daughters were touring Niagara Falls and New York City. At another, he said they had sailed for Europe. He had 16-year-old Alice write letters to her mother in St. Louis, even though he was putting them up blocks apart in Detroit.

Alice's letters are heartbreaking when the Pitezels' actual physical proximity becomes apparent. The 16-year-old asked if her infant brother was talking yet. She begged for a warm coat so she could go outside. She said she longed to share her new experiences with her mother and her grandparents in person—she had eaten a red banana, crossed the Potomac River, and seen an ostrich that was a head taller than her.[10]

On Saturday, November 17, 1894, the Pinkertons made a show of arresting Holmes for insurance fraud in Boston. Holmes's plan B, to flee the country with his unsuspecting third wife, would no longer work.

The detectives held him on an outstanding warrant for horse thievery in Texas. Not wanting to be tried there, Holmes agreed to be extradited to Philadelphia. On the train trip there, he asked one of the detectives if he could hypnotize him. The detective said no. Then Holmes offered him $500 to go under. The detective still refused.[11]

Bound for Philadelphia, Holmes was confident he would get a lighter sentence for insurance fraud there than he would have for the horse theft he pulled in Texas. He might have, too, if it hadn't been for Philadelphia detective Frank Geyer.

Geyer, one of the city's top sleuths, knew instinctively that Holmes's story about carrying a doubled-over cadaver from New York City inside a suitcase didn't ring true. The detective remembered seeing two men carry the corpse from 1316 Callowhill to the morgue—one at the head and one at the feet. When he interviewed Holmes, he asked him how he had crammed the cadaver into the suitcase. Holmes said his medical training enabled him to fold it. In the back of his mind, Geyer thought about the body he saw, stiff enough to be carried by two men positioned at opposite ends. He wondered where Holmes would find a medical man to testify how to tauten a body once rigor mortis had been broken.[12]

And, regrettably for Holmes, Geyer, a loving father of a young daughter, was determined to find the missing Pitezel girls and their little brother. That could only end badly for Holmes, but the prisoner didn't fret. He presupposed the detective's search would go nowhere.[13]

Geyer pored over the letters the children had written to their mother, trawling for even the smallest clues. He crisscrossed the country carrying photos of the Pitezels and one of Holmes. Tireless, he visited hotel clerks and real estate agents in Cincinnati, Indianapolis, Detroit, Toronto, and the small towns that circled them. The keen national interest in the case helped. The Pitezel story was so well-publicized that headline writers began referring to the children by their first names only.

Adults in all walks of life wanted to do whatever they could to help. In Toronto, a real estate agent led Geyer to a lovely gabled cottage on Vincent Street where flowerpots hung from the running trim on the gracious front porch, all brimful with clematis. He said he had leased the place to a man who paid a full month's rent but vanished after just a few days. His tenant resembled the fine-featured man in Geyer's photo.

A neighbor on Vincent Street told Geyer he remembered Holmes because he had borrowed his spade to dig a potato pit in his cellar. The detective borrowed the same shovel and headed for the cellar.

The current lady of the house graciously lifted a large piece of oil-cloth from the kitchen floor and pointed to a tiny trapdoor leading to a pitch-black cellar less than five feet deep. She gave them lamps to light the way.[14]

The deeper Geyer and his helpers dug, the more the sickening odor of decay filled the cellar. Three feet down, a shovel struck the girls' nude bodies.[15]

Holmes had rigged a small trunk as a gas chamber, killed Nellie and Alice inside it, and then dropped their bodies into the deep hole in the dirt floor. One of their toys was found upstairs. When the news got out, Toronto went wild with morbid excitement. Mrs. Pitezel was rushed to the city to identify the bodies.[16]

Unfortunately, the only remains the doctors could clean nicely enough for a mother's glance were Alice's teeth and two plaits of the girls' hair. The coroner covered Alice's head with paper and made a cutout to show the teeth. A freshly washed plait of each girl's hair was displayed nearby.

Carrie Pitezel instantly recognized Alice's teeth and hair. Then she asked, "Where's Nellie?" If she had looked around, she would have seen tears streaming down the faces of the men circling her. Seconds later, when she spotted only a single long black plait of Nellie's hair, she fell apart. Seven months later, Geyer wrote, "The shrieks of that poor, forlorn creature still ring in my ears."[17]

Geyer spent the next six weeks in Indianapolis, following his hunch about where Holmes had separated Mrs. Pitezel's eight-year-old son from his older sisters. He was determined to find Howard, but it wasn't until the final days of August that he caught a break. A real estate man in suburban Irvington recognized Holmes's photo. He said it resembled a young man who had rented a home the previous autumn. It was set back from the road on a large lot. He had a small boy with him.[18]

Detectives searched the empty home until night fell. After dark, two little boys playing detective snuck into the cellar and conducted their own search. One stuck his arm up the chimney and some teeth and bone fell out. When word got out, a large crowd turned out. When the police returned, they found Howard Pitezel's femur, his pelvic bones, and some charred organs stuck in the chimney. They also found some buttons from Howard's little overcoat.[19]

Meanwhile, back in Philadelphia, it was dawning on Holmes that he would be standing trial for murder, not another insurance scam. He was indicted that September. If he were convicted, Moyamensing Prison would be his last address.

In 1896 nearly an entire block of East Passyunk Avenue was ceded to the turreted prison. Since 1977, many Philadelphians have known it only as an Acme Market with an in-house pharmacy, ironic because Holmes worked as a druggist in Chicago.

Moyamensing Prison was designed by Thomas Ustick Walter, the same architect who designed the dome of the US Capitol. The dome was designed to inspire. Moyamensing was designed to frighten.
PENNSYLVANIA PRISON SOCIETY, WIKIMEDIA COMMONS

Thomas Ustick Walter, who designed Moyamensing in the 1830s, is the same architect who, two decades later, conceived of the stunning cast-iron dome of the US Capitol. While the Capitol dome was meant to inspire, Moyamensing was designed to intimidate. Walter intentionally added parapets, ramparts, broad black bars, and steep stone walls to the prison to give it a disquieting air.[20]

Edgar Allan Poe spent a night in the drunk tank there in 1849. When abolitionist Passmore Williamson was jailed there in 1855, his visitors included Harriet Tubman and Frederick Douglass. Gangster Al Capone was processed there in 1929.

But, in 1895, all the buzz on the block was about Holmes, and he reveled in it. When he walked into court one day and saw a packed gallery, he turned to his guard and said, "This is a big crowd, isn't it? I believe the whole of Philadelphia would like to get in here today."[21]

At the desk in his cell, he wrote letters and granted interviews and wrote a hot-selling confessional book full of floridly ornamented lies that netted him $7,500. One detective said all of Holmes's stories were "decorated with flamboyant draperies."[22]

He said he put Alice and Nellie on a steamer headed for Liverpool. He claimed he had chloroform only because it was an ingredient in a new cleaning solution he invented. He said he once dressed Nellie as a boy to throw off detectives. He claimed he had been in a railway collision in the West and woke up in a hospital with his memory erased.[23]

He confessed to sinking a woman's body in a trunk in Lake Michigan. He convinced Georgianna Yoke, Myrta K. Belknap, and Clara Lovering they were each his lawfully wedded wife. He told friends he was an only child with no living relatives, but his brother and sister showed up in court and reported their parents were alive and well in Gilmanton, New Hampshire. He said he murdered 27 people, but many of them later denied that.[24]

Before his trial began, the prosecutor heard from individuals who were so determined to testify against him that they were willing to travel at their own expense from Boston, Detroit, Toronto, Cincinnati, Fort Worth, and Burlington, Vermont.[25]

District Attorney George Graham put the Widow Pitezel on the stand first. Her story about losing her husband and three children to Holmes brought tears across the courtroom.

Holmes, possibly hoping to confuse witnesses, showed up in court with a new bushy beard, but the district attorney displayed large, mounted photographs showing what he looked like at the time the crimes were committed. Witness after witness identified him with surety.[26]

Mrs. Lucinda Burns was positive he was the man who brought Alice and Nellie to her boarding house at 91 Congress Street in Detroit. Hers was the house where Alice wrote her last letter to her mother. "Howard is not with us now," she wrote.[27]

Mrs. Frank Nudel remembered Holmes as the man who said he wanted her house at 16 Vincent Street in Toronto for his widowed sister.[28]

Thomas Ryves of 18 Vincent Street identified Holmes as the new neighbor who borrowed his spade for the potato pit.[29]

Sydney L. Samuels, a Fort Worth lawyer, raised Holmes's ire when he testified. Asked to identify Holmes in the prisoner's dock, Samuels, with clear contempt in his voice, said Holmes was "the individual in the cage." Holmes shot a look of malevolence in the lawyer's direction. A detective who watched it unfold later said it might have boded ill for Samuels if Holmes were free and a bottle of chloroform were handy.[30]

At the trial's close, the judge was straightforward in his charge to the jury members: "Truth is stranger than fiction," he told them.[31]

The jurors told a reporter they had their minds made up before they walked out of the jury box. Their first ballot produced a unanimous guilty verdict. They stayed out for only two hours and 31 minutes, and they said they spent most of that time eating dinner and waiting around so the judge would think they had given the case due deliberation.[32]

Holmes walked into court in high spirits and walked out convicted of murder, but his confidence hadn't cracked. He had lawyers and appeals and the money to pay for them. Life in prison was easy for Holmes. He charmed the guards into letting him wear his own clothes. He even kept his watch. He had money to pay for food and newspapers and magazines brought in from the outside.[33]

First, he petitioned for a new trial on the grounds that his third wife should not have testified because of spousal privilege, but the judge ruled that Georgianna Yoke was not his wife because he was still legally married to the first of his three wives.[34]

With his earthly options fast winnowing, Holmes, always one to think ahead, acquired faith. He spent his last weeks studying to join the Roman Catholic faith. He was baptized in his cell on murderers' row on April 17.[35]

Although he killed his partners' three children, Holmes broke into tears in the weeks leading up to his hanging when he received a brief childish letter from his own six-year-old daughter, who lived with his second wife in the comfortable Chicago suburb of Wilmette, Illinois.[36]

Holmes, who was still not eager to meet his maker, reached out to an unlikely ally to save his life. He offered Carrie Pitezel cash and real estate if she would petition Pennsylvania governor Daniel H. Hastings on his behalf. She would not.[37]

Holmes wrote two of his own letters to the governor. One begged Hastings to commute his sentence because two of his three wives and their children would be rendered penniless if he were executed. The second letter beseeched the governor to at least stall the execution to give Holmes more time to prepare. His timing was off. Another letter on the same subject landed on the governor's desk that same day. It was signed by Rev. Robert Canning, Carrie Pitezel's father and Howard, Alice, and Nellie's grandfather. No allowances were made for Holmes.[38]

He was scheduled to die on May 7, nine days before his 35th birthday.

Detective Geyer must have been pleased. He called Holmes a murder demon. He believed that, if Holmes's Chicago building gave up its guilty secrets, the list of his victims would likely be much longer. Estimates of the numbers killed there vary from 200 to a more likely 9. Either way, after unearthing the bones of the Pitezel children, Geyer said he believed it was not possible to find a more deliberate and cold-blooded villain in the annals of criminal jurisprudence than Holmes.[39]

When it became evident the hanging would proceed, the sheriff was beseeched for tickets. He received more than 1,000 letters requesting them, with some writers offering large sums of money for the privilege. Those who already held tickets were offered exorbitant prices for them.

Dr. Milton Greenman, curator of the Wistar Institute, then a four-year-old biomedical research center, requested more than a ticket. He wanted Holmes's brain.[40]

The Wistar Institute today is known for its trailblazing research on COVID-19 and the hepatitis B virus, but, in the 20th century, it became renowned for its collection of medical specimens.

It was under Dr. Greenman's leadership that scientists there developed and bred the Wistarat—a breed of rat from which more than half of all laboratory rats today are thought to be descended.[41]

Holmes, who bought a dissecting table for his Chicago murder castle, was deathly afraid of being on the other side of the knife. The Wistar Institute would not add his brain to its inventory. In fact, he took an extraordinary measure to ensure his own body would rest in peace. It involved 2,000 pounds of wet cement.

In the days immediately before Holmes's hanging, official visitors from several cities set out for Philadelphia, including professional criminologist Arthur MacDonald, who literally wrote the book on abnormal men. MacDonald had interviewed Holmes several times since his arrest, and he had collected more than 200 letters from the murderer's former schoolmates. Most said they always thought Holmes exhibited some peculiarities, but never criminal tendencies.[42]

Throughout the trial, headlines had highlighted Holmes's cool demeanor, but, as the hours before the execution dwindled, headlines like "Holmes Weeps and Is Afraid" made Philadelphians wonder how Holmes would act atop the gallows.

A portion of each of his last days was spent in prayer and Bible reading. In his last month, his professional visitors were not just attorneys and doctors and real estate men, but also two priests from the Church of the Annunciation, a half block away.[43]

The day before the execution, prison staffers went to work erecting Moyamensing's tall black gallows in a high and wide white-washed corridor about 60 feet from Holmes's cell. They used screws and bolts so the prisoner wouldn't hear them, but two visitors said Holmes's sensitive ears still picked up on the construction.[44]

Weepy, teary, and tired on the night before he was scheduled to die, Holmes stretched himself out on a couch in his cell, looked at his keeper, George Weaver, and said, "I don't know where I'll sleep tomorrow night, but nobody knows that."[45]

Holmes slept so soundly through that last night that Weaver and his fellow keeper John Henry had to shake him twice to get him up. He reported he felt "first rate" and had the best night's sleep of his life.[46]

Holmes did not wear a new suit of clothes for his hanging, as was the custom. He dressed simply in a gray cutaway suit with no collar or tie to get in the way of the noose. He did drape a white silk handkerchief loosely around his shoulders. His shoes were well-shined for the occasion. He had shaved his beard.[47]

He walked to the desk where he wrote his best-selling confession to pen letters to two of his wives and to friends and relatives of his victims. The last thing he wrote on earth was a heartfelt thank you note to his lawyer, Sam Rotan.[48]

By the time he finished writing, Passyunk Avenue was already packed tight with the morbidly curious.

Holmes's last meal waited because the prisoner was fasting to take the sacrament of Holy Communion. It was his first communion—and his last.

He also confessed to his priest. As one newspaperman put it, "His confessor is the only one who knows whether he went into eternity with a lie on his lips."[49]

After the sacraments, Holmes ate heartily, downing eggs, toast, and coffee.[50]

While he ate, invited guests began to gather down the corridor to see him die. Frank Geyer was there. So was an attorney for the Fidelity Mutual Insurance Company. And a city councilman. A physician who had witnessed many hangings stood near a young newspaperman covering his first. There were 51 invited guests, but much to the sheriff's ire, 25 to 30 personal friends of prison officials were also let inside. The sheriff considered ousting them, but he yielded due to the late hour. A prison guard walked the yard, calling, "Hats off and no smoking."[51]

Down the block at the Church of the Annunciation, nuns were already praying for Holmes's soul.

Holmes entered the room with his confessors, the sheriff, the doctors, and his attorney, all men with grave faces walking two by two. The condemned man cradled a small silver crucifix in his hands.

He looked stouter than he had at trial. He was pale faced, his skin slightly yellow. As one guest said, "He looked dead already."[52]

Atop the gallows, the party of six stood for a moment, peeking down. Holmes put his hand on the waist-high railing and stared out at the last human faces he was ever going to see.[53]

In a low voice at first but gradually becoming more audible, he addressed the crowd for two minutes, standing ramrod straight. Speaking with confidence and using hand gestures for emphasis, he denied killing any of the Pitezels. He said the only deaths he was responsible for were those of two women. "They died by my hand as the result of criminal operations," he said, adding no details.[54]

His voice never quavered. His hands did not tremble.

Outside the prison, the minutes dragged by as spectators wondered when the trap would be sprung.[55]

Inside, atop the gallows, Holmes turned to his lawyer, who had worked on his case up until the last minute. Putting his hand on the young man's broad shoulder, he said, "Goodbye, Sam. You have done all you could." Then he hugged him.[56]

When the condemned man released him, Rotan almost ran down the scaffold steps.[57]

Holmes may not have noticed Rotan's uneasy exit, because the priests were motioning to him to kneel with them. For the next two minutes, he was on his knees, holding his crucifix, his lips moving in silent prayer.[58]

Then he rose steadily to his feet and gave a firm handshake to both priests and two officials.

Holmes turned to look at the crowd again, but an official stepped forward, drew both of the killer's hands behind his back, and slipped iron manacles around them. He began to draw a black cap down over

Holmes's face, but, as he did, the prisoner quipped, "Take your time about it. You know I am in no hurry."[59]

As the man prepared the noose, Holmes gibed, "Take your time. Don't bungle it."[60]

He was asked if he was ready. He said yes. Then, in muffled tones from under the cap, his last words came: "Goodbye. Goodbye, everybody."[61]

A prison official said he was the nerviest of the 67 men he had seen hanged. Several older doctors agreed.[62]

The trap was sprung without a hitch at 10:12 a.m. At 10:13 a white handkerchief fluttered from one of the prison windows, signaling to the waiting spectators that the trap had been sprung. A wave of excitement passed through the crowd outside.[63]

Inside, things didn't go exactly as planned. Seconds after the drop, Holmes's legs abruptly swung far outward, toward the 81 assembled guests. One guest tumbled backward.[64]

The body turned round and round in contortions for a full minute, neck twitching, chest heaving, legs swaying back and forth.[65]

Holmes's fingers opened and closed for almost 10 minutes, causing two guests to faint.[66]

His neck never snapped, so six physicians spent 15 minutes checking the still-hanging body for a heartbeat. Two of them put their ears up to the chest of the corpse. The remains hung aloft amid the guests for 33 minutes. All the while the white-robed priests softly chanted in the background.[67]

After death was declared, city patrolmen were allowed to march by the scaffold in a line, examining the hanging body. The face was so contorted that doctors turned away from it, but a reporter said the police seemed to enjoy the spectacle. Their comments were enough to make a person shudder, he said.[68]

After the body was cut down, doctors attempting to remove the hemp noose found the knot jammed tight and the loop burrowed deep into the flesh. They had to turn the head this way and that for several minutes to get the thing off.[69]

THE EXECUTION OF HOLMES—SCENE WHILE HE WAS MAKING HIS FINAL ADDRESS
Sketched in the Prison by a *Times* Artist.

H. H. Holmes was to be hanged before only invited guests, but the guest list expanded at the last minute.
WIKIMEDIA COMMONS

Some spectators headed for the gates, but the large crowd waiting outside peppered them with questions.

A few minutes after noon, the undertaker's wagon rolled into the prison yard to remove the corpse. When the crowd outside got word that the wagon would leave the yard via the back gate, there was a race around the block.[70]

Meanwhile, a letter carrier walked up to the gate to deliver the daily newspaper to an H. H. Holmes. The subscriber would never read that day's stories about him, nor would he see the next day's headlines:

The *New York Times*'s was "Holmes Cool to the End."

The *Miners' Daily Journal* out of Pottsville, Pennsylvania, went with "A Human Fiend Hanged."

The *Macon Telegraph* summed it up thus: "Said Good-Buy [sic] and Then Swung."

And a *Chicago Times-Herald* reporter wrote that Holmes was "a being so unthinkable that no novelist would dare to invent such a character."

The undertaker's wagon exited the prison gate as if it were bound for Holy Cross Cemetery just over the city line, and groups of street kids pounded gleefully on its sides until police drove them away. The wagon made a secret stop at John O'Rourke's funeral home at 10th and Tasker Streets.[71]

O'Rourke's men swiftly removed the corpse from its narrow pine box and transferred it to a strong box with handles, one wide enough for two men of Holmes's size.

They opened five barrels of cement and sand and quickly mixed enough cement to cover the entire bottom of the wider box to a depth of 10 inches. They arranged Holmes's gray-suited body on top. The Pinkertons engaged to guard the body took a last look before a silk handkerchief was placed over the face and more mortar was poured into the box until it was full. Then the lid was nailed down.[72]

The morticians followed Holmes's written orders to a T—or at least they tried. As instructed, O'Rourke's crew did everything they could to thwart graverobbers.

As a reporter for the *Evening Messenger* of Marshall, Texas, wrote, Holmes feared the dissecting table more than he did the grave. That fear was reinforced when one party offered Holmes's lawyer $5,000 for his body—the equivalent of $155,000 today.[73]

When the wagon finished the six-mile trek to Holy Cross, to the undertaker's surprise, cemetery superintendent R. B. Campbell refused to allow the body to be placed in the vault without paperwork from the cathedral. O'Rourke had receipts and permits and a document certifying that Holmes could be buried in consecrated land, but the gatekeeper persisted. They got the additional paperwork, but it took three hours. By then, the cement had hardened.[74]

Three undertakers, two detectives, and two cemetery workers took hold, but the box did not move. They heaved and strained and broke the coffin handles, but nothing happened.

Try as they might, the men couldn't get the cement-filled coffin to budge until they realized the power of the press. Reporters standing nearby pitched in.

Thirteen pairs of arms slowly inched the cement-filled coffin into the vault. The arch murderer of the age was in the ground.[75]

As per Holmes's instructions, two Pinkertons guarded his body the first night. They took turns napping in a white pine coffin.[76]

The next morning, workers poured more cement until the 155-pound remains of H. H. Holmes were safely shrouded in a 2,000-pound cement rectangle.[77]

As a reporter for the *Times* of Philadelphia wrote the next morning, Holmes was unique in life and unique in death.[78]

Holmes did not rest in peace, though. In 2017, producers from the History Channel, with an assist from a Mudgett descendant-turned-author, enlisted a team of nearly 30 to exhume the killer's body with television cameras rolling.

Their goal was to determine, through DNA testing, whether the man in the cement grave was Holmes or if Holmes had somehow cheated the hangman.

Their first discovery was that the undertaker had placed a decoy coffin on top of the real one.

They also learned that the 2,000 pounds of cement Holmes ordered to enclose his body hadn't set correctly. Some of it turned into a heavy gray clay.

When the coffin was opened, Holmes was still wearing a suit coat, a waistcoat, and boots but no pants. One of the archaeologists speculated he may have soiled his pants on the scaffold and the undertaker discarded them.

His trademark brush mustache was still intact until it hit the air and began to disintegrate.

Archeologists found lifts in his shoes that boosted his height by at least three inches.

Lab tests showed the man under the gray clay was a member of the Mudgett clan, and dental imprints were consistent with what is known of Holmes.

H. H. Holmes, whose greatest fear was exhumation and dissection, was returned to his grave after 117 days in laboratories.[79]

CHAPTER TEN

America's First Kidnapping

AMERICA'S FIRST KIDNAPPING FOR RANSOM UNFOLDED IN GERMAN-town. It happened just as Philadelphians were getting into a holiday mood.

Christian Ross could have gotten home in time to thwart it—if he hadn't been preparing for Independence Day. If he had a crystal ball to see into his future, Ross surely would have hurried back to his imposing stone mansion on leafy Washington Lane.

On the afternoon of July 1, 1874, four-year-old Charley Ross vanished from his front yard. He was never seen again.

Parents across the country were bewildered. Up until that sunny, cloudless day, no American child had ever been kidnapped for ransom. No parent worried that would happen. No police officer had ever been assigned a ransom case. Ordinary citizens couldn't imagine anyone would steal a child. The abduction of Charley Ross is the most sensational criminal case in Philadelphia history to this day. It was in the headlines for 50 years.[1]

It was supplanted in the public mind by the 1932 nabbing of Charles A. Lindbergh Jr., another little blond Charley. But, by then, word of the Ross kidnapping had spread as far as Europe and Australia. Almost a half million people assisted in the search for Charley Ross.

George S. Kaufman wrote him into a Broadway play.[2]

A popular song was based on the crime.[3]

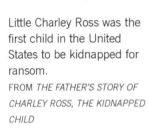

Little Charley Ross was the first child in the United States to be kidnapped for ransom.

FROM *THE FATHER'S STORY OF CHARLEY ROSS, THE KIDNAPPED CHILD*

The publicity inspired killers Richard Loeb and Nathan Leopold Jr. to kidnap 14-year-old Bobby Franks in the case that shocked Chicago in 1924.[4]

And, for almost a century and a half, parents have admonished their children, "Never take candy from a stranger."

Christian Ross was excited when he left his center city shop early on July 1. His mind was on delighting his two younger sons. He had promised four-year-old Charley and five-year-old Walter he'd build them a sand pile where they could safely set off firecrackers together on the Fourth of July. He stopped on Germantown's main street to buy the sand.[5]

While Ross was thinking about his sons, two thieves were, too. They pulled their dilapidated wagon up to the low stone wall that ringed Ross's estate.[6]

The men stepped over the wall and approached Charley and Walter.

Walter Ross was just five when his younger brother was kidnapped, but he dealt with the aftermath of the kidnapping for decades.
FROM *THE FATHER'S STORY OF CHARLEY ROSS, THE KIDNAPPED CHILD*[7]

The graceful old mansion with the wraparound porch no longer stands on Washington Lane in Germantown.
FROM *THE FATHER'S STORY OF CHARLEY ROSS, THE KIDNAPPED CHILD*[8]

One was about the boys' father's size—five foot, nine inches. The other was older, taller, and heavier. His whiskers were bushy and at least three inches long, but his most noticeable feature was his nose. It was pushed upward like a monkey's, little Walter thought.[7]

Walter and Charley weren't alarmed. The same men had stopped by four times in the last week. Each time, they gave the boys some candy. And, each time, they escaped the gaze of the adults inside the house.

This time, the men promised they would take the Ross boys to buy fireworks. In a few fateful minutes, Walter and Charley were spirited away in the speeding wagon, easily snatched from a lawn dotted with so many bushes and thick evergreens that it was impossible to see it all from the wraparound porch.

By nightfall, Walter was back on Washington Lane. Charley never returned. His name became a cautionary tale on three continents.

Everything that happened would seem incomprehensible if it were to happen today, but the Germantown kidnapping was the first of its kind in the United States.

Ross, a father of eight, arrived home about 6 p.m., earlier than usual, excited to see his younger boys, but the nanny said they were playing somewhere outside beyond the trees. When they didn't return home to eat, Ross sent his daughters to knock on neighbors' doors. Then he took off searching in a different direction.

He didn't think there was any real cause for alarm until a neighbor told him she overheard his boys talking to some men and then she saw them ride away in a wagon. At that instant, Christian Ross's life forked forever.[8]

His mind flashed on the piece of white, plaited candy Walter had shown him the previous Saturday. Walter had said two men had given the treats to him and Charley. At the time, Ross thought it was rather pleasant that someone fond of children had offered his boys candy.[9]

The boys' disappearance changed everything. Ross and a neighbor made a beeline toward the police station.

Before they got far, they spied Walter walking toward them with an unfamiliar man who introduced himself as Mr. Henry Peacock. Peacock turned out to be a Good Samaritan who had found Walter crying outside a downtown cigar store and offered to take him home. The boy was still clutching two packages of firecrackers and a bundle of torpedoes in his hands. When his father asked him where Charley was, Walter said, "Why, he is all right. He is in the wagon."

A stunned Ross sent Walter home, collected his nephew Frank Lewis, and took off for the police station. It was nearly 11 p.m. when they arrived at Fifth and Chestnut Streets. The detective on duty gave them the brush-off. Someone had probably taken the child in a drunken frolic, he said, and they'd drop him somewhere as soon as they sobered up.

Exasperated, Ross and Lewis headed to the Kensington neighborhood where Peacock had found Walter. They asked person after person on the streets if they'd seen a small boy with long, blond ringlets, a broadbrimmed straw hat, and a brown linen suit. No one seemed to believe their story that someone had plucked a child from his own yard. One man thought they were jokesters.

At 3 a.m., with no one left to question, Ross and Lewis were ready to head home. The streetcars had stopped running and the livery stables had closed for the night, so they walked about six miles, returning to Washington Lane around 5 a.m.

Ross hadn't told his wife, Sarah Ann, that her baby had been kidnapped. She was in Atlantic City, New Jersey, recuperating from an illness, and he thought it best not to upset her. He believed Charley would be found within hours.[10]

July 1 had been a momentous day for other Philadelphians. Haverford College held its commencement. Mayor William S. Stokley laid the cornerstone for a new city hall in the Second Empire style. The longawaited Philadelphia Zoo opened its black Victorian gates for the first time. A full orchestra played as more than 3,000 people funneled past the 183 animals on display at the nation's first zoo. A crowd favorite was the nearly motionless sloth, so at rest that some viewers speculated it was dead.[11]

Residents were gearing up for the holiday weekend. That day's edition of the *Germantown Telegraph* featured a story on how to make cheap summer drinks to entertain your friends.[12]

When the sun rose on July 2, Christian Ross had been awake more than 24 hours. He anxiously awaited the hour when he could awaken Walter. Even when 7:30 a.m. finally came, his five-year-old seemed so pale and nervous that Ross waited to pepper him with questions.

Walter told his father he and Charley had been driven to a cigar store on Palmer Street in the city. The men gave Walter a quarter to buy fireworks. When he came out of the store with handfuls of fireworks and a pocket full of treats, the wagon was gone. So was his brother.

Walter was able to lead his father on the exact route the kidnappers took to Palmer Street. His memory of landmarks and even street names floored the adults, but there was still no solid clue to Charley's whereabouts.

Ross returned to the police station for information. The officers, still missing a motive for the abduction, began to question him. Did he have family problems? Did he have an angry creditor? Had he served on a jury that convicted someone? Were any servants dismissed from his employ?

Irked, Ross took matters into his own hands. He placed advertisements in the local papers, offering a reward for Charley's safe return.

Then, on the Fourth of July, Ross was talking to detectives at the central police station when his brother came rushing in with a letter for him that had been postmarked in Philadelphia the previous day. The writing was wayward, and the words were wildly misspelled, but it said Charley was safe and the people who had nabbed him wanted $20,000.

After the father read the letter silently, the police captain invited him, his brother, and several detectives into a private room, where the letter was read aloud. Ross said the listeners were so astonished that no one spoke at first. Then, one by one, they expressed their horror that an adult would steal a child.

Ross immediately sensed the note was bona fide because the kidnappers used Charley's middle name, Brewster. He knew they had asked Walter for Charley's middle name.

As the case blew up in the newspapers, Christian Ross knew he could no longer conceal Charley's disappearance from his wife. He rode 70 miles through teeming rain to tell her before she saw a paper. Sarah Ann Ross was so scared she couldn't cry.

Mr. Ros— July 3 be not uneasy you son charly bruster he al writ we is got him and no power on earth can deliver out of our hand— You wil hav two pay us befor you git him from us— an pay us a big cent. to— if you put the cops hunting for him yu is only defeeting you own end— we is got him fitt so no living power can gits him from us a live— if. any aproch is maid to his hidin place that is the signil for his instant aniheleeteon— if yu regard his lif puts no

The kidnappers sent a series of ransom notes in the same handwriting.
FROM *THE FATHER'S STORY OF CHARLEY ROSS, THE KIDNAPPED CHILD*

The ransom note—and the headlines that followed—shocked police into action. Trying to make up for lost time, they searched all boats on the Delaware and Schuylkill Rivers. Officers were sent to every river burg from Trenton to Wilmington. The train stations were put under police surveillance. By early August, they were searching every building in the city. The mayor's office announced a $20,000 reward for information leading to the kidnappers' arrest.[13]

But it was too late.

Police, the family, and concerned citizens all made every effort to recover Charley.

When news broke that Charley had been found in a gypsy camp near Hamburg, residents there ringed the camp so no one could get in or out until police arrived. The Reading Railroad closed the entire Hamburg-Philadelphia line and ran a special train to carry a Ross relative to identify the boy. Crowds circled newspaper offices waiting to read the details as they were posted outside.

It wasn't Charley.[14]

More notes arrived—23 in all. The nabbers repeated that they wanted $20,000 for Charley's safe return—more than $450,000 in today's dollars. They said they had him stashed somewhere safe where only they could reach him.[15]

Leading citizens convinced Ross to withhold the ransom money because paying for Charley might inspire copycats. If he took a chance on saving his boy, he would put all other children at risk, they said. Ross took their advice. It was a decision he would regret to the day he died.

Few people knew it then, but Ross had no choice. Despite appearances, he was deep in debt. The stock market crash of 1873 had cleaned him out.

The mayor offered a reward for the boy's safe return. Citizens raised enough money to hire the fabled Pinkerton Detective Agency. The Pinkertons distributed more than a million fliers with Charley's face and description. They mailed them to three continents, but, in the end, they failed to find Charley.[16]

The kidnap saga made news around the world. Under the headline "Child Stealing in Philadelphia," one newsman wrote: "The new form of crime which is developed in Philadelphia, stealing children from their parental houses, is at once so easy of perpetration and so harrowing that it calls for notice all over the land."[17]

The fliers attracted attention from as far away as London and Australia. Christian Ross heard from sympathetic citizens, cranks, con artists, fortune-tellers, and more than 300 "Charleys." None of them was on the up-and-up. A few parents dressed their girls as Charley in hopes of getting the reward money.[18]

Police regularly fielded calls from ordinary citizens who believed they had spotted Charley. When a Mrs. Jackson of Germantown came to Philadelphia in early August with a small boy with long flaxen ringlets, a couple of ladies became so positive the child was Charley Ross that they went in search of a police officer. An officer arrested the woman and took her and the child to the central police station. Mr. Ross was called to identify his son. When he arrived, he said the boy was not his, although he did allow there was a striking resemblance. Mrs. Jackson was given a certificate, signed by the chief of police, stating that her boy was not Charley Ross.[19]

Christian Ross began giving signed certificates to parents whose children resembled his son, so they wouldn't be waylaid by reward-seekers.[20]

In August, police caught a break in the case. Eager to collect the $20,000 reward, a man named Gil Mosher told police he believed his brother William Mosher and a young man named Joe Douglas had nabbed Charley. He said his brother, a river-pirate-turned-burglar, had once tried to talk him into kidnapping millionaire Cornelius Vanderbilt's grandchildren for ransom. The duo fit the description Walter had given of his kidnappers. To find them, police enlisted the help of Mosher's brother-in-law, a disgraced former policeman named William Westervelt.

In the midst of it all, the *Reading Eagle* published a letter with hard opinions about the Rosses. The headline was "Ross Case All Humbug." The writer claimed that Christian Ross was a bigamist and Charley was his child from his other wife. Christian Ross sued and won a $1,000 judgment against the paper.[21]

The last note from the kidnappers was dated November 6. By then, Christian Ross had suffered a nervous collapse. His wife tried to comply with the kidnappers' demands, but things went haywire. She sent her brother and her nephew to a New York City hotel with a suitcase of money, but no one came to claim it.

After that, there were no more missives from the men who took Charley.

On December 14, Mosher and Douglas broke into an unoccupied bayside vacation home on New York's Long Island. Unbeknownst to the men, the homeowner had wired a burglar alarm that rang at his brother's house next door. The relatives, armed with guns, responded immediately. The thieves were cornered. Shots rang out in the dark.

Mosher was killed instantly. Douglas was mortally wounded, but he held on long enough to confess to kidnapping little Charley Ross.

Richard Herken, a sailor on his way home that night, saw Douglas lying outside the house with his bowels protruding from a shotgun blast to his abdomen. When Herken leaned over to help, Douglas blurted out that he and Mosher had nabbed Charley Ross. There was no point in lying, Douglas said, because he knew he was going to die. Herken asked the question that all of America wanted to know: where was Charley? Douglas said Mosher had him concealed somewhere, but he didn't know where.

Then Herken asked why he would steal a child. Douglas quickly replied, "To make money."

Douglas asked the sailor to fish $40 out of his pocket and use it to give him a decent burial. He said he had made that $40 honestly.

When Philadelphians heard that two men who matched the kidnappers' description had finally been captured in a shootout 166 days after Charley was abducted, they knotted around newspaper buildings, joyously awaiting the good news of the child's return. The crowds turned somber when they learned the kidnapper who knew Charley's location had died without giving it up.

Little Walter was brought to a New York morgue to identify the men. When he saw Douglas, he said, "Oh, that's awfully like him. He's the driver. He was the one that gave me the money to buy the firecrackers." He identified Mosher, too.[22]

The only person left to try was Mosher's brother-in-law, William Westervelt, whom police suspected had helped Mosher more than he helped them. The former police officer was found guilty of conspiracy. He spent six years in prison, but he maintained his innocence and insisted he didn't know Charley's whereabouts.[23]

In 1875, Pennsylvania became the first state to make child kidnapping a felony. In hopes of finding Charley, the legislators included a provision stating the law wouldn't apply to anyone holding a child who was stolen before the act was passed, if they surrendered the child immediately.[24]

Christian Ross wrote a book to raise money for his search for Charley. He laid bare all his regrets in *The Father's Story of Charles Ross, the Kidnapped Child*. It was a bestseller.

One day, while searching for his son in Vermont, he encountered a circus that advertised a wax museum featuring the Charley Ross family. The figures looked nothing like his family. After he introduced himself to the circus manager, the man admitted they had put the exhibit together using figures from discontinued exhibits. He told Ross he'd pay him $1,000 a week if Charley was returned and he were willing to appear in the circus.[25]

Showman P. T. Barnum offered a $10,000 reward for the safe return of Charley Ross—after he extracted a promise from Christian Ross that his son would join Barnum's barn tour or repay the $10,000 if Charley were found alive.[26]

Ross continued to search for his son until he died of heart failure in 1897. He was 73. He spent $60,000 but never found Charley. He did find other lost children.

After Ross's death, his widow, Sarah Ann, continued their quest until 1912.

At 79, she decided to leave the mansion where her son went missing. She purchased a stone house in the manicured suburb where Walter and his family lived. She never moved in. A few days before Christmas, she walked into the foyer of her minister's home for a tea party and collapsed. She died instantly of heart disease.

The fake Charleys kept coming. Walter Ross estimated he and his siblings dealt with more than 500 "Charleys," some from as far away as Germany.[27]

Walter, who went on to be listed in the Social Register and own a seat on the New York Stock Exchange, wrote a requiem for his brother that was published in the Philadelphia papers on July 1, 1924, the 50th anniversary of the kidnapping.

A few weeks later, Charley landed back in the papers when a court psychologist in Chicago said "Dickie" Loeb and "Babe" Leopold copied the Ross kidnapping because they considered it the perfect crime. By kidnapping and killing a wealthy 14-year-old, they hoped to match the notoriety of the Charley Ross case.

Illinois State Attorney Robert Crowe, speaking at the Leopold and Loeb trial, said, "Fifty years ago, Charles Ross was kidnapped. He was never found, and yet we all, even those of us born many years after, still talk about the case of Charley Ross. There is something in the nature of the crime itself that arrests the attention of every person in the land."[28]

As the horror of the Ross kidnapping faded from collective memory, not every person who invoked Charley's name was as kind as Crowe.[29] When the Democratic National Convention came to Philadelphia in 1932, some prankster convinced the announcer whose job it was to call out for lost persons to page "Charles Ross."[30]

And the remaining Ross children's adult lives were regularly interrupted by waves of Charley pretenders. There was a homeless man, a West Virginia farmer, a Phoenix carpenter, a North Carolina mountaineer who remembered a boyhood trip with an itinerant peddler. There was a suburban Philadelphia hermit who lived in a shack with this sign outside: "This place is wired with dynamite. Be careful."

One "Charley" was born six years after the real Charley was nabbed.

Even a California man named Charles E. Ross thought he was Charley Ross.[31]

Gustave Blair, a 69-year-old Phoenix carpenter, petitioned the court to recognize him as the real Charley Ross in 1934. He claimed he grew up in a cave, raised by a man who told him his real name was Charley Ross. Walter Ross called Blair a crank, and the family did not bother to contest the claim. The judge ruled in Blair's favor, but the Ross siblings refused to recognize Blair as family.[32]

Eventually, Blair moved to Los Angeles and tried to sell his story to a movie studio, but he couldn't hook a buyer.

For five decades, any child who had long blond ringlets risked being nicknamed Charley Ross, but, after the Lindbergh kidnapping, the case was largely forgotten.

It returned to the headlines briefly in March 2013 when a Mt. Airy woman searching through a plastic bin of family keepsakes discovered a stack of small envelopes tied together with a black shoelace. She thought they were love letters—until her daughter began reading them. The first one began: "Mr Ros, be not uneasy, you son charley bruster be all writ we is got him and no powers on earth can deliver out of our hand."[33]

Inexplicably tucked away among mementos and saved locks of hair was the first ransom note in American history. The plastic bin yielded 22 of the 23 ransom notes the kidnappers sent Christian Ross—and an original poster emblazoned with Charley's image.

The family members said they didn't know how the items came to be in their basement or how long they had been there, buried under family photographs.

The letters were sold at auction that year. The winning bidder paid $20,000—the same amount the kidnappers wanted Christian Ross to pay in 1874.[34]

CHAPTER ELEVEN

The Assassination of Octavius V. Catto

SAMUEL WANAMAKER HAD A FRONT-ROW SEAT TO MURDER ON ELEC-
tion Day, 1871. From his perch on the back of a streetcar, his eyes
followed a slim, dark-haired assassin as the man fired off four shots at
Octavius Catto on a crowded city street in broad daylight.

Catto, the 32-year-old principal of a nationally renowned Black
school, was steps away from the safety of his boardinghouse when he
passed the short white man on South Street just after 3:30 p.m. The man's
forehead was wrapped in a fresh white muslin bandage, a remnant from
a rumble earlier that day.[1]

A moment after the two passed, the white man twirled around as if
he had just recognized Catto, an amateur baseball player and an activist
who led a successful campaign to allow Blacks to ride city streetcars.

Out of the blue, the man pulled a pistol. A 17-year-old girl saw it.
She shouted to Catto, "Look out for that man!"

Catto turned, but his killer was already firing.

At least two witnesses saw Catto pull a gun, but he did not fire it, and
a later police examination showed its chambers were empty.[2]

The white man's pistol flashed. The first shot hit the principal in his
arm or right thigh.

"What are you doing?" Catto asked.

The streetcar stopped. The gunman didn't. He fired again.

Catto's body was trembling, but, moving with the athleticism of a
skilled second baseman, he dodged around the streetcar to safety.

Wanamaker, a brickmaker and a trustee of 11th Street Methodist Episcopal Church, watched in horror as the shooter gave chase, rounding the streetcar, too.

The pistol flashed again. Catto was hit in the shoulder. The last shot went through his heart sac, felling him in the street.

The first policeman arrived on the scene in seconds because his station was steps away. He ran directly to Catto, lifted him to his feet, and then put a gun to his head.

Wanamaker had had enough.

He jumped off the streetcar, shouting, "This is an outrage!" He pointed to the white man and said, "This is the man who did the shooting."

As the killer quickly slipped his revolver into the right-hand pocket of his dark sack coat, a bystander noticed the number 27 was tattooed on the back of his hand. He seemed unfazed by the killing. Years later, Thomas Higgins, who witnessed it all, said, "There is an expression in his eyes that I carry in my mind yet."[3]

Wanamaker expected the officer to nab the shooter directly. From his perspective a few yards away, it seemed the man could have easily been captured if any of the bystanders on the sidewalk had only reached out their arms. Instead, people on the street yelled to the killer, "Run, Frank. Get out of the way. Don't let them get you."[4]

The 21-year-old zipped around the corner and into a tavern. Wanamaker, 40 years older, sprinted after him, shouting, "Stop, thief!" Isaac Barr and another man joined the chase. Police followed.

Barr was confounded by what happened next. Inside the tavern, he spotted the killer sitting on a barstool. When police arrived, Barr pointed the man out to the first officer. Suddenly, the killer bolted out the back door.

Barr gave chase and nabbed him. "I handed him to the officer and said, 'Here is your man.' They took hold of him, and then I heard someone say, 'Get away! Quick!' I saw the officers going out the back gate . . . and then I lost sight of the man to be arrested."[5]

The man would be recaptured in Chicago more than five years later and returned to Philadelphia for trial.

For Catto, life was over. As writer Harry C. Silcox put it more than a century later, for Catto, the clock froze forever a few minutes after 3:30 p.m.[6]

Wanamaker called it "a cold-blooded assassination of a peaceful, inoffensive man."

The next day Dr. E. B. Shapleigh conducted a post-mortem examination at Catto's boardinghouse at 814 South Street. He found the bullets that traveled through the upper arm, the left shoulder, and the right thigh and the fatal one through the heart sac. Despite his own heart problems, Rev. William Catto traveled from New Jersey to view his son's body. An onlooker said the 61-year-old father wept as though his heart would break. He, too, would be dead before Christmas.[7]

Within hours, the mayor, the sheriff, and the chairman of the Republican Party had all posted $1,000 rewards for Catto's killer.

Later that week, the *Inquirer* called it "the deliberate murder in open daylight of one of Philadelphia's most estimable citizens."[8]

When Election Day was over, Seventh Street was littered with bricks, rocks, and paving stones. Blacks and whites brawled in the voting lines. Police clubbed Black voters. One beating victim was dragged more than a block, leaving a wide blood trail down the street. A razor-wielding attacker cut a man's thumb off.

They were telltale signs of one of the worst election day riots in Philadelphia history. The riot got knocked off the front pages by the Great Chicago Fire, which destroyed 17,500 buildings in that city.

Four men were murdered in the city around that first Election Day after the 15th Amendment gave Black men the right to vote.

The first victim was shot before midnight on election eve. A Black stevedore was shopping for a new pair of shoes when he was shot by a white former police officer. Jacob Gordon, who was shot twice, died the next morning. At trial, his assailant said, "I did it for the cause."[9]

Early in the afternoon, a white man wearing a police uniform shot Levi Bolden, a 22-year-old Black man who was standing near the corner of Seventh and South Streets. He died three weeks later.

A man was shot in the neck while building a bonfire.

By 2 p.m., an African American waiter was killed when he came home to check on his family. Isaac Chase walked out of his house to investigate an uproar near his alley. Two white gunmen attacked him.[10] When Chase's 11-year-old daughter shouted out a window, a man brandished a pistol and ordered her back inside.[11]

Then a 40-year-old hod carrier was shot three times outside a police station.

A random pistol pop would be heard periodically. Black men stood on rooftops and dropped heavy rocks on white policemen in the street. Women and children fled down Lombard Street. Men walked home with bullet holes in their clothing.

A single drugstore at Sixth and Bainbridge treated 16 men for wounds to the head. Forty men were taken to Pennsylvania Hospital with serious injuries. One man hit another with a shovel, and then he shot at the policeman who chased him.

At least twice during the day, Mayor Daniel M. Fox appeared at polling places to quell the disturbances. The street-savvy mayor would appear briefly, asking if police and residents would help him keep order. They'd promise they would. They'd shout three cheers and a tiger, a Civil War–era cheer that would end with a faux growl. As soon as the mayor left, another violent scene would unfold, usually perpetrated by the police.[12]

Amid it all, one 21-year-old citizen who was not allowed to vote registered a formal protest. Miss Carrie Burnham of 1329 Vine Street rolled up to the polls at Broad and Wood Streets and alighted from her carriage in a black silk dress with a lace collar, her hands encased in immaculate white gloves. Her attorney, Damon Y. Kilgore, trailed her, wearing an expensive suit and toting a roll of documents.

Miss Burnham insisted on expressing her right of suffrage. The men in line saw her coming and parted to make a pathway for her. When she was turned away, she said, "Why not, sir? I am a citizen. I pay taxes. I am governed, and I have a right to vote."[13]

One of the most violent Election Days in Philadelphia history ended that midnight, but the killing didn't.

The next day, witnesses testified, four Black men fired shots out of the windows of their union hall. The glass in the windows was gone before the shooting started. White ruffians had broken it on election night.

One of the bullets fired from the union hall struck George Dougherty, a white poll worker who was unpopular with African Americans. He was hit in the right eye and the bullet traveled into his brain. He died eight days later. Almost immediately, the new Republican administration ruled it death by unknown persons, although Irish Americans complained the city had spent time and money investigating each case with an African American victim.

Most of the damage was in the blocks south of the city nucleus, but, to residents, it seemed random and spontaneous. As the *Inquirer* put it, "There appeared to be no organized riot, and not one half of those engaged in the murderous work seemed to know what they were fighting about."[14]

The election ended with a win for the Republicans, the party of the late President Lincoln and the party of Black rights. The mostly white Democrats lost.

The results were projected on a so-called magic lantern in front of the Union League of Philadelphia's graceful French Renaissance building for all to see. The lantern, also known as *lanterna magica*, was an early type of image projector combining lenses, glass plates, and a light source.[15]

People crowded the surrounding streets for several squares, and many built blazing bonfires as they watched the results come in.[16]

The streets were deserted the next day as people stayed in their houses. Some of the housefronts were marred by bullet holes. By that night, the fighting was over, but African American residents still turned down the gas to the lamps on their streets, hoping the darkness would dissuade troublemakers.[17]

Philadelphia, the city that had been called the Athens of America in colonial times, no longer was run by aristocrats with a sense of noblesse oblige. A political machine took charge after the Civil War. Civic order was at a minimum. Neighborhoods were dirty. Outdoor lighting was spotty. Some streets went unpaved. City residents routinely carried pistols. There were nightly brawls at Seventh and Chestnut.[18]

One of the key machine politicians was William McMullen, known as Bull McMullen. A scrappy Democratic alderman, he opposed Catto's aims because he represented another group that was discriminated against—Irish Catholic immigrants. He was an active participant in the Bible riots of 1844, when Catholics had to defend their churches from Protestant hordes who set two churches, two rectories, a convent, and dozens of homes afire. McMullen, a genuine war hero with the First Pennsylvania Infantry during the Mexican War, knew the Black vote would tip city politics against him and his constituents.[19]

If Blacks had the ballot, he thought, they would vote for the party of Lincoln, not the Democrats.[20]

If Blacks could ride streetcars, they could vie for Irish Americans' jobs at the Navy Yard.[21]

If Republicans got control of the city, they could replace the alderman system with a magistrate court, and McMullen would lose his lucrative post.[22]

Like McMullen, many of the white roughs who were busting heads on Election Day had the number 27 tattooed on the backs of their hands. It represented the Moyamensing Fire Company, McMullen's early power base. He was there at its start. As a child, the grocer's son held candles to illuminate the workspace for the men building the firehouse. McMullen scored high enough on a rigorous entrance exam to be admitted to Central High, the city's most prestigious public high school, but he dropped out after a few months.[23]

Catto and his friends were the well-educated sons and daughters of well-to-do African Americans. Many of them attended private schools. Most of them held white-collar jobs. They were political activists. They were what African American sociologist W. E. B. DuBois later termed "better class" Blacks.[24]

They joined literary groups. They sat for formal photographs. They shopped at stores like John Wanamaker, the popular new clothier on Chestnut Street. Catto had recently paid $113.75 there for a jacket, a vest, shirt, pants, gloves, and an overcoat with a plush lapel.[25]

They were Black elites and vocal social activists. Theirs was a parallel world to the white world, but wealthy whites didn't realize it.[26] Catto created a flap when he became the first Black man to purchase a membership in the all-white Franklin Institute, the storied science museum on stately Logan Circle. The dean of Jefferson Medical College, who was scheduled to speak at the institute, threatened to cancel his lecture if a Negro were admitted. The museum welcomed Catto. The medical man canceled.[27]

Catto ran the Institute for Colored Youth, where students studied Latin, Greek, geometry, and trigonometry. The free school was backed by Quakers. Its first graduate went on to the University of Edinburgh, and two other early grads enrolled at the University of Pennsylvania's medical school.[28]

Catto organized Black citizens to campaign for open streetcars. He used a sympathetic group as his example—wounded Black battle veterans and their wives and children.

When Black soldiers were admitted to the city's military hospitals, their families often could not visit because 11 of the city's 19 streetcar and rail companies did not accept Black passengers. The companies that did allow Black riders often restricted them to standing on the platform with the driver, exposed to weather.

Catto spoke of *delicate* Black women—the Victorian word for pregnant—being thrown off streetcars. It worked.[29]

Two companies said their cars would be open to all well-behaved persons. Three said they'd run separate cars for Black riders. The Philadelphia Streetcar Company let their customers vote. Predictably, they voted nay. Another company agreed to admit Black passengers, but it reverted to "colored" cars one month later because of a decline in white riders.

Catto, a gifted orator, kept lobbying. In 1867, the state legislature required all railroads and streetcar companies to carry all passengers.[30] The gunman may have been angered by Catto's success.

As a major in the Pennsylvania National Guard, Catto was buried in his military dress uniform. His casket was trimmed in silver. The hearse was topped by six tall black plumes, like the plumed carriage that had carried President Lincoln to his grave six years earlier. Homes were draped in mourning crape.

Five thousand people reportedly passed by Catto's casket as he lay in state at the city armory. A legacy of the Civil War was America's newfound passion for parades and military displays. Catto's funeral did not disappoint.[31]

The three-mile cortege to Lebanon Cemetery in South Philadelphia featured 125 carriages, riding double through the streets. Two hundred graduates of colored schools and universities marched in the drizzling rain. The Republican Party executive committee walked. The Elephant Club walked. The Colored Odd Fellows walked. The Abraham Lincoln Literary Society of Wilmington, Delaware, walked, too. So did the highway department clerks, the Banneker Literary Society, and a band of city clergymen. Catto's beloved Pythians baseball team walked for their captain. The all-Black team was a precursor to the Negro League teams that formed a decade later.[32]

Mural Arts Philadelphia honored Octavius V. Catto with this Catherine Street mural by artists Willis "Nomo" Humphrey and Keir Johnston.
PHOTO BY STEVE WEINIK FOR MURAL ARTS PHILADELPHIA

Catto was the first African American to be honored with a statue outside City Hall.
PHOTO BY MARK JASON DOMINUS, WIKIMEDIA COMMONS

Catto's fiancée Caroline LeCount was overcome with emotion at the cemetery. LeCount, a school principal who once filed a complaint against a streetcar conductor who wouldn't allow her to ride his car, stepped forward to scatter dirt on the coffin. Then, suddenly, she cried out, "Octavius, Octavius, take me with you."[33]

It was more than five years before the man who got away from Samuel Wanamaker on Election Day, 1871, was back in custody, albeit briefly. Frank Kelly, the man eyewitnesses identified as Catto's killer, was discovered living under an assumed name in Illinois in 1876. He was nabbed while waiting in line at Chicago's Coliseum to watch the high-wire act of Emma Jutau, a world-famous aerialist known for riding down a 20-story wire holding on by her teeth.

Kelly was returned to Philadelphia and tried for the murders of Octavius Catto, Isaac Chase, and Levi Bolden. He was acquitted on the first two, and the jury deadlocked on Bolden.[34]

After one verdict, Blacks and whites crowded Eighth Street so it was nearly impassable. Whites declared, "There will never be a rope made to hang Frank Kelly," and Blacks retorted, "He'll never die in bed," and "Catto's ghost will kill him."[35]

A school was named in Catto's honor, and Caroline LeCount served as its principal. All the teachers were Black.[36]

In 1906, the International Benevolent and Protective Order of the Elks of the World, known as the Black Elks, renamed its Broad Street lodge after Catto.

In 2012, the Pennsylvania National Guard awarded the first two Major Octavius V. Catto Medals to guards for their community service.

A 12-foot bronze statue of Catto was installed in front of City Hall in 2017. It is the first public monument in the city to honor an African American.

CHAPTER TWELVE

The Muffled Murder on Pine Street

THE MURDER OF MARY HILL HAD ALL THE ELEMENTS OF A HIT MYStery novel—a former prostitute who had a child with a US congressman marries a wealthy but penny-pinching Philadelphia landlord. Within months of her hubby's death, she buys a picture-perfect mansion on a pricey corner. Weeks after she moves in, she is tossed from a second-story window to her death.

It took Hill's neighbors seconds to "solve" the murder, and at least one of the culprits was sentenced to hang. The red herring in the case was that the Widow Hill routinely paid workmen from fat bundles of cash stuffed into her bosom—about $37,000 to $55,000 in today's dollars. She did, but that had nothing to do with the crime.[1]

The question that tripped up the killer was, Why didn't the victim's four protective fox terriers make a peep that night? No one heard the pooches yapping. On a busy city corner, no one heard the body hit the brick pavement. Newspapers started calling it "the muffled murder."[2]

An ornate seven-foot, five-inch fence wrapped the four-story white mansion at 10th and Pine Streets in one of Philadelphia's toniest neighborhoods. The front door, with its polished silver nameplate, faced 10th Street. An elegant porch faced Pine Street. A handsome greenery-filled side yard 20 feet wide ran the length of the house, punctuated by a brick sidewalk.

Blood would puddle on that brick sidewalk on Sunday night, November 22, 1868.

View of the mansion at the north-east corner of Tenth and Pine, where Mrs. Mary E. Hill was murdered.

The Hill mansion and outbuildings stretched across a large, beautifully landscaped lot at 10th and Pine.
FROM A FULL AND COMPLETE HISTORY OF THE HILL HOMICIDE

When Hill's maid returned from choir practice around 9 p.m., she waited atop the wide marble front porch in nippy weather for an unusually long time, ringing the doorbell four times. Mrs. Hill usually came immediately.[3]

Finally, she rapped on the door until Hill's son-in-law, George Twitchell Jr., opened it. He was only partially dressed. He said he'd been in bed for an hour and a half, but she noticed he didn't seem like a man roused from sleep.[4]

She asked where Mrs. Hill was. He said he didn't know.

When Campbell walked into the kitchen to put coal on the fire, she noticed something else that was unusual—the side door was open on a chilly November night. Thinking Hill might be in the garden, she went out. There, she saw Hill's petite body lying on the brick pavement beneath the windows of the sitting room. At first, Campbell thought her mistress might have fainted, but then she saw the pool of blood on the bricks. She called for Twitchell.[5]

"My God!" he said. "Will someone assist me in carrying her in?" Twitchell took the shoulders and she took the feet.

After they moved the body to a settee in the kitchen, he told the maid to fetch a wash basin. Then Hill's daughter, Camilla Twitchell, instructed her to run for a doctor. Instead, she went to neighbors' houses and told them of finding Mrs. Hill bloody, battered, and dead.

Mr. Montgomery, the next-door neighbor, and W. N. G. Morrell, who lived around the corner, hurried to the house. The first person they saw in the entryway was Camilla Twitchell, who told them, "Mother has been killed!"[6]

Morrell asked her how it happened. Camilla said her mother fell out of the second-story window.

Morrell, known as a cool and calculating man, was incredulous. "How could she fall out of the window?" he asked.

A policeman came on the scene, but the group of neighbors, which was growing larger, headed straight upstairs to the sitting room to investigate for themselves.

The sitting room curtains were down. There was blood on the widow sash, a smear of it on the widow frame, and a deep pool of it near the old-fashioned sofa next to the window. Curved lines of blood dots covered one wall. A bloody towel rested in between two venetian blind slats.

The pillow Hill had been sleeping on was soaked with blood. There was more blood on a chair, and blood dripped down the exterior of the house directly beneath the window.

Det. William Warnock reasoned someone had recently been sitting in a rocking chair near the sofa, smoking. They had left two cigar stumps.

Hill's eyeglasses were bent and crushed. Gray hair and caked blood stuck to one end of a fireplace poker.

The 110-pound widow had been savagely beaten with the poker. The hole in her right temple was deep enough that a finger could pass through to the brain. She had 13 wounds to her head, one of them 12 inches long. Her right hand was bruised around the knuckles, as if she had tried to fight off her attacker. The back of her left hand was bruised all over, and her second finger had been nearly severed by a blow with a blunt instrument. Her right eye was blackened, and her right cheekbone was fractured. Her body had been heaved from the second-story window to the brick sidewalk.

While neighbors from 10th Street were poking through the mansion's upstairs, Daniel Doster, from several blocks over, went into the yard and inspected the brick path under the window.

Inside, Morrell asked who else was in the house that night. When the Twitchells answered that no one was, he said, "One of you two have committed the murder!"[7]

Camilla Twitchell said her mother routinely carried between $2,000 and $3,000 in her bosom, and many people knew that and might have tried to rob her. One of the neighbors dismissed that. A robber who came for that money would slink away as quietly as possible, he said, not risk discovery by throwing the body out the window on a well-lit city corner.

Camilla Twitchell asked why she would ever kill her own mother. The neighbor said, "For the money."[8]

The detective and the neighbors all remarked that Camilla showed little concern for her mother's death.

Someone asked if Hill's dogs would bark when a stranger came. It was generally agreed they were set yapping by any footfall on the marble steps outside. Montgomery, who lived just one brick away in the next townhouse, said he didn't hear any barking at all.[9]

"I think these people ought to be arrested," one of the neighbors said. "Yes, they ought," said another. One man insisted the detective take charge of the Twitchells until the mystery could be cleared up.[10]

George Twitchell agreed, but he asked to change clothes before he left. The policeman went upstairs with him. He noticed Twitchell had a coat and undershirt on but no collar or cuffs. When the officer saw the collar and cuffs, he noted they were splattered with small blood drops, not smeared with blood as they would be if he had only carried a body in from the yard.[11]

When the Twitchells were jailed and talk of Hill's questionable past hit the papers, the headline writers had a field day, penning, "Low Life Above the Stairs" and "A Lady's Brains Brutally Knocked Out."

Philadelphia reporters hadn't covered such a strange death since the previous July, when Charles Becker, the proprietor of a zoological garden on Ninth Street, had been killed by his newest addition, a large rattlesnake. The rattler had caused no problems until that afternoon, when a visitor wanted to hear the rattle. Becker hit the snake with a stick, making it angry enough to rattle on cue. Minutes later, the snake struck at his index finger. He spent his last 20 minutes on earth writing his will.[12]

The basic facts of the Hill murder were riveting, but, when reporters probed the principals' pasts, they found facts unexpected and revelatory.

One wrote that Hill had run a house of prostitution in Washington, DC, and became pregnant after an assignation with a member of Congress from Ohio.[13]

Another reported that Hill was one of her husband's tenants before they married, and, when he came around to collect rents, carrying thousands of dollars in gold coins on his person, she jokingly offered herself instead of a portion of the rent. He said he would consider it, and they were eventually married.[14]

One paper wrote that Camilla Twitchell, 38, was previously married to a store attendant until she took a job working for George Twitchell Sr., her husband's father. Rumors circulated about her and the elder Twitchell until she suddenly eloped with his 28-year-old son. George Twitchell Sr. was reportedly angry about the marriage.[15]

Agents and landlords began to gossip that Hill and the Twitchells argued about money. Hill intended to put the deed to her $26,800 house in her own name, but the Twitchells switched the deed to theirs. Hill had planned to take them to court the week she was murdered.[16]

The Twitchells would inherit $35,000 from Hill, but they would get none of the fortune her husband had left. His will stipulated that his widow would have access to all his income during her lifetime, but, after her death, the money would revert to his two nieces.[17]

Philadelphia buzzed with every detail of the murder. It was revealed that the victim's four small terriers always guarded her ferociously, but the Twitchells had put them in their room that night.

George Twitchell, whose friends said he was a peach of a man, was in dire financial straits. He was overextended in his roofing shingle business in Camden, New Jersey. Still, court watchers didn't think he could commit such an atrocity because he was a highly esteemed gentleman with correct moral and business habits. He was amiable and generous. He rose early and retired early. He loved children, was an exemplary husband and a friend worth having. He was also an affectionate son-in-law.[18]

Twitchell had plenty of friends and visitors who brought him meals to his cell. He always divided them and sent half to his wife, also jailed.[19] Always, until his wife requested her trial be severed from his, that is.

Camilla Twitchell was found not guilty. Despite his string of character witnesses, it took the jury only 33 minutes to find George Twitchell Jr. guilty. He was sentenced to die.

While he was fighting for a new trial, he sent his wife three confessions and asked her to sign one. They cast blame on her and on others. She was already acquitted and couldn't be tried again due to double jeopardy, but she wouldn't sign any of them.[20]

George Twitchell's hopes were dashed further when the judge rejected all 25 of his lawyer's reasons for a new trial.

The city was thrown into commotion on Saturday, April 3, 1869, when papers reported that George Twitchell had made a full confession from his jail cell. Interest piqued when readers learned it was equal parts confession and accusation.

Twitchell said he was sleeping when his mother-in-law was killed. He said he was roused by repeated calls from his wife. He ran down to the dining room, where he found her in a state of excitement. She told him she had a quarrel with her mother and had killed her.

"I do not know whether she said, 'Save me' or 'Help me hide it,' but we threw the body of Mrs. Hill out the window to make it look as if she fell out," Twitchell said. "I made a solemn vow to the Eternal God that night that I would never reveal it, but I cannot keep it any longer."[21]

Whether Camilla committed the murder or they acted in cahoots, he was still scheduled to hang between 10 a.m. and 3 p.m. on Thursday, April 8. He never climbed the scaffold.

The first word of his death was heard from guards leaving the prison after their shifts that morning. It was carried from lip to lip around the city by streetcar conductors traveling in all directions.

Twitchell was found dead in his cell at 5:20 a.m. on the same morning he was scheduled to hang. He had taken half of a bottle of prussic acid, a quick-acting poison that causes no pain. The rest of the bottle lay on its side in the cell.

Although Camilla Twitchell had been acquitted, her mother and her husband were dead, and she felt she was under a cloud of suspicion.

Hoping for a better ending, she sent a statement to the *Evening Telegraph* about a week after her husband's death. She complained that, although she was found not guilty, Philadelphians continued to denounce her as a murderess.

As proof that she was not involved in the murder, she gave the editors the three confessions she said her husband had sent her. They were not in her handwriting.

Despite her attempt to clear her name, there was no fairytale turnaround for her. The paper published her statement and the confessions, but it savaged her in an editorial.

"She is apparently not content with the verdict of 'not guilty' pronounced by the jury," an editor wrote. "The most fearful feature of this strange case is the singular history of all parties connected with it. Folly, duplicity, falsehood, vice and crime have been so artfully interwoven that there is little room for astonishment at the horrible tragedy which unveiled so many discreditable things to the public gaze."[22]

The tragic case faded from the headlines that summer, but, by that September, it was back.

Rumors that George Twitchell had actually escaped in the nick of time had circulated so widely that Governor John W. Geary called for an investigation. Was there any truth to the whispers that guards had found another prisoner's body and the amiable Twitchell was living happily elsewhere?

Sheriff William B. Perkins said there was no possibility the body of a dead prisoner had been placed in Twitchell's cell so that he could make a clean break. Perkins said not only had he and the coroner identified the body as Twitchell's, but it was also viewed by newspaper reporters who had observed Twitchell throughout his court trial.[23]

Chapter Thirteen

Anton Probst, One
of America's First Serial Killers

Cornelius Carey couldn't have imagined the thumbless farm-hand in the bed next to his was plotting Philadelphia's first mass murder. Or that he had already been chosen as the first victim.

The 17-year-old had no hint his roommate had mentally rehearsed crushing his skull with an axe and hiding his body in a haystack behind the house.

Although the undertaker did what he could to undo what Probst had done, the damage to the bodies was so severe that those who had tickets to view them quickly spread word of the atrocities. Philadelphians became so enraged that Probst feared for his life.

FROM TRIAL OF ANTON PROBST[1]

Carey would be dead by 9:30 a.m. By 10, he would be buried in the tall, wet haystack.

He was the first of eight victims of Anton Probst, one of America's first mass murderers.

In the next 240 minutes, Probst hacked seven unsuspecting members of the Deering family to death in the barn of their cattle farm on a lonely stretch of Jones Lane in the swampy, undeveloped swath of South Philadelphia that locals called "The Neck" in 1866. It is the present-day site of Philabundance's food distribution center, in the shadow of Citizens Bank Park.

Reporters called it the "murder that shocked the world." Newspapers gave it bigger play than a Senate vote on Colorado statehood. A headline writer dubbed it an "octo-homicide."[2]

It all started a week earlier when Probst, a 24-year-old farmhand, eyed Christopher Deering counting a thick stack of dollar bills. He made up his mind right then to kill the family and steal the money. He readied his axe, but he didn't put it to work until the rainy Saturday morning of April 7.

He hit 14-month-old Emily so hard her face flattened like a white china plate. Mrs. Deering's skull was pounded to pieces. Her throat was sliced twice. One of four-year-old Anna's tiny fingers was sliced off when she raised her right hand to protect her face. Thomas, age six, and John, age eight, were nearly beheaded. John's face hung to his neck by one scrap of white skin.[3]

Christopher Deering was a hard-working Irish immigrant.
FROM TRIAL OF ANTON PROBST

The last victims were 38-year-old Christopher Deering and his visiting cousin Elizabeth Dolan, 25. They were cut down minutes after

Deering pulled his wagon up to the house, so quickly that Deering didn't have time to unload the cold beef he had bought in the city.

Dolan was still dressed in her traveling clothes—a half-silk dotted black dress, a black velvet bonnet, a matching muff, and a black crucifix necklace.[4]

The eight bodies lay where Deering dropped them for five days, until a neighbor noticed there was nothing doing at the Deerings' and went to investigate. First, he noticed the Deerings' animals starved and parched. One horse drank nine buckets of water in quick succession.

Then, glancing around the barn, the man spotted a stockinged foot sticking out of a hay mound. He quickly shoveled the hay away and found Christopher Deering's decomposing body still clad in the gray suit he wore into the city on Saturday. His boots were missing. His skull was crushed. His throat was slit side to side.[5]

Police were called. Newspapers printed extra editions. As soon as word got out, Jones Lane was thronged with gawkers. The green meadows around the L-shaped white-frame farmhouse were dotted with newsmen, busybodies, thrill seekers, and society women in elegant dresses. A preacher arrived on horseback. A man on crutches hobbled toward the action. Wagons and carriages clogged the narrow lane to the house. Women holding babies in their arms traipsed through the barn, looking for the blood.

Out front, Elizabeth Dolan's mother sat on a log near the road, dressed in black and weeping bitterly.

Out back, a jokester curled up in the same spot where Carey's bloody corpse was found facedown in the hay.[6]

The scene had the air of a carnival or a holiday excursion, but the levity was mixed with horror, a reporter wrote.

The killer had left on foot around 6:30 Friday night, wearing Deering's clothes and toting Dolan's carpetbag filled with every item of value from the house, even the coins from the children's savings banks.[7]

The Deerings' little yellow dog trailed Probst the entire mile up the road to the train. The killer was spooked. The dog had never followed him before.[8]

Probst was a German immigrant who enlisted in the Union army two hours after his boat docked in America. He collected a $300 bounty and then deserted. He enlisted again and deserted again. Enlisted a third time, he was discharged after he dozed off on picket duty and accidentally fired his gun, shooting his own thumb off.[9]

Probst wound up at the Deering farm in the fall of 1865, but he was soon let go. He returned in early April, penniless. Against his wife's wishes, Deering gave Probst a second chance.

Probst immediately started scheming to steal the cash Deering kept in his first-floor office. Customers said the cattle dealer sometimes had anywhere from $100 to $10,000 on hand.

As soon as Deering left the farm to pick up his cousin that wet Saturday morning, the killer put his plan into action.[10]

Whacking the stout, athletic farmhand was Probst's first hurdle. He stood behind Carey as he chattered about work, drawing the axe up three or four times before he got the courage to deliver a blow to the left side of his head with an axe so sharp it could sever tree roots. That blow felled Carey before he could utter a sound, and it sent his hat aloft into the haystack. The killer struck Carey one or two more times and slit his throat. After that, Probst said, he could have killed 100 men.[11]

Then he went to the house and asked eight-year-old John to help him with something in the barn. He followed the boy inside, felled him with a small axe, and covered him with hay. Then he got Mrs. Deering up from sewing a new pair of trousers for her boy with a ruse about an unruly colt in the barn. One by one, he struck them down and cut their throats. He heaped the little ones next to their mother, covered them with hay, washed their hair off his axe, and walked up to the house to wait out Christopher Deering's return.

When Deering arrived, Probst lured him to the barn with a canard about a sick steer. Then he tricked Dolan by telling her Mrs. Deering and the children were in the barn. Later, when he confessed that ruse, he smiled at his own cleverness.

After Dolan and Deering succumbed, he rifled through their pockets, removed Deering's watch, and ripped off his boots to see if he had stashed any cash inside.

He hadn't.

Probst headed up the lane to loot the Deerings' home. He turned the two-and-a-half-story house inside out looking for valuables, but only turned up two revolvers, some jewelry, and a few trinkets. He expected at least $1,000. He found $17.75, and $4 of that was counterfeit.[12]

Probst's plan was to head for the city, where the bars and brothels would be bustling on a Saturday night. Before he did, he shaved himself with Christopher Deering's straight razor and dressed himself in his boss's shirt, pants, necktie, and boots.

A month later, after he confessed those details to a knot of reporters, a *Brooklyn Daily Eagle* headline blared: "The Monster Shaves Himself with Dearing's Razor."[13]

Probst left the farm on foot around 6:30 p.m., carrying Dolan's carpetbag bulging with stolen items he hoped to sell. He was heedful to make his way through the meadows so he wouldn't be spotted as he made haste to the train.

Only one Deering survived Probst's bloodbath. Ten-year-old Willie was away visiting his grandfather that weekend.

While the killer was carousing in center city, Mayor Morton McMichael offered a $1,000 reward for his capture—equivalent to $17,000 today. Newspapers called Probst "a monster in the shape of a man." With all of Philadelphia on the lookout, it was just days before an alert policeman spotted a man fitting Probst's description and minus one thumb.[14]

When officers searched him, they found items missing from the Deerings' farmhouse. He was arrested and imprisoned awaiting trial.

Meanwhile, on April 14, thousands swarmed Cyrus Horne's undertaking establishment, where seven of the victims were laid out in walnut coffins inscribed with their names and their ages. Although Horne cleaned the remains, there was little he could do to undo what Probst had done. Although only ticket holders were permitted to enter, word of the mashed faces and severed throats spread from lip to lip.[15]

One citizen wanted to torture Probst. Some wanted to mob him. One thought he should be placed in an iron cage and hoisted over a hearty fire. Hanging was too good for him, most agreed.[16]

FARM SCENE OF THE MURDER.

Haystack, where body of the   Dwelling House,   Barn where Mr. Deering and   Corn-crib, rear of barn, where
boy Cornelius was found.   Miss Dolan were found.   mother and children were found.

This sketch shows the distance between the Deering farmhouse and the barn.
FROM TRIAL OF ANTON PROBST

On April 18, Probst was indicted for the murders. He was rushed into the court building to dodge the crowds, but news spread instantly. People who couldn't get seats inside the courtroom stood outside, pressing their faces against the large windows to see whatever they could. Those inside were suddenly surrounded by an eerie glass wall of peering flattened faces.[17]

The day Probst's trial began, more than 2,000 men, women, and children were lined up two hours before the courthouse opened. Probst, who walked crouched down inside a ring of police guards, was lucky the mob was corralled behind an iron fence. He told his jailer, "I know they would kill me in half a minute."[18]

Inside the courtroom, when he raised his right hand to take the oath, a murmur went through the rows like a wave as people noticed his hand was missing a thumb.[19]

The police officer who nabbed the killer was certain he had the right man when he noticed Probst's thumb was missing.

FROM TRIAL OF ANTON PROBST

The prosecution came armed with a small model of the Deering farm, including the ditches where incriminating items were left and a lift-off barn roof so jurors could see where the bodies were stacked.

After chubby 10-year-old Willie Deering took the stand to identify his father's watch and Probst's bloody pants, and after all the facts had been unfurled, the jury took only 15 minutes to return a guilty verdict.

On May 1, Probst was sentenced to die for his crimes.

He took the last ride of his life that afternoon, the two-mile trip back to turreted Moyamensing Prison.

Thousands of spectators had lingered for hours for one glimpse of the round-shouldered, pimple-faced convict. To accommodate them, police seated the five-foot, 11-inch Probst between two officers on the elevated driver's bench, so the dense crowds could get a good long look at him as the vehicle made its way south through the city. Citizens eyed him as if he were a wild beast, a *Philadelphia Inquirer* reporter wrote.[20]

Probst was assigned to the "murderers' cell" at Moyamensing, the same drab second-floor cell where at least four other killers spent their last days. His left leg was chained to a ring on the floor. Sunlight was meted out through one narrow window. But Probst's jailers acted kindly toward him, and he looked forward to regular visits from the German-speaking pastor of a nearby Roman Catholic parish.

On Monday, May 7, just more than a month before he was scheduled to hang, newsmen learned Probst had made a full confession to his priest and he was willing to give the same to them.

The ax murderer sat on his mattress, his big hands fingering a thin black rosary, as he recollected his crimes in gruesome detail. He spoke in such low tones that reporters bent to catch every word. Occasionally his face would glow with suppressed laughter as he told them how he had outwitted his victims. He smiled when he recalled assuring Elizabeth Dolan, his last victim, that she'd find the others in the barn. One of the reporters later wrote that his nerves trembled as he took down Probst's words.[21]

Philadelphians of all stations applied to watch Probst hang. The hanging of the Lincoln conspirators 11 months earlier had been a hot ticket. With midday temperatures soaring over 100 in Washington that day, barkers sold lemonade outside the prison. At Moyamensing, though, spectators were limited to 40, many of them prison officials.

The warden had the scaffold constructed 20 feet from the prison wall, where it couldn't be seen from any window in the prison or from any high elevation in the city.

The day before Probst's judicial execution, one of the jailers brought him an orange. The ax murderer thanked him and said, "You are one of my best friends."

In the lead-up to his last day, Probst arranged for an acquaintance to send a lock of his hair and a photograph to his family in Germany. One of the last things he would do on earth was to pen a letter to them on note-size paper. "May we meet again in a better world," he wrote in German.[22]

Hardly anyone at the corner of 10th and Chestnut Streets on June 8 knew that the special railroad car that stopped there at 9:45 a.m. would ferry the official witnesses to the Probst execution. They quietly boarded the car with the closed blinds.

When they arrived at the prison at 10 a.m., refreshments awaited them. After a few moments of social intercourse, the party proceeded, two by two, to the main door of the prison. At 10:20, the death warrant was read aloud.[23]

They awaited the arrival of Probst, who had been up since 4 a.m., reading and praying and polishing off two eggs with bread and butter and coffee. Probst appeared, holding a crucifix and accompanied by his confessor. He appeared plumper than he had been at his arraignment. During his eight-week prison stint, he had gained eight pounds.[24]

As they started their march to the scaffold, a jailer named Clayton piped up. "Goodbye, Probst," he said. The killer's eyes suffused with tears.[25]

Probst, who had told people he was anxious to die, kissed the crucifix repeatedly. As the priest prayed aloud, Probst walked right up to the trap so that the noose dangled in his face.

Then, in an almost inaudible and tremulous voice, he said, "Forgive me. I hope God will forgive me. I am sorry for what I have done. I thank you officers of the prison and friends for all the kindness you have shown me."[26]

Probst and his priest fell to their knees on the scaffold and recited the Act of Contrition in German. When the prayers were over, the condemned man stood up and stretched his neck to the side to accommodate the jailer whose job was to put the noose in place.[27]

Before the sheriff covered his face with a white cotton cap, Probst looked up to the heavens, but the oppressively hot sun was too blinding.[28]

At 10:45 a.m., he dropped four feet to his death. His body turned round and round for almost 30 minutes before it was cut down at 11:13 a.m.[29] The *Juniata Sentinel* put it this way: "Anton Probst hung dangling twixt heaven and earth."[30]

Probst's corpse was covered with a white cloth and a crucifix. The priests recited Mass and sprinkled holy water.

Then the body was hurriedly removed to the prison paint shop, where surgeons examined the eye to determine whether the last image a person sees before death is imprinted on the retina.[31]

It was not.

CHAPTER FOURTEEN

The Bible Riots—Catholics vs. Protestants

A PARISH PRIEST BOLTED FROM HIS BURNING RECTORY TO THE SAFETY of a horse-drawn cab waiting outside St. Michael's Catholic Church at Second and Master Streets. It was May 8, 1844, the day a Protestant mob tried to burn his parish out of business in the City of Brotherly Love.

Tall flames consumed the Gothic church. When the heavy cross atop the roof fell to the street with a deafening thud, rioters gave three cheers, and their fifers and drummers tuned up an anti-Catholic song.[1]

Just yards away from the merry mob, two Catholics rushed to bury their dead infant in the parish graveyard. With the logs of their church crackling behind them, the parents offered quick prayers over their child because there was no priest to conduct a proper funeral. As they knelt, the wall of the rectory, buckling against the flames, arched over the walkway.[2]

The 10-year-old church was reduced to blackened walls. The convent was burned to the ground. The rectory was a ruin.

In the parish lot, Catholic women clung to furniture they saved from their torched parlors. Families walked the streets aimlessly, carrying bundles. Bedsteads and tables proven too heavy to carry littered the streets.[3]

Some Irish immigrants put American flags in their windows in hopes the rioters would believe they were native born and pass by their doors. Some abandoned their homes and all their possessions and ran for their lives.

The Bible Riots—which vexed the city for 11 bloody weeks in 1844—tested Philadelphia's lofty image of itself. Far from the ideal of

Catholics and Protestants fought each other with cannons in the streets during the Bible Riots of 1844.
DIGITAL LIBRARY@VILLANOVA UNIVERSITY

William Penn's City of Brotherly Love that welcomed religions of every stripe, Philadelphia had turned lethal.

Churchgoers pointed cannons at each other. One church was breached with a battering ram.

Two Catholic churches were set afire. At least 14 men were killed. More than 50 people were injured. Rioters threw thousands of religious books into a blazing bonfire. Two hundred people lost their homes to arson.

Families by the dozen slept outdoors, often with no food and no blankets. One woman gave birth there.

The lawlessness shocked city residents of all religions. The riots were dubbed "the Bible Riots" because Protestant pamphleteers said Catholics wanted to kick the Bible from public schools.

Catholic Bishop Francis P. Kenrick had written a letter to the school board in 1842, complaining that the Protestant's King James Bible was being used for reading instruction and school days were being opened and closed with Protestant hymns and Bible readings.[4]

In response to the bishop's letter, the school board ruled that students could be excused from daily Bible readings and that any version of the Bible without note or comment could be used in schools. So, the bishop got half of what he wanted—Catholic students could be excused, but they could not read the Catholic Douay-Rheims Bible because it included comment.

The riot's roots were more widespread. Protestants, fearing the Pope would dictate how Irish Catholics would vote, wanted to restrict the vote to native-born citizens and immigrants who had lived in the US for a minimum of 21 years.

Cutthroat competition for jobs pitted Catholics and Protestants against each other. The General Trades Union, which included workers of all faiths, was losing ground.

Everyone wanted something in the struggle between the faiths. Protestant employers backed temperance laws, hoping they would control the Catholic workforce. Ministers hoped to woo the city's 100,000 unchurched. Anti-immigrant sentiment swelled as Philadelphia's Irish population doubled and Irish Catholics formed their own businesses and savings-and-loan associations.[5]

Twenty-six Protestant clergymen, alarmed by growing Catholicism in Philadelphia, formed the American Protestant Association.

Added to all that, there was a lingering historic hatred between the Catholics and Protestants who had emigrated from Ireland.

The riots began in Kensington, a mixed neighborhood of 22,314 residents working as weavers, tradesmen, and factory workers. It all started on the first Friday in May when S. R. Cramer, publisher of an anti-Catholic newspaper, staged a rally less than a block from St. Michael's Catholic Church. About 100 angry Catholics drove him off.

Cramer returned the next Monday with thousands of nativists from around the city. Lewis Levin, a popular orator who edited a nativist newspaper, kicked off the high-spirited rally. The weather had been iffy that week. A tornado had passed over Kensington just two days earlier, knocking over a wall and killing a man.

The rally had barely begun when a sudden heavy thunderstorm drove the speakers inside an open-air market where Irish Catholics were shopping. Levin climbed up on some packing boxes and held forth on "Popish influence" in elections. Shoppers hit him with vegetables, then fists, then bricks.[6]

The fight spilled into the street. More armed men joined the fray on both sides. The nativists broke into the nearby Hibernia Hose House, then into the homes of two weavers they said harbored snipers who had fired on them.

Because the Protestants were shooting from the streets and the Catholic rifles were posted in the upper stories, seven Protestants were shot. A young leatherworker was mortally wounded in the chest and carried off to a drugstore to die. At 19, George Shiffler became the nativist movement's first martyr.

More armed men kept arriving for both sides. By the end of the night, two more Protestants were dead and a Catholic was severely beaten.[7]

Ironically, the Catholics fired from a seminary building, and the nativists holed up inside a temperance grocery store, a business that adhered to the goals of temperance societies and did not sell liquor.[8]

The next day, 3,000 militiamen flooded into Kensington, but the destruction accelerated. By midnight, dozens of Catholic homes would be looted, and two Catholic churches, two parsonages, a convent, and a religious library would be in flames. Ash, dust, smoke, and sparks would cover the streets.

Packs of Protestants roamed Catholic neighborhoods, searching for illegal guns. When they did find weapons, they often burned the homes and beat the homeowners.

The mob busted into Patrick Murphy's three-story house on Jefferson Street, smashed the furniture, heaved looking glasses into the street, and looted whatever they could carry away.

At a Master Street home, rioters sliced the featherbeds and tossed them out of windows, scattering feathers everywhere.

The home of a suspected sniper was riddled with gunfire until everything inside was destroyed.

J L MAGEE LITH

DEATH OF GEORGE SHIFLER

BORN JAN 24 1825   IN KENSINGTON   MURDERED MAY 6 1844

Pub by Wm Smith 106 So Third St Phil.a

Protestants cast 19-year-old George Shiffler as a martyr after he was one of the first to be killed.

The mob surrounded St. Michael's and cheered its demise.

Then a rumor passed that St. Augustine Catholic Church would be next. Mayor John Morin Scott rode through the streets on horseback to calm the crowd, but a rioter's rock hit him in the chest.

Police rushed to protect the area's largest Catholic church, the one church some Protestants had tender feelings toward because the pastor had opened his home to cholera victims during the epidemic that killed 10 to 71 people a day in 1832. Sisters of Charity ministered to the 370 patients there, and 9 out of 10 of them were Protestants.[9]

Even though policemen were posted around the church, a 14-year-old boy pussyfooted into the vestibule minutes before 10 p.m. and set it afire. Dense black smoke quickly curled out of every window. In minutes, the flames reached the belfry and burst out in broad sheets. Soon flames wrapped the three-story cupola.[10] A shower of gold cinders fell to the street.

Protestants set two Catholic churches afire, including St. Augustine Church, the area's largest Catholic church.

The blinding firelight made the gas streetlamps look dim, and the heat was so intense that onlookers had to back away a full block. When the cross at the top fell intact to the ground with a loud crash, many spectators applauded.[11]

Then rioters heaved thousands of religious books from the church library onto a blazing bonfire.[12]

Only the blackened walls of the church were standing. One still bore three words outlined in black grime: "The Lord Seeth."[13]

The city seemed calm for the next eight weeks, but both sides were anxious.

In the Protestant stronghold of Southwark, a Catholic priest's brother started stockpiling guns in the basement of St. Philip de Neri Church.[14]

Meanwhile, the nativists' clout caught politicians' attention when 4,500 of them marched with banners and floats in the Independence Day parade and 50,000 people lined the parade route.

To protect St. Philip de Neri, a rumored target for burning, the governor allowed parishioners to draw some muskets from the Philadelphia Arsenal. Someone saw the muskets being carried into the church, and word spread that St. Philip's was an armed Catholic fortress. The sheriff showed the crowd there were just 12 unloaded muskets, but then the large cache of weapons the priest's brother had hidden in the church was discovered. When word got out, more than 1,000 nativists gathered.

Two hundred militiamen marched down Second Street, but the bigger nativist mob didn't back down. They threw stones. One got hold of a soldier's sword. A battle ensued, and this time both the militia and the rioters were armed with cannons.

A melee of stoning, bottle-throwing, brick-throwing, gunfire, and cannon fire went on for hours. By morning, four militiamen and many rioters were dead, and many more were wounded. One wall of the church had been breached with an impromptu battering ram.[15]

Militia from Lancaster and Harrisburg arrived to patrol the city. Marines and sailors were called in to circle the arsenal. The collapse of public order shocked Philadelphians.

The riots and anti-immigrant fears became an issue in the next election, buoying the nativist candidates, but their reign was short-lived.

The longest-lasting effects of the riots were on city government and public education.

In less than a year after the riots, the city beefed up its police force and the sheriff was given the power to call up the militia to handle riots.

In 1854, the City of Philadelphia was consolidated with the six boroughs, 13 townships, and nine districts that made up the rest of Philadelphia County—places like Kensington, Southwark, and Northern Liberties.

The loss of life and property in the riots showed that law enforcement was much more difficult when more than one municipality was involved, and the population had shifted into the areas north of the city boundaries, bringing tax revenue north, too. With tax revenue from the consolidation, the city could modernize with a trained professional police force, a paid fire service, and water and sewage expansion.

When administrators would not agree to Bishop Kenrick's request to excuse Catholic students from the compulsory reading of Protestant prayers in public schools, the Catholic Church established its own parochial school system that permanently removed hundreds of thousands of students from the city system.

Philadelphia schools continued mandatory Bible readings until 1963.

CHAPTER FIFTEEN

America's First Bank Robbery

AMERICA'S FIRST BANK ROBBERY ENDED WITH AN INNOCENT GENIUS jailed, a guilty man set free, and some bank executives caught with egg on their faces.[1]

The haul was $162,821 in 1798—equal to about $3.4 million today.[2]

The whodunnit solved itself when one of the robbers raised suspicions by depositing his newfound wealth in the same bank he had robbed.

It came off in August 1798, right after the Bank of Pennsylvania moved its office to Carpenters' Hall. The bank was in the basement of the same iconic building where Sam Adams, Patrick Henry, and George Washington had met for the First Continental Congress 24 years earlier. Ironically, it was an attempted break-in at its last address that had prompted the bank's move.[3]

Patrick Lyon, a well-regarded local blacksmith, was hired to install new locks on two iron vault doors. Lyon told the bankers the locks they wanted really weren't fit for a vault, but he didn't argue much because he was anxious to get out of town with his young apprentice, James M'Ginley.[4]

The duo had booked passage on a boat to Lower Delaware. Philadelphia was in the throes of its second yellow fever epidemic in five years, and they were eager to leave. The first wave killed 5,000 people in 1793, and Lyon had already lost his wife and infant daughter to the second wave.

Sometime on the weekend of August 31, robbers entered the bank's basement vault and made off with the cash and banknotes.

This *Century Magazine* illustration shows Patrick Lyon at his forge. The prison where he was incarcerated during the yellow fever is visible through the window at the rear.

A bank runner discovered the heist when he went to the bank to do some work he had left unfinished. He found the back door open, and, when he entered, he saw the open vault doors.

The bankers pinned it on the locksmith because there was no forced entry and he had left town.

When the vault was being emptied, Lyon was already 100 miles away, sailing down the Delaware coastline. He spent the entire weekend nursing M'Ginley, who started showing yellow fever symptoms after they put to sea. Four days later Lyon would be buying a coffin for him.[5]

Lyon stayed in Delaware after M'Ginley's death, waiting for the epidemic to ebb in the city and working on a diving bell for a water salvage operation. He saw news of the Bank of Pennsylvania robbery in a Delaware newspaper and thought to himself that the thief could be a man who had spent an inordinate amount of time fiddling with the locks while waiting for his carpenter friend.[6]

A few days later, Lyon ran into his old landlord from Philadelphia. Something seemed off about the landlord, especially when the two talked about the robbery. It got more awkward when they had a drink together the next day. The landlord repeated the same story, but, this time, he alluded to the fact that many innocent people were suspects. Lyon asked if his name had come up. The landlord said it had. Flabbergasted, Lyon asked why he hadn't told him sooner. The landlord said he didn't want to affront him.

A reward-conscious constable was already searching for Lyon in New Jersey, according to the landlord. The two men agreed Lyon's best option was to return to the city and share his own suspicions about the robbery with the bank director.[7]

Lyon tried to book passage to Philadelphia the next day, but the best he could find was a captain sailing as far as northern Delaware. He walked the other 28 miles into Philadelphia. Hot and tired, he arrived at the country estate of bank director John Stocker.[8]

Lyon explained his weeks-long absence. It was not unusual for anyone who could afford passage out to leave the city during a yellow fever epidemic. During the 1793 fever, when people were dying at the rate of 20 a day, both George Washington and Thomas Jefferson had left the city. John Adams, who was out of town, stayed away.[9]

After explaining, Lyon shared his suspicions about the man he'd seen trying and retrying the keys. Instead of welcoming Lyon's information, Stocker had him arrested.

The blacksmith's bail was set uncommonly high at $150,000—$3.1 million today. He was locked up in a moldy 4-by-12-foot space in Walnut Street Prison, where yellow fever was rampant. He had no bed for the first three weeks. Often, he had no food for 24 hours.[10]

His sadistic guard would die of the fever himself in a few weeks, but not before he withheld Lyon's food so frequently that the blacksmith became dizzy and started seeing double.[11]

Some of Lyon's friends wouldn't come to the fever-infested prison. One friend brought Lyon a piece of meat, but the man took sick with the fever shortly afterward. Another visited twice but never returned. Lyon later learned that the missing friend had died of the fever.[12]

He tried to contact other old friends, only to find out they had died of the fever, too.

Lyon was convinced he would soon contract the fever in the prison and die—until another man's stupidity turned out to be a lucky break for him.

Isaac Davis, the man Lyon recalled fiddling with the keys, decided to put his stolen money in the bank for safekeeping. He deposited large amounts in three banks—including the bank he had robbed.[13]

The large deposit in Bank of Pennsylvania raised the suspicions of bank officers, who checked to see if he had made deposits in the Bank of the United States and the Bank of North America, too. He had. His total deposits were suspiciously close to the $162,821 haul from the heist.

Davis confessed.

Luckily for him, Governor Thomas Mifflin had issued a proclamation in the newspapers on the day the caper was made public. He promised a free and entire pardon to any perpetrator who turned in his or her associates.[14]

Davis turned in his accomplice, Thomas Cunningham, the armed bank employee who served as the inside man. He said Cunningham plotted the robbery and had the extra keys made. Initially, they had split the money.[15]

It was one of the last things Cunningham did on earth. The next day, he took sick with yellow fever. He was dead within a week.

After his partner's death, Davis helped himself to the other half of the money.

Davis was set free with a governor's pardon, but authorities kept Lyon in prison for three more weeks under suspicion as an accomplice.

Lyon was finally released in January when a grand jury declined to indict him.

The blacksmith hatched a plan to restore his reputation and retaliate against the officials who had locked him in a prison where the disease that killed his wife and daughter was raging.

He wrote a bestselling short book with a long title: *Narrative of Patrick Lyon, Who Suffered Three Months Severe Imprisonment in Philadelphia Gaol on Merely a Vague Suspicion of Being Concerned in a Robbery of the Bank of Pennsylvania with His Remarks Thereon.*

The book cast Lyon as a working-class genius who studied mechanics at age 11, as an immigrant who left Britain on his own to make his fortune in America, as a successful smithy who opened his own shop, as a new husband who lost his young family to yellow fever, and as a master designer who fashioned a fire apparatus that could "throw" water for the first time.[16]

Reviewers loved it. The *Aurora General Advertiser*, the newspaper published by Benjamin Franklin's grandson, pointed out that Lyon received "no pecuniary recompence" for the "unmerited sufferings" he had experienced.[17]

It was the dawn of the Patrick Lyon legend. Eventually, there would be a play about him, a youth novel, a board game, a serialized story of his life, even Patrick Lyon parade hats for firefighters.

Lyon filed a civil lawsuit against three bank officials and the constable who mishandled his case. His lawyers were a colonial dream team—Alexander Dallas, a future secretary of the treasury, and Joseph Hopkinson, a skilled attorney whose father was a signer of the Declaration of Independence. The bankers hired Jared Ingersoll, a signer of the Constitution, and William Rawle, who was named a US attorney by George Washington.[18]

It took the jury just four hours to award Lyon $12,000—$264,585 today. The packed courtroom cheered.

The defendants were granted a new trial on appeal, but they agreed to settle the case by paying Lyon $9,000.[19]

Lyon went on to win fame and fortune designing fire apparatuses. In 1804, he engineered an innovative hose wagon that hooked to Philadelphia's gravity-fed municipal water system. It eliminated the need for bucket brigades.

He created dozens of pieces of fire apparatus, including the Diligent, a pumping wagon that, in a publicity stunt, threw water 196 feet in the air over a doctor's office on Chestnut Street. The Diligent was so popular that it was pictured on firemen's parade hats.[20]

Lyon sprang for a portrait of himself painted by top Philadelphia portraitist John Neagle, who would later paint politician Henry Clay, actor Junius Booth, and portraitist Gilbert Stuart. While most of Neagle's subjects struck regal poses, Lyon did not want to be sketched as an aristocrat. He told Neagle he did not want to be portrayed as something he was not.

Neagle portrayed Lyon as a brawny-chested blacksmith at his forge in an open shirt, rolled-up sleeves, and a stiff brown leather workman's apron. In the background, a shop window revealed the cupola of the Walnut Street Prison. The 1827 painting, titled *Pat Lyon at the Forge*, is Neagle's best-known work. It is on view at the Pennsylvania Academy of Fine Arts.

Lyon died a wealthy man on April 15, 1829.

A week later, the *National Gazette* carried a notice that his furniture would be sold at auction.[21]

Four days after that, another ad appeared, this time for an upcoming auction of his valuable book collection.[22]

CHAPTER SIXTEEN

The Fatal Witch Hunt During the 1787 Constitutional Convention

IF GEORGE WASHINGTON PICKED UP A NEWSPAPER WHEN HE STAYED IN Philadelphia for the Constitutional Convention in 1787, he would have seen a report of a grim crime that happened a few streets over from the mansion where he was staying.

A frail, elderly woman named Korbmacher was set upon by a vicious crowd convinced she was a witch.[1]

Philadelphia, the largest city in America with 60,000 inhabitants, was home to scientists and artists and the learned American Philosophical Society. The country's first two magazines were published there, along with eight newspapers.[2]

Almost as if it were 95 years earlier during the Salem witch frenzy, an excited mob seized a sick old woman, cut a mark in her forehead, and paraded her through the streets with no one stopping it. It is not known whether any of the delegates saw it.

The woman, realizing her life was in danger, begged for help. The *Pennsylvania Packet* said she was the victim of some vengeful individuals who abused her.[3]

Then, on July 10, while 57 delegates were writing the document that guaranteed "the blessings of liberty," another mob carried the same old woman through the streets of Newmarket. It happened just a few blocks from the meeting room where James Madison, Alexander Hamilton,

At the same time the Founding Fathers were meeting at Independence Hall to write the document that would guarantee rights to Americans, a few blocks away a mob stoned a frail, old woman and cut her face to identify her as a witch.
SCENE AT THE "SIGNING OF CONSTITUTION" BY HOWARD CHANDLER CHRISTY

and Benjamin Franklin were working, in the most sophisticated city in America.

Spewing insults at her, the mob pelted her with objects and invited spectators to pelt her, too. One woman triggered more abuse when she cried that her only child was sickened and died because of Korbmacher's charms. A crowd gathered to hear the tormentors who made claims against the woman. When a gentleman moved in to help her, the spectators insulted him.[4]

Several citizens who witnessed it unfold vowed to testify to what they'd seen in court. The *Freeman's Journal* reported that Korbmacher had again been attacked by "an ignorant and inhuman mob."[5]

The old woman never recovered.

On July 23, the papers reported that Korbmacher had died of her injuries on July 18.[6]

The case came to trial on October 22, after the final draft of the Constitution had been signed and sent to the states for consideration.

When the woman who incited the terror testified, she said Korbmacher had put a charm on her child that caused the child to sicken and die. The judge flippantly called the late Korbmacher a poor wretch wrinkled with extreme old age. He said young, beautiful women might be able to charm and bewitch, but the aged and infirm could not. Newspapers did not report the final disposition of the case.[7]

Americans link "Salem" and "witch," but Philadelphians held a witch trial long before the ones in Salem, Massachusetts. In 1683, Margaret Mattson and Yeshro Hendrickson were charged with casting spells on cows and oxen. William Penn presided at the trial.

The jurors returned a guilty verdict, but Penn did not sentence the women to death.

Instead, he required the defendants' husbands to post 50 pounds to guarantee the good behavior of their wives for six months.[8]

Acknowledgments

Researching this book introduced me to Philadelphia's greatest reporters of the 1930s and 1940s, chief among them Owen F. McDonnell and, especially, George M. Mawhinney. I'm grateful for their detailed reporting that allowed me to re-create crimes and punishments just as they unfolded decades ago.

I'm grateful to 21st-century Philadelphians, too. Due to COVID-19, I met most of them only by email, but they did everything possible to help as institutions were closing around us.

This book would not have the vivid photographs it does without the curation of Josué Hurtado at Temple's Special Collection Research Center. I thank Michael Foight at Villanova's Falvey Memorial Library for helping me access the library's stunning collection of art depicting the Bible Riots of 1844. I'm also grateful for the kindness of Jane Golden and Amy R. Johnston at Mural Arts Philadelphia.

Historic research becomes fun when the staff at institutions shares your enthusiasm for the subjects and for history in general. I was fortunate to encounter that in Kenneth E. Rice at the Philadelphia City Archives, Renee Garvin Johnson at the Philadelphia Free Library, Alex Bartlett and Irv Miller at the Germantown Historical Society, and Zarek Faago and Renee Pauls at the University of Delaware's Morris Library.

At the Federal Bureau of Investigation, I thank Linda Miller. At Eastern State Penitentiary Historic Site, I'm grateful for the help I received from Nicole Frankhouser, Annie Anderson, and Erica Harmon.

I owe a special debt to Parry Desmond, a local historian with an encyclopedic knowledge of bootlegging entrepreneur Max "Boo Boo" Hoff.

I'm also grateful to Jonathan Eaker at the Library of Congress and Susan McNaughton of the Pennsylvania Department of Corrections.

And, at Lyons Press, I thank Sarah Zink, Ellen Urban, Stephanie Scott, and Rick Rinehart.

I owe much to my friend Rachel Simon, best-selling author of six books, including *The Story of a Beautiful Girl* and *Riding on the Bus with my Sister*. Despite her own schedule and deadlines, Rachel always took time to cheer me on toward my deadline.

I am grateful to Philadelphia's top crime writer George Anastasia, author of *Blood and Honor*, *Gotti's Rules*, and *The Last Gangster*, for his generosity in reading the manuscript of an unknown writer.

I thank Ciro Poppiti III for his help. I also thank Frank Smith and Anne Slaton for sharing their knowledge of the Pottsville, PA, area in the 1950s and 1960s.

I'm indebted to Greg Sweeney for his careful reading of the manuscript.

I also thank Matt Sweeney who reminded me of Elmore Leonard's advice to writers—leave out the parts nobody reads.

And I thank John Sweeney, who grew up in Port Richmond and graduated from Temple. He was my guide to a city I knew only as a place where I occasionally reported and volunteered as a dinosaur docent. Everything is easier when you have a real Philadelphian on hand.

Notes

Chapter One

1. "Lillian 'Tiger Lil' Reis Dies," *Philadelphia Inquirer*, 13 December 2009, A1, B11; "Miller Tells of 45 Cent Role in Heist," *Philadelphia Daily News*, 17 March 1961, 3; "Tiger Lil's Twisted Tale," *New York Daily News*, 23 May 1968, 53; "The Great Pottsville Heist," *Philadelphia Daily News*, 27 July 1999, 12; America's Obituaries and Death Notices, *Philadelphia Inquirer*, 13 December 2009, 20 April 2020; "*Saturday Evening Post* Sued," *New York Times*, 10 January 1964.

2. Pamela C. MacArthur, *The Genteel John O'Hara* (New York: Peter Lang, 2009), 22.

3. "Intriguing Case of the Nightclub Owner," *St. Louis Post-Dispatch*, 5 March 1962, 36; Alfred G. Aronowitz, "They Call Me Tiger Lil," *Saturday Evening Post*, 26 October 1963, 28.

4. "Miller Tells of 45 Cent Role in Heist."

5. "Shovel Goes to Work," *Republican and Herald* (Pottsville, PA), 12 August 1957, 1.

6. "From Chorus to Crime Spotlight," *New York Daily News*, 15 May 1966, 135; "Accused Fingerman Tells," *Philadelphia Daily News*, 17 March 1961, 70; "Liquor, Pillowcase Figure in Rich Theft," *Pottsville (PA) Republican*, 7 April 1961, 16; "Coal Firm Heads Face Tax Charge," *Republican and Herald* (Pottsville, PA), 14 July 1964, 1.

7. Aronowitz, "They Call Me Tiger Lil"; "From Chorus to Crime Spotlight"; Ron Avery, *City of Brotherly Mayhem* (Philadelphia: Otis Books, 1997), 103.

8. "Accused Fingerman Tells."

9. "Past Weather in City of Pottsville, Pennsylvania," TimeandDate.com, https://www.timeanddate.com/weather/@5207082/historic.

10. Superior Court of Pennsylvania, Commonwealth v. Staino, 204 Pa. Super. 319, CourtListener, https://courtlistener.com/opinion/1504551/commonwealth-v-staino; "Admit Statements," *Pottsville (PA) Republican*, 17 March 1961, 2; Aronowitz, "They Call Me Tiger Lil."

11. "Admit Statements"; Aronowitz, "They Call Me Tiger Lil."

12. "2 Confessions Read at Trial in Pottsville," *Sunbury (PA) Daily Item*, 17 March 1961, 1; Superior Court of Pennsylvania, Commonwealth v. Staino; "Admit Statements"; Aronowitz, "They Call Me Tiger Lil."

13. Superior Court of Pennsylvania, Commonwealth v. Staino; "Admit Statements."

14. Superior Court of Pennsylvania, Commonwealth v. Staino; "Admit Statements"; "Berkery-Lil Romance Revealed," *Philadelphia Daily News*, 13 April 1961, 41.

15. "Miller, Not Lillian, Masterminded Theft, Lawyer Tells Jurors," *Philadelphia Inquirer*, 14 October 1961, 1;" Liquor, Pillowcase Figure in Rich Theft;" "They'll Kill Me If I Talk," *New York Daily News*, 8 May 1966, 253.
16. "Philadelphia, PA, Weather History," Weather Underground, https://www.wunder ground.com/history/monthly/us/pa/philadelphia/KPHL/date/1959-8.
17. "They'll Kill Me," *New York Daily News*, 8 May 1966, 253.
18. "They'll Kill Me"; "Admit Statements"; "Berkery Spree Recounted by Witness," *Morning Call* (Allentown, PA), 13 April 1961, 12; "Says Berkery's Home Like Rich's," *Pottsville (PA) Republican*, 13 April 1961, 23; "Defense Attacks Credibility of State's Chief Witness," *Plain Speaker* (Hazleton, PA), 13 April 1961, 13; "Berkery-Lil Romance Revealed."
19. Superior Court of Pennsylvania, Commonwealth v. Staino.
20. "Lillian 'Tiger Lil' Reis Dies," *Philadelphia Inquirer*; "Intriguing Case of the Nightclub Owner."
21. "Lillian Reis, Famous Philly Showgirl, Dies at 79," *Philadelphia Inquirer*, 14 December 2009, https://www.inquirer.com/philly/obituaries/20091214_Lillian_Reis__famous_Philly_showgirl__dies_at_79.html.
22. Aronowitz, "They Call Me Tiger Lil."
23. "Other Woman Sought," *Philadelphia Daily News*, 21 February 1961.
24. "Violent Life," *Philadelphia Daily News*, 28 July 1961, 12.
25. Ibid.
26. "Richie Blaney in Gossipy Day on the Stand," *Philadelphia Daily News*, 14 April 1961, 14; "Fearful Poulson Key to Blaney Bomb Death," *Philadelphia Daily News*, 28 July 1961, 14; "Ferguson Bitter; 'Knows' Slayers," *Philadelphia Inquirer*, 28 July 1961, 3.
27. "Eyewitness," *Philadelphia Daily News*, 28 July 1961, 9; "Blaney Killed as Bomb Wrecks Auto," *Philadelphia Inquirer*, 28 July 1961, 3.
28. Ibid.
29. "Lil Back at Old Grind Minus Bumps," *Philadelphia Daily News*, 23 May 1961, 3; "Intriguing Case of the Nightclub Owner"; "Lil's Defense," *New York Daily News*, 11 October 1961, 398.
30. Aronowitz, "They Call Me Tiger Lil."
31. "Lil's Ex-Sugar Masterminded Job," *New York Daily News*, 14 October 1961, 135.
32. "Lil's Ex-Sugar Masterminded Job"; "Miller, Not Lillian, Masterminded Theft"; "Retrial," *Bristol (PA) Daily Courier*, 14 October 1961, 3.
33. "Tiger Lil's Twisted Tale"; "Bonds in Safe Not Stolen," *Pottsville (PA) Republican*, 7 April 1961, 1.
34. Aronowitz, "They Call Me Tiger Lil."
35. "Court Admits Previous Testimony of Rich," *Philadelphia Inquirer*, 18 March 1964, 11.
36. "Fergy the Fabulous Retires," *Philadelphia Daily News*, 5 February 1970, 3; "Tiger Lil's Twisted Tale"; "The Great Pottsville Heist."
37. "Porkpie's Back—Fergy's Under It," *Philadelphia Daily News*, 20 October 1970, 3.
38. "Fergy Was Good Cop Led Astray, Lil Purrs," *Philadelphia Daily News*, 6 February 1970, 4.

39. "Proud to Be Mom of Fergy's Child," *Philadelphia Daily News*, 18 March 1972, 5; "Fergy Wills Estate to Daughter," *Philadelphia Daily News*, 17 March 1972, 5; "Fergy's Widow Owns 17 Properties," *Philadelphia Daily News*, 21 March 1972, 32; "Attorney Expects Mrs. Ferguson to Get Joint Real Estate," *Philadelphia Inquirer*, 19 March 1972, 32; "Fergy: 'I'm Tired,'" *Philadelphia Daily News*, 8 November 1971, 3.

40. "The Great Pottsville Heist."

41. Abbe Art Cinema ad, *Philadelphia Inquirer*, 12 April 1964, 78.

42. "Lillian Reis, Famous Philly Showgirl, Dies at 79."

43. "Coal Firm Heads Face Tax Charge"; "Rich Must Pay $90,740 Fine," *Republican and Herald* (Pottsville, PA), 13 May 1965, 1; "Rich Changes Tax Case Plea to No Defense," *Philadelphia Inquirer*, 22 September 1964, 35.

CHAPTER TWO

1. "Broker's Wife Slain in Oak Lane Home," *Philadelphia Record*, 8 December 1944, 1.

2. "Maid Traced in Oak Lane Murder Case," *Philadelphia Record*, 9 December 1944, 1.

3. "Broker's Wife Slain in Oak Lane Home."

4. "New Hired Maid Vanishes along with Jewelry and Money," *Philadelphia Inquirer*, 8 December 1944, 1.

5. Ibid.

6. "Broker's Wife Slain in Oak Lane Home: Main Line Housemaid Held in 50 Robberies," *Philadelphia Inquirer*, 12 November 1944, 21

7. "Twins 81 Hours Apart," *Philadelphia Bulletin*, 7 December 1944, 1.

8. "Broker's Wife Slain in Oak Lane Home."

9. "Nickname Led Cops to Murder Suspect," *Courier Post* (Camden, NJ), 11 December 1944, 1.

10. "Daughter of Murdered Woman Gave Two Tips That Trapped Maid Slayer," *Philadelphia Record*, 11 December 1944, 1.

11. "Maid Traced in Oak Lane Murder Case."

12. Joseph W. Laythe, *Engendered Death: Pennsylvania Women Who Kill* (Bethlehem, PA: Lehigh University Press, 2011).

13. "Maid Is Accused in Fatal Stabbing," *Morning News* (Wilmington, DE), 21 December 1944, 9; "Daughter of Murdered Woman Gave Two Tips That Trapped Maid Slayer," *Philadelphia Record*, 11 December 1944, 1.

14. Harry M. Wodlinger US Draft Registration Card, Ancestry.com.

15. "Confession," *Doylestown (PA) Intelligencer Journal*, 11 December 1944, 4.

16. "Maid, a Killer, Admits Taking Job to Steal," *New York Daily News*, 11 December 1944, 25, 1.

17. "Maid Trapped by Nickname," *Morning Post* (Camden, NJ), 11 December 1944, 1.

18. "Maid Now Accuses Man as Killer of Mrs. Wodlinger," *Philadelphia Evening Bulletin*, 11 December 1944, 1.

19. "Daughter of Murdered Woman Gave Two Tips."

20. "Death Asked for Maid in Murder," *Philadelphia Inquirer*, 17 March 1945, 9.

21. "Maid Now Accuses Man as Killer of Mrs. Wodlinger"; David A. Canton, *Raymond Pace Alexander: A New Negro Lawyer Fights for Civil Rights in Philadelphia*

(Jackson: University Press of Mississippi, 2013), 85. "Daughter of Murdered Woman Gave Two Tips That Trapped Maid Slayer," *Philadelphia Record*, 11 December 1944, 1.

22. "Cover Story," *Philadelphia Daily News*, 4 February 1985, E12–15.

23. "Maid Now Accuses Man as Killer of Mrs. Wodlinger."

24. "Second Man Hunted," *Philadelphia Inquirer*, 21 December 1944, 1; "Crazed Servant Stabs Housewife," *Philadelphia Inquirer*, 9 May 1945, 1.

25. "Nickname Trapped Slayer of Woman," *Morning Post* (Camden, NJ), 11 December 1944, 1, 3; "Cover Story." "Maid Blames Man As Wodlinger Slayer," *Philadelphia Inquirer*, 12 December 1944, 1.

26. "Crazed Servant Stabs Housewife," *Philadelphia Inquirer*, 9 May 1945, 1; "Cover Story;" Pennsylvania and New Jersey town records, 1669-2013, Ancestry.com.

27. Canton, David A., "Raymond Pace Alexander, A New Negro Lawyer Fights for Civil Rights in Philadelphia," (Jackson, MS: University Press of Mississippi, 2013) 84; "Men and Things," *Philadelphia Tribune*, 24 September 1946, 5.

28. Ibid, "Men and Things."

29. Canton.

30. "Men and Things," *Philadelphia Tribune*, 24 September 1946, 5.

31. "Murder Knife Identified at Maid's Trial," *Philadelphia Inquirer*, 15 March 1945, 19. Canton, 82.

32. "Murder Knife Identified at Maid's Trial," *Philadelphia Inquirer*, 15 March 1945, 19.

33. "Housemaid Collapses on the Stand," *Philadelphia Inquirer*, 16 March 1945, 21; "Maid Gets Chair for Slaying," *Philadelphia Inquirier*, 18 March 1945, 18.

34. Ibid, "Murder Knife;" "Maid Doomed to Die in Chair for Knife Slaying" *Philadelphia Inquirer*, 18 March 1945, 17.

35. Ibid, *Philadelphia Inquirer.*

36. Canton, David A., "Raymond Pace Alexander, A New Negro Lawyer Fights for Civil Rights in Philadelphia," (Jackson, MS: University Press of Mississippi, 2013) 84.

37. "Maid Screams in Court as She Is Doomed to Die," *Philadelphia Inquirer*, 8 June 1945, 21.

38. Supreme Court of Pennsylvania, Commonwealth v. Sykes, 353 Pa. 392, 7 January 1946; *Baltimore Afro-American*, 19 May 1945; "Corrine Sykes Dies in Chair," *Amsterdam News*, (New York, NY) 19 October 1946, 1.

39. "Corrine Sykes Loses Pleas to Escape Chair," *Philadelphia Tribune*, 16 June 1945; Roland, Ruth, "Corrine Sykes First Black Woman Executed in Pa.," *Philadelphia Tribune*, 3 October 1978, 4.

40. "Last Plea Made to State on Maid," *Philadelphia Inquirer*, 11 October 1946, 3; "Two Empty Chairs," *Philadelphia Afro-American*, 9 October 1946, 1; "Tripping Blamed in Bride's Death," *Philadelphia Inquirer*, 8 October 1946, 3.

41. "That's That," *Philadelphia Tribune*, 3 November 1959, 5; "Housemaid Executed for Robbery Slaying," *Pottsville Republican*, 14 October 1946, 1; "Corrine Sykes Dies in Chair," *Mt. Carmel Item*, 14 October 1946, 1.

42. "That's That;" "Housemaid Doomed to Death in Chair," *Morning Post* (Camden, NJ), 12; "Housemaid Executed for Robbery Slaying," *Pottsville Republican*, 14 October 1946, 1.

43. "Housemaid Executed," "Corrine Sykes Dies in Chair," *Mt. Carmel Item,* 14 October 1946, 1; "Corrine Sykes Dies in Electric Chair, First Woman Executed in Fifteen Years," *Philadelphia Afro-American* (Philadelphia, PA), 19 October 1946, 1.

44. "Corrine Sykes Dies in Chair;" "Corrine Sykes Dies in Electric Chair, First Woman Executed in Fifteen Years," *Philadelphia Afro-American* (Philadelphia, PA), 19 October 1946, 1; "Corrine Sykes, 22, Ready for Execution at Rockview," *Morning Call* (Allentown, PA), 14 October 1946, 1; "House Maid Pays Supreme Penalty," *Harrisburg Telegraph* (Harrisburg, PA), 14 October 1946, 11; "Negress, 22, Dies Calmly in Chair at State Prison," *Daily Item* (Sunbury, PA), 14 October 1946, 1.

45. Commonwealth of Pennsylvania, Department of Health, Bureau of Vital Statistics, file 85113, Ancestry.com.

46. "Two Empty Chairs," *Philadelphia Afro-American,* 9 October 1946, 1.

47. "Final Rites Held for Corrine Sykes," *Baltimore Afro-American,* 26 October 1946. (The number of mourners may have been higher than the *Afro-American* reports, but in my search of 11 general circulation and African American newspapers, I was unable to find a 1946 story to verify a *Philadelphia Tribune* columnist's 1950 assertation that the funeral service drew thousands of mourners. An NPR broadcast in 1998 used the same numbers the Philadelphia columnist used in 1950.)

48. "Ghost of Corrine Sykes Walks Streets of City," *Philadelphia Tribune,* 31 January 1950.

49. "Ghost of Corrine Sykes Walks Streets of City;" Avery, Ron, *City of Brotherly Mayhem* (Philadelphia, PA), Otis Books, 1997, 79.

CHAPTER THREE

1. James O'Shea, "How Irish American Willie Sutton Became America's Most Famous Bank Robber," *Irish Central,* 24 March 2020, https://www.irishcentral.com/roots/history/willie-sutton.

2. Steve Cocheo, "The Unexpurgated Search for Willie Sutton," Banking Exchange, 2 August 2012, https://m.bankingexchange.com/sections/reporter-s-notebook/item/256-the-unexpurgated-search-for-willie-sutton.

3. "Willie Sutton: The Man Who Loved Robbing Banks," domain-b.com, https://www.domain-b.com/finance/banks/20090724_willie_sutton.html.

4. Amy Farber, "Historical Echoes: That's Where the Celebrity Advertising Was, or the Gentleman Bank Robber," 19 August 19, https://libertystreeteconomics.newyorkfed.org/2016/08/historical-echoes-thats-where-the-celebrity-advertising-was-or-the-gentleman-bank-robber.html.

5. Quentin Reynolds, *I, Willie Sutton* (New York: Farrar, Straus and Giroux, 1953), 110.

6. Peter Duffy, "Willie Sutton, Urbane Scoundrel," City Lore, *New York Times,* 17 February 2002, 3.

7. Reynolds, 28.

8. David J. Krajicek, "Bank Robber's Legacy: Willie Sutton Didn't Snitch, Kill—or Stay in Prison," *New York Daily News,* 17 July 2011.

9. Willie Sutton and Edward Linn, *Where the Money Was* (New York: Broadway Books, 1976), 376–77.

10. "History of Eastern State: Timeline," Eastern State Penitentiary, https://www
.easternstate.org/research/history-eastern-state/timeline.

11. Sutton and Linn, 246.

12. "1941 Willie Sutton Prison Escape Head and Hand," *Antiques Roadshow*, PBS,
2017, https://www.pbs.org/wgbh/roadshow/season/22/harrisburg-pa/appraisals/1941
-willie-sutton-prison-escape-head-hand--201701A45.

13. Jimmy Stamp, "The Daring Escape from the Eastern State Penitentiary," *Smithsonian*, 13 November 2013, https://www.smithsonianmag.com/arts-culture/the-daring
-escape-from-the-eastern-state-penitentiary-180947688.

14. Sutton and Linn, 243–44.

15. Ibid., 244–45.

16. Ibid., 245.

17. Stamp, "The Daring Escape."

18. Sutton and Linn, 270–71.

19. Ibid., 272–73.

20. "Five Convicts in Prison Break," *The Philadelphia Inquirer*, 11 February 1949, 2.

21. Ibid., 3.

22. Krajicek, "Bank Robber's Legacy."

23. Sutton and Linn, 321.

24. "Willie Sutton's 'Landlady' Will Remain in Cell," *New York Daily News*, 28 March
1950, 5.

25. Reynolds, 229.

26. "Willie Sutton," Famous Cases and Criminals, FBI.gov, https://www.fbi.gov/his
tory/famous-cases/willie-sutton.

27. "Public Duty," *New York Daily News*, 11 September 1998, 204; Reynolds, 241–43.

28. Reynolds, 244; Duffy, "Willie Sutton, Urbane Scoundrel."

29. Duffy, "Willie Sutton, Urbane Scoundrel."

30. Ibid.

31. Jay Maeder, "The Shocking Murder of Police Tipster Arnold Schuster," *New York
Daily News*, 14 August 2017, https://www.nydailynews.com/news/crime/shocking-mur
der-police-tipster-arnold-schuster-article-1.806885.

32. Ibid.

33. Ibid.

34. Peter Maas, *The Valachi Papers* (New York: William Morrow), 1968, reprint edition
2003, 185–86.

35. Maeder, "The Shocking Murder."

36. Meyer Berger, "Sutton, Bank Thief, Captured," *New York Times*, 19 February 1952,
1, 21.

37. Cocheo, "The Unexpurgated Search for Willie Sutton"; Reynolds, 14.

38. "A Jail Term Lifted, Sutton Cries in Joy," *New York Times*, 2 December 1969, 42.

39. Albin Krebs, "Willie Sutton Is Dead at 79," *New York Times*, 19 November 1980,
31.

40. Reynolds, 4.

41. Ibid., 19.

42. Farber, "Historical Echoes."

43. Sutton and Linn, 191.

44. Stamp, "The Daring Escape."

45. "Midnight Gun Duel," *Philadelphia Inquirer*, 6 September 1927, 1; "Hundreds of Prisoners Escape from Eastern State Penitentiary," NJ.com, https://www.nj.com/indulge/2015/04/hundreds_of_prisoners_escape_from_eastern_state_penitentiary_learn_about_them_all_at_pop-up_museum_e.html; Anne Anderson interviewed by Kathy Canavan, 20 August 2020; "Ex-Policeman Held as Pen Fugitive," *Philadelphia Inquirer*, 10 October 1934, 16; "Convict Slain in Boiler Room," *Evening News* (Harrisburg, PA), 25 April 1938.

Chapter Four

1. L. Stuart Ditzen, "Where Saints and Sinners Shared the Halls," *Philadelphia Inquirer*, 17 December 2000, 61.

2. "Arsenic Score Board," *Philadelphia Inquirer*, 20 October 1957, B26.

3. George M. Mahwhinney, "Doctor Admits Playing Part in Poison Ring," *Philadelphia Inquirer*, 5 May 1939, 1, 6; Owen McDonnell, "Bolber Tells of Starting Practice as a Witch Doctor Here," *Philadelphia Inquirer*, 5 August 1939, 4.

4. Frank H. Weir, "Witch Doctor's Confession Helped Break Arsenic Ring," *Philadelphia Inquirer*, 21 October 1957, 1, 11.

5. "Bolber Says Petrillo Lost $1,000," *Philadelphia Inquirer*, 8 August 1939, 7; "Three More Confess," *Philadelphia Inquirer*, 7 May 1939, 2.

6. Roger D. Simon, "Great Depression," Encyclopedia of Greater Philadelphia, https://philadelphiaencyclopedia.org/archive/great-depression; "Weird Rites Described by Widow," *Philadelphia Inquirer*, 23 January 1941, 1.

7. "Poison Slayers Appeal Death," *Plain Speaker* (Hazelton, PA), 20 May 1941, 22.

8. "Widow Brands Petrillo Demon," *Philadelphia Inquirer*, 30 June 1939, 19.

9. "Poison Widow Fearing Death Tells of Plots," *Philadelphia Inquirer*, 25 April 1939, 1; Simon, "Great Depression"; Robert James Young Jr., "Arsenic and No Lace: The Bizarre Tale of a Philadelphia Murder Ring," *Pennsylvania History: A Journal of Mid-Atlantic Studies* 67, no. 3 (2000): 406, www.jstor.org/stable/27774276 "Mass Murder Ringleader Dies in Chair," *Sunbury (PA) Item*, 31 March 1941, 1, 5; "Poison Slayers Appeal Death."

10. "Free or Not Free," *Philadelphia Inquirer*, 23 April 1939, 32; "The Black Widows," *New York Daily News*, 14 May 1939, 396, 194; Young, "Arsenic and No Lace," 405–406.

11. David G. Wittels, "Police Officer's Hunch Led to War on Band of Killers," *Times Tribune* (Scranton, PA), 15 May 1939, 1.

12. "Six New Poison Murder Charges Follow Inquest," *Philadelphia Inquirer*, 20 July 1939, 1.

13. "Poison Slayers Appeal Death"; Young, "Arsenic and No Lace," 397; "Potato Chip Undid Death's Evil Genius," *Philadelphia Inquirer*, 20 October 1957, B26.

14. "Potato Chip Undid Death's Evil Genius."

15. "Counterfeiters Led to Murder Ring," *Philadelphia Inquirer*, 4 May 1941, 94.

16. Young, "Arsenic and No Lace," 397.

17. Young, "Arsenic and No Lace," 397; Owen Mc Donnell, "Doomed Prisoner Tells Whole Story of Insurance Murder Conspiracies: Three More Women Accused," *Philadelphia Inquirer*, 27 April 1939, 1, 11.

18. Young, "Arsenic and No Lace," 398.

19. Ibid.

20. Ibid., 397–402.

21. Ibid., 398.

22. "How Does Arsenic Kill?" Live Science, December 2, 2010. https://www.live science.com/32880-how-does-arsenic-kill.html.

23. "Bail Denied Pair," *Philadelphia Inquirer*, 29 October 1938, 3; Young, "Arsenic and No Lace," 398.

24. "Riccardi Gambles on a Hunch and Wins," *Philadelphia Inquirer*, 20 October 1957, B26; "Mrs. Favato Faces Trial," *Philadelphia Inquirer*, 5 April 1939, 19.

25. "Riccardi Gambles on a Hunch."

26. "Eighteen Efforts to Insure Poison Victim Bared," *Philadelphia Inquirer*, 3 February 1939, 1.

27. "Riccardi Gambles on a Hunch."

28. Ibid.

29. Young, "Arsenic and No Lace," 402–404.

30. Ibid.

31. "The Black Widows."

32. "Mass Indictments in Poison Murders," *Philadelphia Inquirer*, 20 May 1939, 7.

33. "Neighbors Defend the Rose of Death," *Philadelphia Inquirer*, 29 April 1939, 2; Owen F. McDonnell, "Kiss of Death Talks," *Philadelphia Inquirer*, 19 May 1939, 1.

34. "Modernist Icon Is Highlight of School of Architecture Exhibit," *Yale Bulletin and Calendar* 33, no. 1 (August 27, 2004), http://archives.news.yale.edu/v33.n1/story8.html.

35. Stefano Luconi, "The Changing Meaning of Ethnic Identity among Italian Americans in Philadelphia during the Inter-War Years," *Pennsylvania History: A Journal of Mid-Atlantic Studies* 63, no. 4 (1996): 562, 563, www.jstor.org/stable/27773932.

36. Simon, "Great Depression"; Louis C. Jones, "The Evil Eye among European-Americans," *Western Folklore* 10, no. 1 (1951): 11–25, doi:10.2307/1496629.

37. Jones, "The Evil Eye," 18.

38. Jones, "The Evil Eye," 12–13

39. Young, "Arsenic and No Lace," 406.

40. "Poison Ring's Messenger Gets 2-to-20 Year Term," *Philadelphia Inquirer*, 13 December 1939, 29; "The Black Widows."

41. "Housewife Heads Poison Plot Jury," *Philadelphia Inquirer*, 15 March 1939, 21.

42. "Detective Attacked by Petrillo's Son," *Philadelphia Inquirer*, 16 March 1939, 4.

43. "Convict Names Two Petrillos as Murder Ring Heads," *Philadelphia Inquirer*, 18 March 1939, 1.

44. Owen F. McDonnell, Ibid, 28.

45. "Poison Death Plots Denied by Petrillo," *Philadelphia Inquirer*, 22 March 1939, 1.

46. Ibid., 16.

47. Owen F. McDonnell, "Petrillo Found Guilty; Death Penalty Urged," *Philadelphia Inquirer*, 23 March 1939, 1, 5.

48. Ibid.
49. Ibid.
50. Ibid.
51. Young, "Arsenic and No Lace," 408.
52. Howard Gillette, "City Hall (Philadelphia)," Encyclopedia of Greater Philadelphia, https://philadelphiaencyclopedia.org/archive/city-hall-philadelphia.
53. "State Will Demand Death Penalty," *Philadelphia Inquirer*, 19 April 1939, 2.
54. Ibid.
55. "Mrs. Favato Confesses," *Philadelphia Inquirer*, 23 April 1939, 5.
56. "Efforts to Insure Poisoned Boy Bared," *Philadelphia Inquirer*, 20 April 1939, 4.
57. "Woman on Trial Confesses Three Arsenic Murders," *Philadelphia Inquirer*, 22 April 1939, 1, 5; "The Black Widows."
58. "Woman on Trial Confesses Three Arsenic Murders"; "Poison Widow Fearing Death"; "Poison Ring Threatens Mrs. Favato's Son," *Philadelphia Inquirer*, 24 April 1939, 1.
59. "Dorothy Lamour Sued for Divorce," *Philadelphia Inquirer*, 22 April 1939, 3; "Princess Elizabeth," *Philadelphia Inquirer*, 22 April 1939, 3; "Al Capone Denied Release," *Philadelphia Inquirer*, 22 April 1939, 3; "LaFollette Bares Nazi Persecution," *Philadelphia Inquirer*, 22 April 1939, 3.
60. "Poison Ring Threatens Mrs. Favato's Son."
61. Ibid.
62. Young, "Arsenic and No Lace," 406; "Fifteen More Poisoners Face Arrest," *Philadelphia Inquirer*, 28 April 1939, 4.
63. "Dr. Perlman Admits Aid in Poisoning," *Philadelphia Inquirer*, 29 May 1940, 21; "Poison Ring's Messenger Gets 2-to-20 Year Term."
64. McDonnell, "Kiss of Death Talks."
65. George M. Mawhinney, "Herman Petrillo Linked to 21 Arsenic Murders," *Philadelphia Inquirer*, 30 April 1939, 1.
66. "Herman Petrillo to Die Tomorrow," *Philadelphia Inquirer*, 19 October 1941, 11.
67. Mawhinney, "Herman Petrillo Linked to 21 Arsenic Murders."
68. Mawhinney, "Doctor Admits Playing Part in Poison Ring."
69. "Murder Probe Aids Boy to Find Mother," *Star Tribune* (Minneapolis, MN), 15 May 1939, 1; "CCC Youth," *Carlsbad Current-Argus* (Carlsbad, NM), 14 May 1939, 2; "Carlsbad Camp Enrollee, Victim of Poison Ring, Finds Long-Lost Mother," *Philadelphia Inquirer*, 14 May 1939, 1.
70. "Carlsbad Camp Enrollee."
71. "Arsenic Boarder Does Own Cooking," *Philadelphia Inquirer*, 17 May 1939, 8.
72. Owen F. McDonnell, "Widow Foiled on Suicide in Arsenic Case," *Philadelphia Inquirer*, 9 May 1939, 1; Owen F. Mc Donnell, "Girl Foils Suicide in Arsenic Inquiry," *Philadelphia Inquirer*, 9 May 1939, 5; "Woman Wins Inquirer's Hero Award for First Time," *Philadelphia Inquirer*, 5 June 1939, 13.
73. "Widow Brands Petrillo Demon."
74. "Poison Ring's Eerie Drama Is Unfolded," *Philadelphia Inquirer*, 27 April 1939, 1.
75. "Creditors Demand Payments," *Philadelphia Inquirer*, 11 June 1939, 57.
76. "Courtroom Theft Solved," *Philadelphia Inquirer*, 9 June 1939, 21.

77. "Petrillo Attacked by Arsenic Orphan," *Philadelphia Inquirer*, 12 September 1939, 6.

78. "Bolber Linked Paul Petrillo to Three Poison Murders," *Philadelphia Inquirer*, 23 September 1939, 15.

79. "Three Judges Hear Petrillo Plea," *Philadelphia Inquirer*, 1 November 1939, 1.

80. "Two Offered Jobs as Executioners," *Reading (PA) Times*, 15 May 1939, 1; "Slayer Now Pastor Freed from Parole" *Daily Independent Journal* (San Rafael, CA), 30 March 1957, 3; "The Rev. John Cacopardo," *Philadelphia Inquirer*, 31 October 1961, 6.

81. Frank O'Gara, "Paul Petrillo Executed for Poison Deaths," *Philadelphia Inquirer*, 31 March 1941, 1, 3.

82. "Ebbets Field Hosts Football History," Pro Football Hall of Fame, https://www. profootballhof.com/football-history/the-1930s-and-the-first-televised-game.

83. "Widow Put on Trial in Poison Ring," *Philadelphia Inquirer*, 24 October 1939, 19; "Women on Jury Refused," *Mercury* (Pottstown, PA), 24 October 1939, 2.

84. "Mrs. Alfonsi in Poison Trial Today," *Philadelphia Inquirer*, 23 October 1939, 13; "Free Widow in Mass Murders," *Plain Speaker* (Hazelton, PA), 28 October 1939, 1; "Poison Jury Deliberates on Fate of Mrs. Alfonsi," *Philadelphia Inquirer*, 28 October 1939, 17.

85. "Poison Jury Deliberates on Fate of Mrs. Alfonsi."

86. "One Woman Died in Chair," *Philadelphia Inquirer*, 26 October 1940, 4.

87. "Widow Is Free in Murder Plot," *Lancaster (PA) New Era*, 28 October 1939, 1.

88. "Mrs. Alfonsi Freed," *Courier Post* (Camden, NJ), 4 November 1939, 3.

89. "Stella Alfonsi Is Freed," *Harrisburg (PA) Telegraph*, 4 November 1939, 3.

90. "Mrs. Alfonsi Freed," *Philadelphia Inquirer*, 4 November 1939, 8.

91. "Jurors Acquit Mrs. Carina in Arsenic Case," *Philadelphia Inquirer*, 3 December 1939, 1; "Acquitted of Charges of Poisoning Husband," *Morning Call* (Allentown, PA), 3 December 1939, 1.

92. "Mrs. Carina Faces Second Trial," *Philadelphia Inquirer*, 4 December 1939, 1.

93. "Life Term in Drowning Ralph Caruso," *Public Opinion* (Chambersburg, PA), 2 November 1939, 10; "Man Carried Egg in Armpit Nine Days," *Bristol (PA) Courier*, 8 November 1939, 1.

94. "Arsenic Widow Feared Victim of Same Poison," *Philadelphia Inquirer*, 31 July 1939, 1; "Women Admit Murder Guilt," *Philadelphia Inquirer*, 9 December 1939, 21.

95. L. Stuart Ditzen, "Where Saints and Sinners Shared the Halls," *Philadelphia Inquirer*, 17 December 2000, 61.

96. "Dies in Electric Chair for Part in Insurance Deaths," *Intelligencer Journal* (Lancaster, PA), 31 March 1941, 1, 9.

97. Frank O'Gara, "Paul Petrillo Executed for Poison Deaths," *Philadelphia Inquirer*, 31 March 1941, 1, 3.

98. "Herman Petrillo Dies in Chair, Pleading for Mercy," *Gettysburg (PA) Times*, 20 October 1941, 4.

99. "Herman Petrillo Dies in Chair"; "Slayer Meets Doom Claiming Innocence," *Republican and Herald* (Pottsville, PA), 20 October 1941, 4.

100. "Petrillo Pays Death Penalty," *Mt. Carmel (PA) Item*, 20 October 1941, 9.

101. "Petrillo Pays Death Penalty"; "Herman Petrillo Dies in Chair"; "Slayer Meets Doom Claiming Innocence"; "Herman Petrillo Dies in Electric Chair for Arsenic Ring Murder," *Philadelphia Inquirer*, 20 October 1941, 2; "Pardon Board Denies Pleas," *Shamokin (PA) News-Dispatch*, 17 October 1941, 3.

102. "Pardon Board Denies Pleas"; "Murder Ring Head Pays for Crimes," *Evening Times* (Sayre, PA), 20 October 1941, 3.

103. "Insurance Fight Left by Petrillo's Death," *Courier Post* (Camden, NJ), 3 December 1941, 19.

104. Pennsylvania (state) death certificates, 1906–1967, certificate number range 061201–63900, Pennsylvania Historical and Museum Commission, Harrisburg, PA; "The Industrial Home for Women at Muncy, Pennsylvania," *Another Century* blog, https://anothercenturyblog.wordpress.com/2018/01/23/the-industrial-home-for-wom en-at-muncy-pennsylvania.

105. Pennsylvania (state) death certificates, 1906–1967, certificate number range 013801–016500, Pennsylvania Historical and Museum Commission, Harrisburg, PA; "Bolber, Arsenic Ring Witch Doctor, Dies," *Philadelphia Inquirer*, 16 February 1954; Frank H. Weir, "Witch Doctor's Confession Helped Break Arsenic Ring," *Philadelphia Inquirer*, 21 October 1957, 1, 11.

106. "Mother of 5 Sentenced in Arsenic Ring," *Philadelphia Inquirer*, 11 December 1945, 21.

107. J. Jerry Cacopardo and Don Weldon, *Show Me a Miracle: The True Story of a Man Who Went from Prison to Pulpit* (New York: E. P. Dutton, 1961).

108. "Samuel Riccardi, 80, Homicide Detective," *Philadelphia Inquirer*, 7 July 1973, 26; "Shakeup Affects Four Inspectors," *Philadelphia Inquirer* 20 September 1952, 26.

109. "Willie Jones, Martyr," *Daily Item* (Sunbury, PA), 25 November 1941, 4; "Clemency Denied Two Slayers," *Mount Carmel (PA) Item*, 22 November 1941, 2; "Pardon Board Denies Pleas."

110. "Pardon Board Denies Pleas."

111. "Two Slayers Die," *Shamokin (PA) News-Dispatch*, 24 November 1941, 1.

112. Romaine "Raymond" Mandiuk death certificate, Find a Grave, https://www.finda grave.com/memorial/152656932#view-photo=128806127.

113. "Lt. Thomas G. McDaniel, Criminal Investigations Commander, State Police at Reading," *Reading (PA) Eagle*, 23 December 2009, http://www2.readingeagle.com/arti- cle.aspx?id=179579.

114. "The Amazing Story of the Arsenic Ring," *Philadelphia Inquirer*, 20 October 1957, 50.

CHAPTER FIVE

1. Peter Levins, "Justice and the Rise and Decline of Philadelphia's Most Feared Mob," *New York Daily News*, 16 July 1939, 134.

2. Jeff Laughead, "Main Line History: Mobsters on the Main Line," *Main Line Times* (Exton, PA), 10 September 2009.

3. John Wallace, *The Boardwalk Empire A-Z* (online: John Blake, 2012).

4. Levins, "Justice and the Rise and Decline."

5. Ibid.

6. Ibid.

7. Ibid.

8. "Lanzetti Never Kidded Self," *Morning Post* (Camden, NJ), 1 January 1937, 2.

9. "Gangland Rule by Lanzetti Clan Ends in Death of Its Head Man," *Philadelphia Inquirer*, 2 July 1939, 6; "Catholic Information," *Spokesman-Review* (Spokane, WA), 5 October 1947, 8.

10. Gordon Mackay, "Is Zat So," *Courier Post* (Camden, NJ), 2 January 1937, 2.

11. "Unity of Lanzettis Shattered Only by Their Foes' Bullets," *Philadelphia Inquirer*, 2 July 1939, 1, 2.

12. Levins, "Justice and the Rise and Decline."

13. "Twenty-Two Arrests, Four Convictions for Willie," *Philadelphia Inquirer*, 2 July 1939, 1, 2.

14. "Freedom Is Won by Lucian Lanzetti on Vagrant Charge," *Philadelphia Inquirer*, 5 August 1933, 5.

15. "Lanzetti Never Kidded Self."

16. "Gangsters Kill Three Men in Last Five Days," *Philadelphia Inquirer*, 23 August 1925, 1, 4.

17. 1910 United States Federal Census, Philadelphia, PA, Ward 3, Roll T624_1387, Page 35A, Enumeration District 004, FHL microfilm 1375400, Ancestry.com.

18. "Unity of Lanzettis Shattered."

19. Mark H. Haller, "Philadelphia Bootlegging and the Report of the Special August Grand Jury," *Pennsylvania Magazine of History and Biography* 137, no. 4 (October 2013), 219; "Potable Power: Delaware Valley Bootlegging During Prohibition," Temple University Library Digital Exhibits, http://gamma.library.temple.edu/exhibits/exhibits/show/potable-power--delaware-valley.

20. Russell F. Weigley, ed., *Philadelphia: A 300-Year History* (New York: W. W. Norton, 1982), 578, 639; Annie Anderson, "Prohibition," Encyclopedia of Greater Philadelphia, https://philadelphiaencyclopedia.org/archive/prohibition.

21. "Gang War Victim Keeps Lips Sealed," *Philadelphia Inquirer*, 28 November 1925, 6.

22. "Gangsters Kill Three Men in Last Five Days."

23. "Lanzetti, Two Pals Get 5-Year-Terms," *Philadelphia Inquirer*, 24 September 1936, 15.

24. "Long Vigil Traps Man," *Philadelphia Inquirer*, 7 April 1927, 1.

25. "Lanzetti Boys Crash Camden Numbers Game," *Morning Post* (Camden, NJ), 25 June 1932, 1.

26. "Lanzetti, Two Pals Get 5-Year-Terms."

27. "500,000 to Cheer Mummers' Revels on Broad Street Today," *Philadelphia Inquirer*, 1 January 1937, 1.

28. George M. Mawhinney, "Pius Lanzetti Shot to Death by Gang Foes," *Philadelphia Inquirer*, 1 January 1937, 1.

29. "Pius Lanzetti Shot Dead by Gang Gunner," *Morning Post* (Camden, NJ), 1 January 1937, 1.

30. "Police Say One Victim Numbers Game King-Pin," *Wilkes-Barre (PA) Record*, 1 January 1937, 15.

31. Mawhinney, "Pius Lanzetti Shot to Death."

32. "Hunt Newark Killers in Lanzetti Murder," *Philadelphia Inquirer*, 3 January 1937, 26.

33. "Lanzetti Plagued Police for 15 Years Before Gang Death," *Morning Post* (Camden, NJ), 1 January 1937, 2.

34. "200 Guard Lanzetti While 15 Kin Mourn," *Philadelphia Inquirer*, 4 January 1937, 3.

35. Ibid.

36. "Numbers Racket Led to Lanzetti Slaying," *Philadelphia Inquirer*, 4 January 1937, 3.

37. "Numbers Racket Led to Lanzetti Slaying"; Levins, "Justice and the Rise and Decline."

38. "Lanzetti Slaying Laid to Numbers," *Philadelphia Inquirer*, 4 July 1939, 1.

39. Ibid.

40. "Lanzetti Slaying Laid to Numbers"; George M. Mawhinney, "Willie Lanzetti Is Slain," *Philadelphia Inquirer*, 2 July 1939, 1, 2.

41. George M. Mawhinney, "Murdered Willie Lanzetti's Body Found," *Philadelphia Inquirer*, 2 July 1939, 2.

42. Ibid.

43. "Unity of Lanzettis Shattered."

44. "$30 Saves Lanzetti from a Pauper Grave," *Philadelphia Inquirer*, 5 July 1939, 6.

45. Ibid.

46. Ibid.

47. "Slain Phila. Racketeer Has Modest Funeral," *Journal Every Evening* (Wilmington, DE), 6 July 1939, 16.

48. "Three Philadelphia Slayings Laid to Hirelings," *Courier Post* (Camden, NJ), 5 April 1940, 4.

49. National Archives and Records Administration, Electronic Army Serial Number Merged File, 1938–1946: ARC 1263923. World War II Army Enlistment Records; Records of the National Archives and Records Administration, Record Group 64, Ancestry.com.

50. Dearborn Michigan City Directory, US City Directories, 1822–1995 database, Ancestry.com.

CHAPTER SIX

1. "Al Capone's Cell," Eastern State Penitentiary, https://www.easternstate.org/explore/exhibits/al-capones-cell).

2. "Chicago's Own Scarface Held," *Philadelphia Inquirer*, 17 May 1929, 1; "Al Capone Chronology," *Tribune* (Coshocton, OH), 17 May 1929, 1; "Capone Starts Fight to Regain Lost Freedom," *Chicago Tribune*, 19 May 1929, 2.

3. "Armed Guards Escort Capone to Holmesburg," *Philadelphia Inquirer*, 19 March 1930, 8.

4. Ibid.

5. Ibid.

6. "Scarface Al Gets One Year," *Province* (Vancouver, British Columbia, Canada), 17 May 1929, 1.

7. "Armed Guards Escort Capone to Holmesburg."

8. Fred D. Pasley, *Al Capone: Biography of a Self Made Man* (Garden City, NY: Star Books, 1930), part 7; "Scarface Al Capone Tells His Own Story," *Philadelphia Inquirer*, 18 May 1929, 8.

9. "Scarface Al Capone Tells His Own Story."

10. Pasley, *Al Capone*, part 7.

11. "Capone in Jail Garb," *New York Times*, 19 May 1929, 24; "Al Capone Gets One Year in Jail," *Morning News* (Wilmington, DE), 18 May 1929, 1.

12. Pasley, *Al Capone*, part 7.

13. "Sentencing of Al Capone Gives Gangland Laugh," *Shamokin (PA) News-Dispatch*, 18 May 1929, 1.

14. Pasley, *Al Capone*, 336.

15. Lily Rothman, "Read Al Capone's Obituary from 1947," *Time*, January 25, 2017, https://time.com/4639795/al-capone-obituary.

16. Daniel Okrent, *Last Call: The Rise and Fall of Prohibition* (New York: Scribner 2010), 321.

17. "Jail Sentence for Capone So Well Oiled," *Brooklyn (NY) Daily Eagle*, 26 May 1929, 85.

18. "Capone Starts Fight"; "Capone Sealed in Prison Gloom," *Chicago Tribune*, 20 May 1929, 5.

19. "Capone in Jail Garb Loses Good Cheer," *New York Times*, 19 May 1929, 24; "Armed Guards Escort Capone," *Philadelphia Inquirer*, 18 May 1929, 1, 8.

20. "Capone in Jail Garb."

21. Ibid.

22. "Capone in Jail Garb"; "Capone Hires Only Gentlemen," *New York Times*, 10 July 1929, 14.

23. Pasley, *Al Capone*, 230.

24. "Armed Guards Escort Capone," *Philadelphia Inquirer*, 19 May 1929, 8.

25. "Scarface Gloomy Amid Jail Routine," *Philadelphia Inquirer*, 21 May 1929, 3.

26. Ibid.

27. "Menace Magistrate Who Jailed Capone," *New York Times*, 22 May 1929.

28. Wall text, brochure, and tour, Eastern State Penitentiary, Philadelphia, PA, 11 September 2020.

29. Ibid.

30. Deirdre Bair, *Al Capone: His Life, Legacy and Legend* (New York: Nan Talese, 2016).

31. Laurence Bergreen, *Capone: The Man and the Era* (New York: Simon & Schuster, 1994), 340.

32. "Very Comfortable, Says Capone, in Luxurious Cell at Eastern 'Pen,'" *Public Ledger* (Philadelphia, PA), 20 August 1929.

33. Eastern State Penitentiary Historic Structures Report, City of Philadelphia, PA, 1994, Vol. 1, 182.

34. Bergreen, 340.

35. "Capone's Stars Beat Lockports," *Brooklyn (NY) Citizen*, 6 June 1918, 5.

36. "Capone Likes Pen," *Philadelphia Inquirer*, 10 August 1929, 22.

37. Bergreen, 353.

38. "Sister of Capone, His Chief Defender, Eagerly Awaits Him," *Chicago Tribune*, 17 March 1930, 6.

39. "A Line O' Type or Two," *Chicago Tribune*, 18 March 1930, 14.

40. Bill Morrison, "On March 17, 1930, Crowd Assembled Outside Eastern State," Vimeo, https://vimeo.com/38540558; "Al Capone Freed at Graterford in Surprise Move," *Philadelphia Inquirer*, 18 March 1930, 17.

41. Ibid.

42. "Mystery Locks Departure of Al Capone," *Republican and Herald* (Pottsville, PA), 18 March 1930, 8; Robert P. Loughran, "Capone Under Cover," *Pittsburgh Press*, 18 March 1930, 2.

43. Bergreen, 354; "Al Capone Freed at Graterford."

44. "Al Capone Freed at Graterford."

45. "Assails Capone Favor," *Philadelphia Inquirer*, 23 Mar 1930, 12.

46. "Capone Speeds for Chicago," *Chicago Tribune*, 18 March 1930, 1.

47. "Sister of Capone, His Chief Defender."

48. Loughran, "Capone Under Cover."

49. "Capone Freed Secretly," *Morning Post* (Camden, NJ), 18 March 1930, 1; "Capone Reaches Chicago," *Philadelphia Inquirer*, 19 March 1930, 4.

50. "Capone Reaches Chicago by Air," *Philadelphia Inquirer*, 19 March 1930, 1, 4.

51. "Black Hills Offer Haven to Al Capone," *Post-Crescent* (Appleton, WI), 28 March 1930, 1; "Capone Gets 50 Votes," *Philadelphia Inquirer*, 3 April 1930, 3.

52. Bergreen, 319.

53. "Capone's Story: By Himself," *Chicago Tribune*, 18 September 1930, 1.

54. "Gangster King's Career Told as Al Capone Dies," *Reno (NV) Gazette-Journal*, 27 January 1947, 8; "Capone Dies Broke Said," *Indiana (PA) Gazette*, 27 January 1947, 1.

55. "It's Francis . . . Not Capone," *Miami Herald*, 10 May 1966, 56.

56. Tom Nicholas and David Chen, "Al Capone," Harvard Business School Case 809-144, April 2009, https://www.hbs.edu/faculty/Pages/item.aspx?num=37240.

57. Nicole Frankhouser, director of Marketing and Communications, Eastern State Penitentiary Historic Site, September 21, 2020.

58. Jake Rossen, "Oral History: When Geraldo Rivera Opened Al Capone's Vault," *Mental Floss*, 21 April 2016, https://www.mentalfloss.com/article/78842/oral-history-30-years-ago-geraldo-rivera-opened-al-capones-vault.

59. Rosemary Rossi, "Seventeen Actors Who've Played Al Capone: From Tom Hardy to Robert De Niro," The Wrap, 11 May 2020, https://www.thewrap.com/actors-played-al-capone-tom-hardy-to-robert-de-niro-photos.

Chapter Seven

1. "Policeman's Widow Faces Bank Bandit," *Philadelphia Inquirer*, 13 May 1926, 8.

2. Ibid.

3. Ibid.

4. "News of the World," *Philadelphia Inquirer*, 6 May 1926, 19; Frank H. Weir, "One More Routine Day," *Philadelphia Inquirer*, 27 October 1959, 42.

5. Weir, "One More Routine Day"; "Policeman's Widow Faces Bank Bandit," 8.

6. Weir, "One More Routine Day."

7. "Four Taken Fleeing with $80,000; Bluecoat Killed," *Philadelphia Inquirer*, 6 May 1926, 6; "Four Bandits Indicted in Olney Holdup," *Philadelphia Inquirer*, 6 May 1926, 1.

8. "Four Taken Fleeing with $80,000."

9. "Four Bandits Indicted in Olney Holdup."

10. "Four Taken Fleeing with $80,000."

11. "Jury Convicts Bandit to Chair," *Philadelphia Inquirer*, 14 May 1926, 8.

12. "Policeman's Widow Faces Bank Bandit."

13. Frank H. Weir, "He Sees His Duty," *Philadelphia Inquirer*, 27 October 1959, 42; "Four Taken Fleeing with $80,000."

14. Weir, "He Sees His Duty."

15. "Jury Convicts Bandit to Chair."

16. Weir, "He Sees His Duty."

17. Ron Avery, *City of Brotherly Mayhem* (Philadelphia: Otis Books), 1997, 59.

18. "Four Taken Fleeing with $80,000"; Weir, "He Sees His Duty."

19. Weir, "He Sees His Duty."

20. "Slain Policeman Given Last Rites," *Philadelphia Inquirer*, 9 May 1926, 5.

21. "Four Taken Fleeing With $80,000."

22. "Four Bandits Indicted in Olney Holdup."

23. "Four Olney Bandits Pace Tiny Cells," *Philadelphia Inquirer*, 7 March 1927, 5.

24. Avery, 60.

25. "Fifth Olney Bandit," *Philadelphia Inquirer*, 7 March 1927, 5.

26. "Four Olney Bandits Pace Tiny Cells"; "Olney Bandits Die in Death Chair," *Philadelphia Inquirer*, 8 March 1927, 1, 5.

27. "Four Olney Bandits Pace Tiny Cells."

28. "Bandits Keeping Up Nerve," *Philadelphia Inquirer*, 5 March 1927, 11.

29. "Four Olney Bandits Pace Tiny Cells."

30. Ibid., 1.

31. Ibid., 1, 5.

32. "Four Olney Bandits Pace Tiny Cells"; "Olney Bandits Die in Death Chair."

33. Avery, 62.

34. "Olney Bandits Die in Death Chair."

35. "Four Olney Bandits Pace Tiny Cells."

36. Ibid.

37. "Olney Bandits Die in Death Chair."

38. Ibid.

39. Ibid.

40. Ibid.

41. Ibid.

42. Ibid.

43. "Olney Bandits Awaiting Doom," *Philadelphia Inquirer*, 6 March 1927, 21.

44. Arthur H. Lewis, *The Worlds of Chippy Patterson* (New York: Harcourt, Brace, 1960), 294.

45. "Olney Bandits Die in Death Chair."

46. "Crowds See Funerals of Two," *Philadelphia Inquirer*, 11 March 1927, 7.

47. "Bandits Dynamite Armored Pay Car," *New York Times*, 12 March 1927, 1.

CHAPTER EIGHT

1. Fred D. Baldwin, "Smedley D. Butler and Prohibition Enforcement in Philadelphia, 1924–1925," *Pennsylvania Magazine of History and Biography* 84, no. 3 (1960): 352–68, www.jstor.org/stable/20089312.

2. "Mr. Paul Crompton," The Lusitania Resource, https://www.rmslusitania.info/peo ple/saloon/paul-crompton.

3. Jacob Downs, "World War I," Encyclopedia of Greater Philadelphia, https://phila delphiaencyclopedia.org/archive/world-war-i.

4. Dan Barry and Caitlin Dickerson, "The Killer Flu of 1918: A Philadelphia Story," *New York Times*, April 10, 2020, https://www.nytimes.com/2020/04/04/us/coronavi rus-spanish-flu-philadelphia-pennsylvania.html; Kenneth C. Davis, "Philadelphia Threw a WWI Parade That Gave Thousands of Onlookers the Flu," *Smithsonian*, 21 September 2018, https://www.smithsonianmag.com/history/philadelphia-threw-wwi -parade-gave-thousands-onlookers-flu-180970372; Thomas Wirth, "Influenza ('Spanish Flu' Pandemic, 1918–19)," Encyclopedia of Greater Philadelphia, https://philadelphia encyclopedia.org/archive/influenza-spanish-flu-pandemic-1918-19.

5. Margaret Newman, *Philadelphia at the Beginning of the Twentieth Century: Incorpo-rating the Automobile into an Urban House Type* (unpublished master's thesis, University of Pennsylvania, 1999), 15–28.

6. Edgar Williams, "Family's Story Is a Twisted Tale," *Orlando Sentinel*, 12 May 1988, https://www.orlandosentinel.com/news/os-xpm-1988-05-12-0040080229-story.html.

7. *Billy Sunday*, Smithsonian National Portrait Gallery, https://npg.si.edu/object/npg_ NPG.74.69 ; "Famous 'Booze' Sermon," Billy Sunday Online, https://www.billysunday. org/sermons/booze3.html (accessed 21 August 2020).

8. "1921–Philadelphia's 'Dance Cop,'" *The Philadelphia Dance History Journal*, 22 Janu-ary 2012, https://philadancehistoryjournal.wordpress.com/tag/1920s.

9. "Harry Blitman," Philadelphia Jewish Sports Hall of Fame, http://phillyjew ishsports.org/2014/08/harry-blitman; Anne Margaret Anderson and John J. Binder, *Philadelphia Organized Crime in the 1920s and 1930s* (Charleston, SC: Arcadia, 2014), 33.

10. "Dempsey Claims Fight Was Fixed," *Intelligencer Journal* (Lancaster, PA), 19 Sep-tember 1927, 10.

11. "Boo Boo's Rod," *New Yorker*, 30 September 1935..

12. "Max (Boo Boo) Hoff Dies Broke at 48," *New York Times*, 28 April 1941, 17, http://timesmachine.nytimes.com/timesmachine/1941/04/28/85485318.html.

13. "Boo Boo Hoff, Ex-King of the Rackets, Dies," *Philadelphia Inquirer*, 28 April 1941, 3.

14. "Max Hoff Did Boy Favor," *Nashville Banner*, 28 July 1924, 10.

15. "Dempsey Claims Fight Was Fixed;" Harry Blitman.

16. Perry Desmond, "Remembering Max 'Boo Boo' Hoff," DVRBS.com, http://www. dvrbs.com/history-local/InterestingPeople-MaxBooBooHoff.htm.

17. Annie Anderson, "Bootlegging," Encyclopedia of Greater Philadelphia, https:// philadelphiaencyclopedia.org/archive/bootlegging; Mark H. Haller, "Philadelphia Bootlegging and the Report of the Special August Grand Jury," *Pennsylvania Magazine of History and Biography* 137, no. 4 (October 2013), 228.

18. Perry Desmond, letter from Michael Adams, 21 March 2005.

19. Perry Desmond letter; Desmond, "Remembering Max 'Boo Boo' Hoff.

20. Okrent, Daniel, "Last Call: The Rise and Fall of Prohibition" (New York: Scribner) 2010, 202, 322.

21. "Boo Boo Hoff Silent After Surrender in Shooting of Bondsman," *Philadelphia Inquirer,* 27 March 1940, 8.

22. Interview with John B. Summers, February 15, 1984, Louie B. Nunn Center for Oral History, University of Kentucky Libraries, Charles Hardy, Interviewer—2014OH184 GN 036.

23. "Boo Boo Hoff, Ex-King of the Rackets, Dies," *Philadelphia Inquirer*, 28 April 1941, 3; Daniel Okrent, *Last Call, The Rise and Fall of Prohibition* (New York: Scribner) 2010, 203.

24. Daniel Okrent, 203.

25. "Boo Boo Hoff, Ex-King of the Rackets, Dies," *Philadelphia Inquirer,* 28 April 1941, 3.

26. "Prominent Quaker City Fans to See Fight," *Philadelphia Inquirer,* 7 September 1924, 23.

27. "W. Freeland Kendrick, Former Mayor Dies," *Philadelphia Inquirer,* 21 March 1953, 1, 16.

28. Baldwin, Fred D. "Smedley D. Butler and Prohibition Enforcement in Philadelphia, 1924–1925." *The Pennsylvania Magazine of History and Biography* 84, no. 3 (1960): 352–68, www.jstor.org/stable/20089312.

29. Anne Anderson and John J. Binder, *Philadelphia Organized Crime in the 1920s and 1930s* (Charleston, SC), Arcadia, 2014, 9–28.

30. Ibid, 22.

31. Ibid, 11.

32. Okrent, 203.

33. "Butler Plans War on Hotel Parties," *Philadelphia Inquirer*, 5 December 1925, 3.

34. Ibid, Okrent, 203; Anne Anderson, 9–28.

35. "Butler Quits Job, But Goes Out Fighting," *Fort Worth Record-Telegram,* 24 December 1925, 1.

36. Ibid, "Butler Quits;" "Philadelphia Mayor Issues Statement," *The Daily Notes* (Canonsburg, PA), 24 September 1924, 1.

37. Fred Baldwin, "Smedley D. Butler and Prohibition Enforcement in Philadelphia 1924–1928, *Pennsylvania Magazine of History and Biography,* 84, no. 3, July 1960, 352–368.

38. Ibid, Baldwin, Fred D. "Smedley D. Butler and Prohibition Enforcement in Philadelphia, 1924-1925."

39. Interview with John B. Summers; "Some Born Lucky," *Boston Globe*, 24 September 1926, 27.

40. "Thongs Gay, Move Calmly, Despite Rain," *Philadelphia Inquirer*, 24 September 1926, 1; "Some Born Lucky, *Boston Globe*, 24 September 1926, 27.

41. "Dempsey Claims Fight Was Fixed," *Intelligencer Journal* (Lancaster, PA), 19 September 1927, 10.

42. "Max (Boo Boo) Hoff Dies Broke at 48."

43. "Letters," *New Yorker* 6, no. 50, 10 December 1973, 6.

44. "The Murder of Hugh McLoon and the 1928 Special August Grand Jury," Temple University Libraries, http://gamma.library.temple.edu/exhibits/exhibits/show/potable -power—delaware-valley/mcloon; Annie Anderson, "Prohibition," *Encyclopedia of Greater Philadelphia*, https://philadelphiaencyclopedia.org/archive/prohibition.

45. Ibid.

46. Ibid.

47. "Elliott Accepted Gift from Hoff," *Evening Sun* (Baltimore, MD), 15 September 1928, 1.

48. Amy Cohen, "Bootleggers and Back Alley Bars: Philadelphia During Prohibition a City 'Soaked in Alcohol,'" Hidden City, 4 September 2019, https://hiddencityphila .org/2019/09/bootleggers-back-alley-bars-philadelphia-during-prohibition-a-city -soaked-in-alcohol.

49. "Sailor Fredman Wanted by Police," *Daily Journal*, Vineland, NJ, 1.

50. "Max Hoff's Wife Dies of Worry over Inquiry," *Courier Post* (Camden, NJ), 21 January 1929, 2.

51. "Los Angeles Abandons Quest for Lost Fliers," *Philadelphia Inquirer*, 29 March 1929, 1; "Wind Wrecks Blimp," *Philadelphia Inquirer*, 29 March 1929, 1.

52. Anderson and Binder, 28.

53. Robert Michael, *A Concise History of Antisemitism* (Lanham, MD: Rowman & Littlefield, 2005), 138.

54. "Boo Boo Hoff, Broke, Called Philanthropist," *New York Daily News*, 2 November 1928, 40.

55. "Boo Boo Hoff, Prohibition Millionaire, Dies Broke," *New York Daily News*, 28 April 1941, 312.

56. "Max (Boo Boo) Hoff Left Estate of $500," *Philadelphia Inquirer*, 3 July 1941, 9.

57. "Boo Boo Hoff, Prohibition Millionaire, Dies Broke."

CHAPTER NINE

1. Frank P. Geyer, *The Holmes-Pitezel Case: A History of the Greatest Crime of the Century and of the Search for the Missing Pitezel Children* (Philadelphia: Publishers Union, 1896), 319.

2. "Holmes Found Guilty," *Times* (Philadelphia, PA), 4 November 1895, 2.

3. Geyer, 13–16.

4. Ibid., 13.

5. Ibid., 16.

6. Ibid., 16, 313.

7. Ibid., 22–27.

8. Ibid., 134.

9. Ibid., 44, 51.

10. Ibid., 353–60.

11. Ibid., 130.

12. Ibid., 134.

13. Erik Larson, *The Devil in the White City* (New York: Vintage Books, 2004), 352.

14. Geyer, 229–231.

15. Ibid., 230–33.

16. Ibid., 234.

17. Ibid., 245–46.

18. Ibid., 256–91.

19. Ibid., 296–97.

20. Jennifer Rogers, "Then and Now: 11th and East Passyunk Avenue," *Hidden City*, July 12, 2015, https://hiddencityphila.org/2015/07/then-and-now-11th-passyunk-avenue.

21. "Holmes Found Guilty," *Times* (Philadelphia, PA), 4 November 1895, 2.

22. "Fiend Hangs," *Fort Wayne (IN) News*, 7 May 1896, 1; "Holmes Cool to the End," *New York Times*, 8 May 1896, 1; Geyer, 53.

23. Geyer, 148, 320, 330.

24. "Holmes Cool to the End"; Geyer, 325–28.

25. Geyer, 337.

26. Ibid., 338.

27. Ibid., 338–40.

28. Ibid., 341.

29. Ibid., 341.

30. Ibid., 342.

31. Ibid., 327.

32. "Holmes Found Guilty," *Fall River (MA) Daily News*, 4 November 1895, 2; "Holmes Found Guilty," North Adams (MA) Transcript, 4 November 1895, 4.

33. Larson, 351.

34. "Holmes' Doom Fixed," *Philadelphia Inquirer*, 5 March 1896, 1.

35. "Holmes Cool to the End."

36. "Holmes Pays Penalty," *St. Albans (VT) Daily Messenger*, 7 May 1896, 1; "A Letter from His Child," *Philadelphia Inquirer*, 7 May 1896, 1.

37. "In the Shadow of Death," *Philadelphia Inquirer*, 6 May 1896, 3.

38. "Holmes' Last Hope Is Gone," *Times* (Philadelphia, PA), 30 April 1896, 10.

39. Geyer, 7.

40. Larson, 386.

41. "Our Story," The Wistar Institute, https://wistar.org/about-wistar/our-story.

42. "Holmes Weeps and Is Afraid," *Times* (Philadelphia, PA), 7 May 1896, 1.

43. "Hanging of Holmes," *Evening Star* (Washington, DC), 7 May 1896, 1.

44. "Holmes Weeps and Is Afraid."

45. "As Holmes Chose to Die," *Times* (Philadelphia, PA), 8 May 1896, 4.

46. Ibid.
47. "Holmes Cool to the End."
48. "As Holmes Chose to Die."
49. "Hanging of Holmes."
50. "Holmes Cool to the End."
51. "A Human Fiend Hanged," *Miners' Daily Journal* (Pottsville, PA), 8 May 1896, 1; "As Holmes Chose to Die."
52. "As Holmes Chose to Die."
53. Ibid.
54. "Holmes Cool to the End."
55. "Crowds Watched the Prison," *Times* (Philadelphia, PA), 8 May 1896, 4.
56. "As Holmes Chose to Die."
57. Ibid.
58. "Hanging of Holmes"; "Holmes Cool to the End."
59. "As Holmes Chose to Die."
60. "Holmes Cool to the End."
61. "As Holmes Chose to Die."
62. Ibid.
63. Ibid.
64. Ibid.
65. Ibid.
66. Ibid.
67. Ibid.
68. Ibid.
69. Ibid.
70. "Crowds Watched the Prison."
71. "Hanging of Holmes;" "Unique Method of Internment Devised by the Murderer to Protect His Body from Ghouls," *Times* (Philadelphia, PA), 8 May 1896.
72. "Unique Method of Internment Devised."
73. "Holmes Body Buried," *Evening Messenger* (Marshall, TX), 9 May 1896, 1; Larson, 386.
74. "Unique Method of Internment Devised."
75. Ibid.
76. Ibid.
77. Larson, 35.
78. Unique Method of Internment Devised."
79. Bob McGovern, "The Measure of a Killer: When DNA Can't Provide a Positive ID," *Philly Voice*, 20 December 2017, https://www.phillyvoice.com/the-measure-of-a-killer-when-dna-cant-provide-a-positive-id.

CHAPTER TEN

1. Paula S. Fass, "Abduction Stories That Changed Our Lives," Chapter 3, in *American Behavioral History, An Introduction*, ed., Peter M. Stearns (New York: NYU Press, 2005).
2. Steven Suskin, *Broadway Yearbook 2000-2001: A Relevant and Irreverent Record* (New York: Oxford University Press, 2002), 24–25.

3. "Bring Back Our Darling," Keffer Collection of Sheet Music 1790–1895, Library of Congress, https://www.loc.gov/resource/sm1874.12564.0?st=gallery.

4. Peter N. Steams, ed., *American Behavioral History: An Introduction* (New York: NYU Press, 2005), 44.

5. Ross, 27.

6. Ross, 31–33.

7. "Kidnapping: Heartless Abduction of a Child—A Ransom of $20,000 Asked," *Philadelphia Inquirer*, 14 July 1874, 3; Christian K. Ross, *The Father's Story*, 33.

8. Christian K. Ross, *The Father's Story of Charley Ross, the Kidnapped Child* (Philadelphia: JE Potter, 1876), 28, Germantown Historical Society, Philadelphia, PA, and Hathi Trust Digital Library, https://catalog.hathitrust.org/Record/006514213.

9. Christian K. Ross, *The Father's Story*, 26.

10. Ross, 48.

11. "Our Zoo," "Haverford College," and "The New Public Buildings," *Philadelphia Inquirer*, 1 July 1874, 3

12. "How to Make Cheap Summer Drinks," *Germantown Telegraph* (Philadelphia, PA) 1 July 1874.

13. Christian K. Ross, *The Father's Story of Charley Ross, the Kidnapped Child* (Philadelphia: JE Potter, 1876) 111.

14. Christian K. Ross, *The Father's Story of Charley Ross, the Kidnapped Child* (Philadelphia: JE Potter, 1876), 123–124, Germantown Historical Society, Philadelphia, PA, and Hathi Trust Digital Library, https://catalog.hathitrust.org/Record/006514213.

15. Ross, 116–118.

16. Thomas Everly, "Searching for Charley Ross," *Pennsylvania History: A Journal of Mid-Atlantic Studies* 67, no. 3 (2000): 378.

17. "Child Stealing in Philadelphia," *Philadelphia Bulletin*, 15 July 1874.

18. Carrie Hagen, "The Story Behind the First Ransom Note in American History," SmithsonianMag.com.

19. Germantown Historical Society, Philadelphia, PA, scrapbook of unidentified newspaper clippings.

20. "Another Disappointment," *Philadelphia Inquirer*, 5 August 1874, 2.

21. Ross, 94.

22. Ross, 251.

23. "Charley Ross: A Just Retribution. Two of His Abductors Killed while Attempting a Burglary," *Philadelphia Inquirer*, 15 December 1874, 1; Ross, 335.

24. Thomas Everly, "Searching for Charley Ross," *Pennsylvania History* 67, no. 3 (Summer 2000), 380.

25. Edward W. Hocker, *Germantown 1683–1933* (privately published, 1933), 268; Ross, 178.

26. "$10,000 for Charley Ross," *Pacific Rural Press* (San Francisco, CA), 9 June 1877, California Digital Newspaper.

27. *Germantown 1683–1933*, 268.

28. Avery, 33.

29. Paula S. Fass, *Kidnapped: Child Abduction in America* (Oxford: Oxford University Press, 1997), 54–55.

30. Marion Elizabeth Rodgers, *The Impossible H. L. Mencken* (New York: Doubleday, 1991), 327–29.

31. Everly, "Searching for Charley Ross," 382.

32. Ibid., 388–390.

33. Jeff Gammage, "'Jon Benet' Case of Its Time—in 1874—at Germantown Exhibit," *Philadelphia Inquirer*, 27 February 2014.

34. Ibid.

CHAPTER ELEVEN

1. "The Fifth Ward Murders," *Philadelphia Inquirer*, 14 October 1871, 3.

2. Ibid.

3. "The Fifth Ward Murders"; *The Trial of Frank Kelly, for the Assassination and Murder of Octavius V. Catto on October 10, 1871* (Philadelphia: Philadelphia Daily Tribune Publishing Co.).

4. *The Trial of Frank Kelly*, 16.

5. "The Fifth Ward Murders."

6. Harry C. Silcox, "The Black 'Better Class' Political Dilemma: Philadelphia Prototype Isaiah C. Wears," *Pennsylvania Magazine of History and Biography* 113, no. 1 (January 1989): 45–66, https://www.jstor.org/stable/20092282.

7. "The Fifth Ward Murders"; *The Trial of Frank Kelly;* Ancestry.com. Philadelphia, PA, US, Death Certificates Index, 1803–1915 [database on-line]. Provo, UT, USA: Ancestry.com Operations, Inc., 2011; Philadelphia City Directories, 1871, Ancestry. com. US, City Directories, 1822–1995 [database on-line]. Provo, UT; "Prominent Colored Man Shot," *Philadelphia Inquirer* (Philadelphia, PA) 11 October 1871, 2; Henry H. Griffith, *The Trial of Frank Kelly for the Assassination and Murder of Octavius Catto.*

8. "Indignation," *Philadelphia Inquirer*, 14 October 1871, 2.

9. "Matters in the Courts," *Philadelphia Inquirer*, 27 November 1871, 7.

10. "The Fifth Ward Murders."

11. "The Fifth Ward Murders"; "On Trial Again," *Philadelphia Inquirer*, 19 June 1877, 8.

12. William S. Walsh, *Literary Curiosities* (Philadelphia: J. B. Lippincott, 1901), 1053; "Voting and Rioting," *Philadelphia Inquirer*, 11 October 1871, 2; Silcox, "The Black 'Better Class' Political Dilemma."

13. Woman's Rights," *Philadelphia Inquirer*, 11 October 1871, 2.

14. "Voting and Rioting," *Philadelphia Inquirer*, 11 October 1871, 2.

15. Harry C. Silcox, *Philadelphia Politics from the Bottom Up* (Cranbury, NJ: Associated University Presses, 1989), 80–81; "Coroner's Inquest," *Philadelphia Inquirer*, 24 October 1871, 2.

16. Voting and Rioting, *Philadelphia Inquirer,* 11 October 1871, 2.

17. Ibid.

18. Russell F. Weigley, ed., *Philadelphia: A 300-Year History* (New York: W. W. Norton, 1982), 413–15.

19. Harry C. Silcox, "William McMullen, Nineteenth-Century Political Boss," *Pennsylvania Magazine of History and Biography* 110, no. 3 (July 1986): 389–412, www.jstor.org/stable/20092022.

20. Ibid.

21. Daniel Biddle and Murray Dubin, *Tasting Freedom: Octavius Catto and the Battle for Equality in Civil War America* (Philadelphia: Temple University Press, 2010), 331–32.

22. Biddle and Dubin, 331–32; Silcox, "William McMullen, Nineteenth-Century Political Boss."

23. Ibid.

24. Silcox, "The Black 'Better Class' Political Dilemma"; Biddle and Dubin, 331–32.

25. Biddle and Dubin, 412.

26. Independence Hall Association, "Catto and American Civil Rights," https://catto.ushistory.org/catto-and-american-civil-rights.

27. Biddle and Dubin, 412.

28. J. O. White and Octavius V. Catto, "Our Alma Mater: An Address Delivered at Concert Hall on the Occasion of the Twelfth Annual Commencement of the Institute for Colored Youth," 10 May 1864, Daniel Murray Pamphlet Collection, Library of Congress.

29. Weigley, 412–15.

30. Ibid.

31. Dennis Clark, *The Irish in Philadelphia* (Philadelphia: Temple University Press, 1973), 127.

32. Biddle and Dubin, 436–40.

33. Ibid.

34. Ibid., 466–67.

35. "Kelly Walking the Streets," *Times* (Philadelphia, PA), 12 July 1877, 3; Silcox, "William McMullen, Nineteenth-Century Political Boss."

36. "The Public Schools," *Philadelphia Inquirer*, 9 October 1878, 2; "Under the Gaslight," *Philadelphia Inquirer*, 9 October 1886, 3.

Chapter Twelve

1. *The Trial and Conviction of George S. Twitchell, Jr., for the Murder of Mrs. Mary E. Hill* (Philadelphia: Barclay & Co., 1869), 2, http://lawcollections.library.cornell.edu/trial/catalog/sat:0804.

2. Winfred Van Duzer, "Dramatic Clue in Muffled Murder," *Philadelphia Inquirer*, 16 November 1941, 158.

3. Ibid.

4. Ibid.

5. *The Twitchell Tragedy: More about the Crime* (Philadelphia: C. W. Alexander, 1869), 32.

6. *The Trial and Conviction of George S. Twitchell, Jr.*, 21, 22.

7. *The Twitchell Tragedy*, 22–28.

8. Ibid., 22.

9. Ibid., 22.

10. Ibid., 22–23.

11. Ibid., 22.

12. "Death from a Snake Bite," *Evening Telegraph* (Philadelphia, PA), 31 July 1868, 3.

13. *The Twitchell Tragedy*, 37.

14. *The Trial and Conviction of George S. Twitchell, Jr.*, 37.

15. *The Trial and Conviction of George S. Twitchell, Jr.*, 38; "The Hand of Blood," *Evening Telegraph* (Philadelphia, PA), 23 November 1868, 1.

16. Van Duzer, "Dramatic Clue in Muffled Murder"; *The Trial and Conviction of George S. Twitchell, Jr.*, 30.

17. *The Trial and Conviction of George S. Twitchell, Jr.*, 60.

18. Van Duzer, "Dramatic Clue in Muffled Murder."

19. *The Trial and Conviction of George S. Twitchell, Jr.*, 37.

20. "Twitchell: Further Curious Developments," *Philadelphia Inquirer*, 14 April 1869, 1.

21. *The Trial and Conviction of George S. Twitchell, Jr.*, 91.

22. "Mrs. Twitchell's Statement," *Evening Telegraph* (Philadelphia, PA), 14 April 1869, 4.

23. "Governor Geary's Letter," *Philadelphia Inquirer*, 17 September 1869, 4.

CHAPTER THIRTEEN

1. A. Probst and W. B. Mann, *Trial of Anton Probst, for the Murder of Christopher Dearing and Family* (Philadelphia: T. B. Peterson and Bros., 1866), Hathi Trust Digital Library, https://catalog.hathitrust.org/Record/100633090.

2. "Probst," *Evening Telegraph* (Philadelphia, PA), 9 May 1866, 1.

3. "The Horror of the Age," *Brooklyn (NY) Daily Eagle*, 8 May 1866, 2; "The Great Tragedy," *Philadelphia Inquirer*, 13 April 1866, 8.

4. "The Trial of Anton Probst," *Philadelphia Inquirer*, 28 April 1866, 1.

5. Ibid.

6. *Anton Probst: The Murderer of the Deering Family* (Philadelphia: Barclay & Co., 1866), 44–47, 66–67, 84; "The Great Tragedy."

7. "When Justice Triumphed Completely," *Knoxville (TN) Journal*, 22 February 1942, 32; "Confession of Eight Murders," *Anglo-American Times* (London), 2 June 1866; "The Horror of the Age."

8. "The Horror of the Age."

9. "When Justice Triumphed Completely."

10. "The Trial of Anton Probst," *Philadelphia Inquirer*, 27 April 1866.

11. Probst and Mann, *Trial of Anton Probst: for the Murder of Christopher Dearing and Family*.

12. "The Horror of the Age."

13. Ibid.

14. "Reward," *Philadelphia Inquirer*, 13 April 1866, 8.

15. "The Great Tragedy."

16. Ibid.

17. "The Murderer Probst," *Philadelphia Inquirer*, 19 April 1866, 1.

18. "The Trial of Anton Probst," *Philadelphia Inquirer*, 28 April 1866, 1.

19. "The Murderer Probst."

20. "The Trial of Anton Probst," *Philadelphia Inquirer*, 26 April 1866, 1.

21. "Confession of Probst," *Philadelphia Inquirer*, 8 May 1866, 1; "The Horror of the Age."

22. "The Deering Murderer," *Chicago Tribune*, 13 June 1866, 2.

23. Ibid.

24. Ibid.

25. Ibid.

26. Ibid.

27. Ibid.

28. "The Execution of Probst," *Bedford (PA) Inquirer*, 15 June 1866, 2.

29. "The Deering Murder," *Janesville (WI) Daily Gazette*, 14 June 1866, 2; "The Execution of Probst"; "The Deering Murderer."

30. "Crime Punished in the Death of Probst," *Philadelphia Inquirer*, 9 June 1866, 1–2; "The Execution of Probst," *Juniata Sentinel* (Mifflintown, PA), 13 June 1866, 2.

31. "Ax Murders Made for Trial of the Century," *Philadelphia Daily News*, 6 September 1995, 12.

CHAPTER FOURTEEN

1. "Local Affairs," *Public Ledger* (Philadelphia, PA), 9 May 1844, 2; "Destruction of Catholic Churches," *Chaos in the Streets: The Philadelphia Riots of 1844*, Falvey Memorial Library, Villanova University, https://exhibits.library.villanova.edu/chaos-in-the-streets-the-philadelphia-riots-of-1844/churches.

2. Ibid.

3. "Local Affairs," *Public Ledger* (Philadelphia, PA), 9 May 1844, 2, and 10 May 1844, 2; "Destruction of Catholic Churches."

4. Bruce Dorsey, "Bibles, Public Schools and Philadelphia's Bloody Riots of 1844," *Pennsylvania Legacies* 8, no. 1 (2008): 12–17; Mary Ann Meyers, "The Children's Crusade: Philadelphia Catholics and the Public Schools, 1840–1844," *Records of the American Catholic Historical Society of Philadelphia* 75, no. 2 (1964): 103–127.

5. David Montgomery, "The Shuttle and the Cross: Weavers and Artisans in the Kensington Riots of 1844," *Journal of Social History* 5, no. 4 (1972): 411–66; Russell F. Weigley, ed., *Philadelphia: A 300-Year History* (New York: W. W. Norton, 1982), 356.

6. Montgomery, "The Shuttle and the Cross"; "Local Affairs," *Public Ledger* (Philadelphia, PA), 9 May 1844, 2.

7. Ibid.

8. Ibid.

9. Ibid. William Watson, "The Sisters of Charity, the 1832 Cholera Epidemic in Philadelphia and Duffy's Cut," *US Catholic Historian* 27, no. 4 (2009): 1–16, www.jstor.org/stable/40468598.

10. "Local Affairs," *Public Ledger* (Philadelphia, PA), 9 May 1844, 2; "Destruction of Catholic Churches."

11. "Local Affairs," *Public Ledger* (Philadelphia, PA), 9 May 1844, 2.

12. Ibid.

13. Ibid.

14. "Destruction of Catholic Churches."

15. "Destruction of Catholic Churches"; "The Philadelphia Anti-Catholic Riots of 1844," *American Catholic Historical Researches* 7, no. 3 (1911), 233; Zachary M. Schrag, "Nativist Riots of 1844," *Encyclopedia of Greater Philadelphia*, https://philadelphiaency clopedia.org/archive/nativist-riots-of-1844; "Local Affairs," *Public Ledger* (Philadelphia, PA), 9 May 1844, 2.

CHAPTER FIFTEEN

1. "Pat Lyon, Pioneer Builder of Fire Engines," *Pottsville (PA) Republican*, 1 September 1927, 4.

2. "Interesting Electrical Reminiscences," *Brookville (PA) Jeffersonian*, 2 July 1857, 2.

3. "Pennsylvania Legislature," *Aurora General Advertiser* (Philadelphia, PA), 4 September 1798, 3; "Pennsylvania Legislature," *Philadelphia Inquirer*, 8 February 1799, 3.

4. "America's First Bank Heist Was Nearly Perfect," *History Things*, 16 November 2020, https://historythings.com/1798-americas-first-bank-heist-nearly-perfect.

5. Lyon, *Narrative of Patrick Lyon*.

6. Ibid.

7. Lyon, *Narrative of Patrick Lyon*; Ron Avery, "America's First Bank Robbery," Carpenters' Hall, https://www.carpentershall.org/americas-first-bank-robbery.

8. Lyon, *Narrative of Patrick Lyon*.

9. Ron Chernow, *Washington: A Life* (New York: Penguin Press, 2010), 701; David McCullough, *John Adams* (New York: Touchstone, 2001), 446; John B. Boles, *Jefferson: Architect of American Liberty* (Philadelphia: Basic Books, 2017), 252–53; Russell F. Weigley, ed., *Philadelphia: A 300-Year History* (New York: W.W. Norton, 1982), 181–89.

10. Avery, "America's First Bank Robbery"; Lyon, *Narrative of Patrick Lyon*.

11. Lyon, *Narrative of Patrick Lyon*.

12. Ibid.

13. P. Lyon, T. Lloyd, J. Haines, J. Stocker, J. Clement., J. Smith, and S. M. Fox, *Robbery of the Bank of Pennsylvania in 1798: The Trial in the Supreme Court of the State of Pennsylvania* (Philadelphia: Pennsylvania Supreme Court, 1808); "America's First Bank Heist Was Nearly Perfect."

14. "Proclamation," *Aurora General Advertiser* (Philadelphia, PA), 4 September 1798, 3.

15. Lyon et al., *Robbery of the Bank of Pennsylvania*; Lyon, *Narrative of Patrick Lyon*.

16. Lyon, *Narrative of Patrick Lyon*.

17. "Communication," *Aurora General Advertiser* (Philadelphia, PA), 20 June 1799, 2.

18. Lyon et al., *Robbery of the Bank of Pennsylvania*; Lyon, *Narrative of Patrick Lyon*.

19. "Today's Story in Pennsylvania History," *Pottsville (PA) Republican*, 1 September 1927, 4; Avery, "America's First Bank Robbery."

20. George G. Heiss, *Diligent Fire Engine*, Library Company of Philadelphia, https://digital.librarycompany.org/islandora/object/digitool%3A64232.

21. "Sales at Auction," *National Gazette* (Philadelphia, PA), 23 April 1829, 3.

22. "Sales at Auction," *National Gazette* (Philadelphia, PA), 27 April 1829, 3.

CHAPTER SIXTEEN

1. "Philadelphia, May 11," *Pennsylvania Packet* (Philadelphia, PA), 11 May 1787; Richard Beeman, *Plain, Honest Men: The Making of the American Constitution* (New York: Random House Trade Paperbacks, 2009), xxxiii–xxv, 34–35.
2. Edmund S. Morgan, "The Witch & We, the People," *American Heritage* 34, no. 5 (August-September 1983).
3. "Philadelphia, May 11."
4. "Philadelphia, July 16," *Independent Gazetteer* (Philadelphia, PA), 16 July 1787, 3.
5. "Philadelphia, July 18," *Freeman's Journal* (Philadelphia, PA), 18 July 1787, 2.
6. "Philadelphia, July 23," *Pennsylvania Packet* (Philadelphia, PA), 23 July 1787, 3.
7. "Philadelphia, October 29," *Independent Gazetteer* (Philadelphia, PA), 29 October 1787, 2.
8. Craig R. Shagin, "The 'Fame' of a Witch," *Pennsylvania Lawyer*, September-October 2016.

Index